ARTHURIAN STUDIES XV

LOVE'S MASKS

ARTHURIAN STUDIES

ISSN 0261-9814

LOVE'S MASKS

IDENTITY, INTERTEXTUALITY, AND MEANING
IN THE OLD FRENCH TRISTAN POEMS

Merritt R. Blakeslee

D. S. BREWER

First published 1989 by D. S. Brewer, Cambridge

D. S. Brewer is an imprint of Boydell & Brewer Ltd
PO Box 9, Woodbridge, Suffolk IP12 3DF
and of Boydell & Brewer Inc.
Wolfeboro, New Hampshire 03894-2069, USA

ISBN 0 85991 264 7

British Library Cataloguing in Publication Data
Blakeslee, Merritt, 1946–
    Love's masks : identity, intertextuality,
    and meaning in the Old French Tristan poems.
    – (Arthurian studies, ISSN 0261-9814; 15).
    1. Poetry in Old French. Special subjects:
    Tristan – Critical studies
    I. Title   II. Series
    841'.1'09351
    ISBN 0-85991-264-7

    Library of Congress Cataloging-in-Publication Data
Blakeslee, Merritt R., 1946–
    Love's Masks: identity, intertextuality, and meaning in the
Old French Tristan poems / Merritt R. Blakeslee.
        p.   cm. – (Arthurian studies, ISSN 0261–9814; 15)
    Bibliography: p.
    Includes index.
    ISBN 0–85991–264–7 (alk. paper)
    1. Tristan (Legendary character) – Romances – History and
criticism.   2. French poetry – To 1500 – History and criticism.
3. Identity (Psychology) in literature.   4. Disguise in literature.
5. Love in literature.   I. Title.   II. Series.
PQ1543.B55   1989
841'.1'09351–dc19   88–22225
                                                       CIP

∞ The paper used in this publication meets the minimum
requirements of American National Standard for Information
Sciences – Permanence of Paper for Printed Library Materials,
ANSI Z39.48–1984.

Printed in Great Britain by
St Edmundsbury Press, Bury St Edmunds, Suffolk

This book is dedicated to
Martha Adkins Blakeslee
Q'en lieis es la seignoria
de pretz e de cortesia,
de gens dos
e de far que ben l'estia
and to
Richard Austin Blakeslee
gen parlan e gran donador
e tal qi sapcha far e dir
fors e dinz son estatge
segon lo poder qi l'es datz.

CONTENTS

Acknowledgements

I wish to express my deep gratitude to those whose advice and insights have played a part in shaping this study: Francis L. Lawrence and Charles T. Davis of Tulane University and Scott Bates of the University of the South, who read and commented on this manuscript in its earliest stages, Deborah H. Nelson and Susan Clark of Rice University, Donald Maddox of the University of Connecticut, Glyn Burgess of the University of Liverpool, and Joseph T. Snow of the University of Georgia. I am much indebted to Paul Schach of the University of Nebraska and to B. C. Barker-Benfield of the Bodleian Library, who generously placed at my disposal otherwise unobtainable information bearing on problems addressed herein. I owe a special debt of gratitude to the late William S. Woods of Tulane University, under whose patient guidance the initial version of this work was written, and to Emmanuèle Baumgartner of the University of Paris (Nanterre), whose continuing interest, encouragement, and suggestions have been invaluable. Portions of this work have appeared previously in a different form in *Tristan et Iseut, mythe européen et mondial. Actes du Colloque des 10, 11 et 12 janvier 1986, Arthurian Literature, Romania, Philological Quarterly, Cultura Neolatina,* and the *Michigan Academician.*

INTRODUCTION

Preface

The corpus that will serve as the object of this study comprises the extant French verse versions of the Tristan legend composed in the twelfth and early thirteenth centuries: the *Tristran* of Beroul (*B*), the *Tristan* of Thomas of Britain (*T*), the *Folies Tristan* of Bern (*Fb*) and Oxford (*Fo*), the *Lai du Chevrefoil* of Marie de France (*Ch*), the episode of *Tristan rossignol* from the *Donnei des amanz* (*Tros*), and the episode of *Tristan ménestrel* from Gerbert de Montreuil's continuation of Chrétien's *Perceval* (*Tmen*).[1] It includes five episodic texts and two 'full' (Fr. *totalisantes*) versions of the Tristan narrative – versions, that is, that set out to recount the entire narrative of Tristan's life and death. While the full versions, the romances of Thomas and Beroul, have survived only in fragmentary form and while it is not certain that Beroul's romance was ever finished, the episodic versions are all complete. Three of the episodic poems, *Fb*, *Fo*, and *Ch*, are independent compositions, while the other two, *Tros* and *Tmen*, belong to larger works. Three parameters unite these texts: their metrical form, the date of their composition, and their provenance. All are composed in rhymed octosyllabic couplets, all date from the second half (and probably the last third) of the twelfth or the first third of the thirteenth century, and all (save *Tmen*) were composed in Norman or Anglo-Norman (Legge, 'Problème' 372).[2]

In view of the frequent allusions to the Tristan legend in the literature of the twelfth and thirteenth centuries, it is notable that there are within the Old French Tristan poems of the same period only a tiny number of explicit allusions to texts outside of the Tristan matter. Leaving aside the invocation of saints and the Deity, there are only three explicit biblical allusions

---

[1] In addition to the French Tristan poems, reference will be made as needed to other, closely allied Tristan texts, whose names will be abbreviated as follows: Eilhart von Oberge's *Tristrant* [*O*], the dominant version of the French prose *Tristan* [*R*], the variant version of the French prose *Tristan* preserved by Paris, MS. B.N.fr. 103 and the fifteenth century imprints based on it [MS. B.N.fr. 103], Brother Robert's Old Norse *Tristrams saga ok Ísöndar* [*S*], Gottfried von Strassburg's *Tristan* [*G*], and the Middle English *Sir Tristrem* [*E*].

[2] It is relevant to note in this regard that all of the extant manuscripts of *T*, *B*, *Fo*, *Fb*, and *Tros* were preserved outside of France: in Germany, in Italy, and above all in England.

in the corpus (*Fb* 353, *B* 41, 1461).[3] With the exception of those references to
Arthur and the members of his court who make episodic appearances in *B*,
T, and *Tmen*, the Tristan poems contain only a handful of allusions, of
varying degrees of explicitness, to contemporary non-Tristanian works:
the *Roman de Renart* (*Malpertis*: *B* 4286), the epic *cycle de Guillaume* (*roi
Otran*: *B* 1406), the *Chanson de Roland* (*Guenelon*: *B* 3138, etc.), the lost 'lai
Guirun' (*T*Sn[1] 783–90), and two unspecified Arthurian romances (*Yvain*: *B*
1155–270; *Yder* and *Guenievre*: *Fb* 234–37).[4] Because each is a part of a larger
work, *Tmen* and *Tros* constitute special cases of intertextual referentiality,
but the episodes themselves contain no explicit allusions to works beyond
the Tristan matter.[5] The Tristan poems contain a number of silent borrowings from non-Tristanian texts, most prominently Thomas' borrowings
from Ovid, the Old French Ovidian poems, and Wace.[6] As the rarity of
these allusions and reminiscences demonstrates, the referentiality of the
Tristan poems is essentially internal rather than external. That is to say,
they are primarily the product of a tradition that the Tristan poets apparently thought of as self-contained (if not necessarily unified) and self-
referential. Nowhere is this self-referentiality more apparent than in the
episodic poems, *Fb*, *Fo*, *Tros*, *Tmen*, and *Ch*, which depend for their comprehensibility on a knowledge of the canonical narrative. *Fb* and *Fo* are,
moreover, extended allusions to the aforegoing events in the lives of the
lovers.

While numerous studies of the medieval Tristan legend have examined
the relation of a given Tristan text or textual element to the traditional body
of narrative material that it continued, these have for the most part been
source studies whose object was genealogical rather than semiotic. In
seeking to delineate the relation of a given narrative element in the poems
to the canon within which it was composed, my own intention has been
very different. I have sought to elucidate certain of the conscious thought
processes and unconscious associations of the Tristan poets as they re-

---

[3] *T* D 1323–33 is an amplified paraphrase of Ecclesiastes 25: 22, while Sn[2] 805 is an oblique
allusion to the biblical metaphor of the bitter chalice (Matthew 26: 39; John 18: 11; see below,
'The Intoxicating Potion').
[4] It is not unlikely that the allusion to Yvain refers to Chrétien's romance, an assumption
permitted by the relative chronology of Beroul, which was composed after 1176–1180 (Blakeslee, 'Date'), and the *Chevalier au Lion*, probably composed between 1176 and 1181 (Frappier,
Chrétien de Troyes 145). The last allusion, perhaps to the *Roman d'Yder*, is of interest, since in its
form it anticipates an entire body of similar allusions to Tristan's suffering.
[5] However, in keeping with the clerical bent of the narrator, the *Donnei des amanz* contains
numerous allusions to biblical and classical authorities (e.g. 153–54, 164, 217–18); the episode
of *Tristan rossignol* represents the most extensive of a series allusions and counter-allusions to
the romances of *Tristan*, *Enéas*, *Thèbes*, *Troie*, and *Amadas et Ydoine* (391–93, 399–418,
663–714).
[6] On Thomas' literary sources, see Delpino; Zingarelli; Bédier 2: 99–101; Pelan 72–97.

interpreted the narrative matter in light of the aforegoing canon. Specifically, I have sought to explicate those portions of the poems whose meaning depends on the metaphorical development of a narrative detail found in an earlier version of the legend or in the literary ethos in which the poems were composed.

In a recent study of Chrétien's *Chevalier au Lion*, Peter Haidu, arguing from principles first enunciated by Robert Guiette, affirmed the existence of an 'écart symbolique' between *sen* and *matiere* in Chrétien's romance. Following Guiette, Haidu assumed that an important mystical element, maintained by deliberate ambiguity, is fundamental to Chrétien's work. Far from seeking to resolve this ambiguity, the poet cultivates a ' "'climat d'énigme" qui forme le charme spécial de ces romans' (Haidu 12).[7] Haidu suggested, however, that it is the largest symbols in Chrétien's work, the grail in *Perceval*, for example, that exhibit most fully what Guiette had called a 'symbolisme sans senefiance'. Haidu postulated the existence of another order of symbols whose meaning is both entire and accessible, 'des symboles moins ambitieux, moins resplendissants, des symboles dont la valeur et la portée se définissent à l'intérieur du texte, explicitement ou indirectement, par des manoeuvres narratives contextuelles' (14).

The differences between Chrétien's *oeuvre* and the French Tristan poems of the twelfth and early thirteenth centuries are legion. The poems are more firmly grounded in an antecedent tradition than are Chrétien's more innovative creations. With the exception of Thomas of Britain, the Tristan poets also differ from Chrétien in their lesser degree of self-conscious artistry, and none indulges in the 'jeu de l'énigme insoluble', which, Guiette suggests (49), is a hallmark of Chrétien's art. These differences notwithstanding, Haidu's formulation of the problem of meaning and its discovery in Chrétien's romances is relevant to the Tristan poems. As in the *Conte del Graal*, there is in the Tristan poems a central, structuring mystery, whose key is to be sought not, as in Chrétien's texts, in the *sens de l'aventure et de l'amour* but in the *sens de l'amour et de la mort*. The most ambitious and least successful attempt to demystify this mystical content is Denis de Rougemont's *L'Amour et l'Occident*, a work whose final lesson is perhaps the danger of attempting to explicate the inexplicable. Yet, there exists in the Tristan poems a system of symbols grounded in the narrative context and accessible to analysis and explication of the sort proposed by Haidu and practiced more recently by John L. Grigsby in 'L'Empire des signes chez Béroul et Thomas', a sober and fruitful reading of the poems in the light of modern semiotic principles.

---

[7] On the cultivation of ambiguity in twelfth-century French romance, see Duggan. On ambiguity in *T*, see Bruckner, 'Open Text'.

The present study adopts certain elements of the methodologies of both Haidu and Grigsby, but its scope is broader than theirs. It seeks through a study of Tristan's identities in the French poems to elucidate not a single, transcendent meaning for each poem or even for each identity but the process through which meaning and meanings are invented or, in the case of a pre-existing and subliminally perceived meaning, through which signs are discovered to clothe and embody that meaning. It seeks, then, not the meaning but the meanings of the Tristan poems. Unlike Grigsby's method, which operates at the level of the individual sign, my own permits the recognition and exploration of systems of signs attaching to a given narrative element – one of the identities of the protagonist – and linking it with others. Unlike de Rougemont's, my intent is not to extract from this diverse body of texts a single, transcendent meaning, still less to analyse the functioning of the myth in Western culture. Rather, I describe a number of *réseaux* of meaning that are elaborated within the poems and that collectively constitute, if not their ultimate sense, at least an effort to point towards that ultimate and ultimately ineffable meaning. In order to avoid a ponderous and overly subtle technical vocabulary, I have chosen to speak of 'metaphorical elements', a phrase that encompasses all of the constitutent elements of symbolic meaning: icon, sign, emblem, symbol, and allegory. Moreover, this phrase permits the discussion of the significance of different orders of narrative elements: objects, actions, places, and identities. Like Haidu, I have chosen to study those metaphorical elements that are the product of a narrative contextualization on the part of the poet, although I have enlarged the definition of context to include not only the text proper but the pretextual canon of the Tristan legend, the extratextual literary and non-literary ethos, and the intertextual tradition of the extant poems.

Methodological and Critical Presuppositions

Even in this era of critical sophistication it is sometimes forgotten that conclusions are dictated as much by methodology as by the object of study, and the obligation of the literary critic to make explicit the methods upon which his conclusions rest is honored more often in the breach than in the observance. It is presently the fashion in Tristan scholarship to limit one's study to a single Tristan text or, more narrowly still, to the extant fragments of that text, should it be defective. Comparative studies of the various versions of the Tristan matter have fallen into disfavor, and the same concern with reducing the hypothetical element in the critical endeavor is responsible for the current skepticism with which the use of modern reconstructions of lost portions of texts is viewed. The methodology utilized in this study, while unfashionable in these two respects, is not, I think, unsound; for it has been employed with an understanding of its limitations and dangers but also with an awareness of its potential for providing insights not possible through other means.

In the present work I focus on the figure of Tristan but make no attempt to study systematically the figure of Iseut, a task already accomplished by Pierre Jonin in his monumental study of the female characters in the Tristan poems. Perhaps because of the realities of medieval gender roles, perhaps simply because of the narrative tradition within which the Tristan poems were composed, Iseut does not adopt the range of identities assumed by Tristan, whose kaleidoscopic changes of form and identity are at once a major theme of the poems and a powerful tool of metaphorical development and of literary invention and variation. Rather, Iseut represents the element of stability that permits the mutability of Tristan's persona, a contrast that is nowhere more marked than in *T* (see below, 'Mutability and Shape-shifting in Thomas' *Tristan*'). She is the constant against which the variables of the narrative are set in motion.

The present work is a study of meaning in the French Tristan poems, particularly as that meaning is transmitted from version to version of the corpus. While each poem differs substantially from the others, all are concerned with a single protagonist and share a common set of narrative premises; this commonality of narrative material permits us to measure the innovations of a given author. Earlier versions of the legend, now lost, were known to the poets of the surviving texts, who were conscious of writing within a coherent tradition. Frequently, a poet may be observed to react to prior developments in the legend, shaping his own material in response to the work of his predecessors. Yet, the canonical narrative is modified only within certain limits and in accordance with the received understanding of the structure and significance of the traditional matter. I examine these poems within a unified perspective, a methodology that makes it possible to study the relations that exist among these texts and that link each with the literary and cultural milieu in which it was composed.

In this study, which is an examination of the metaphorical use of narrative detail, I rely for certain of my conclusions on the narrative of closely allied texts to replace the lost portions of the poems of Thomas and Beroul. Because both the full versions of the French Tristan matter are fragmentary, any discussion of this question that does not take account of their lost narrative content is perforce incomplete, while any that does is necessarily speculative. The present study is founded on two assumptions concerning this lost content: Eilhart's *Tristrant* reflects *dans ses grandes lignes* the lost beginning of Beroul's romance, while the Old Norse *Tristrams Saga* is a faithful, if abridged rendering of the *narrative* of Thomas' poem. I make no assumptions concerning the lost ending of Beroul's text and draw no conclusions based on its missing content, although it has been persuasively argued that Beroul followed the conclusion given by the dominant version of the French prose *Tristan* (Ewert *Romance of Tristran* 2: 260–261; Adams-Hemming, 'Fin').[8]

The conformity of Eilhart and Beroul in recounting the episodes of the tryst in the garden, the *fleur de farine*, Iseut and the lepers, the leap from the chapel, the life in the forest, and the restitution of Iseut to Mark suggests that there existed a similar conformity between the lost beginning of *B* and the corresponding portions of *O* (Ewert, *Romance of Tristran* 2: 59–60). This assumption is further strengthened by the allusions in *Fb*, whose narrative model was presumably either Beroul or Beroul's immediate source, to episodes from the beginning of the narrative that are conserved in *O*: Tristan's combat with Le Morholt, the two voyages to Ireland, and the drinking of the potion (e.g. 97–103, 126–27, 172–77, 183, 309–19, 397–424, 426–41). Since, as I contend below, in all of the extant twelfth and early thirteenth-century versions of the Tristan legend the early episodes were the most stable and most uniform portion of the narrative, this was presumably the case for *B* as well.[9]

Modern Tristan scholars are justly skeptical of the accuracy of Joseph Bédier's reconstruction of the lost portions of Thomas' *Tristan*. I share this skepticism and hence rely on the Old Norse *Tristrams Saga*, which I shall quote in the English translation of Paul Schach, as a guide to the lost portions of Thomas' romance. Were my study concerned with lexical or linguistic questions, even this procedure would be open to question. However, because it studies the narrative elements of *T* (and the metaphoric associations attaching to them), its reliance on *Tristrams Saga*, which reproduces faithfully the narrative material *that it retains* from Thomas' poem, is justified. I have discussed more fully elsewhere the question of the fidelity of *Tristrams Saga* to the narrative content of his

---

[8] In any event, the text of *B* certainly continued beyond the point at which it presently breaks off in MS. B.N.fr. 2171, for the last folio (32d) of that manuscript contains a catchword for the next gathering.
[9] Two theories have been proposed to explain *B*'s sudden divergence from the narrative of Eilhart's *Tristrant*, its episodic character, and its minor narrative inconsistences. A number of scholars have postulated that the poem is the work of two authors (for a summary of this question, see Ewert, *Romance of Tristran* 2: 1–3 and Shirt B.d. 1–26), while others have surmised that the single poet was a minstrel whose text was a working draft of a work intended for episodic performance before a variety of audiences (Ernest Muret, in the Roques-Foulet edition of *B*, viii–ix; Ewert, *Romance of Tristran* 2: 3; Ditmas).

source ('*Mouvance*' 130–36), a discussion that I briefly summarize here. Certain generalizations may be made concerning Robert's practices as translator and adaptor of Thomas. Essentially he is an abridger, although the figure given by Bédier (*Thomas* 2: 75, 93–4), who estimates that Robert reduces Thomas' poem to one half of its original 17,000–20,000 lines, is excessive. On one hand, his estimate of the length of *T* is too high by a quarter or a third; on the other, the majority of those passages of *T* that have survived to permit comparison with Robert's translation show the Anglo-Norman poet at his most prolix and would consequently have been most condensed by the Old Norse adaptor. The missing portions of *T*, like the lost beginning of *B*, contained a stable narrative; Thomas' drastic innovations *vis-à-vis* his model are generally confined to the second half of his poem, the majority of which is preserved in the extant fragments (Blakeslee, 'Structure and Sense').

Robert tends to economize in descriptive passages, to minimize monologue and dialogue, to suppress passages of psychological analysis, especially those treating love, and to eliminate authorial interventions and references to his source. Yet he is faithful in his fashion to the text that he renders. While he omits much narrative material, he translates with accuracy those details of plot that he retains. His additions are few and with one exception, Ísönd's prayer (Ch. 101), touch only the surface of a work whose *narrative* content they do not significantly modify (Bédier, *Thomas* 2: 64–75; Gunnlaugsdóttir 212–20, 329–32; Shoaf 21–54). His originality, such as it is, resides in his skillful use of rhetorical and metrical embellishment at the level of the word or phrase (Schach, 'Style'; Gunnlaugsdóttir 212–13, 216).[10] Robert's additions, all minor, fall into four categories. A number arise from his penchant for providing occasional explanations not found in his model, either to recapitulate, to clarify, or to instruct. Thus, where Thomas' text has none, Robert will frequently invent an explicative detail (Gunnlaugsdóttir 213). Robert also adds details that would hold a special interest for a Scandinavian audience. His predilection for using alliterating word pairs for stylistic effect leads him to add words not found in his model. Elsewhere, Robert simply exaggerates, presumably to retain the interest of an audience used to the action-filled narratives of the native sagas.

What is more, it is clear that the earliest manuscripts fragments of *Tristrams Saga* reflected more accurately the narrative of their source than do the later manuscripts that preserve the entire work. A comparison of the

[10] This is not to imply that Robert does not substantially alter his model. In fact, as Shoaf has shown, he effects important changes in the theology and ideology of his source. However, his tool in doing so is omission and not addition, for he respects the letter of his model while markedly altering its spirit (Shoaf 15).

oldest fragments, three fifteenth-century vellum leaves preserved in
manuscript AM 567 4to and one in the fifteenth-century Reeves fragment
of the Library of Congress, with the two seventeenth-century and one
eighteenth-century paper manuscripts (AM 543 4to, ÍB 51 fol., and JS 8 fol.)
shows that the later texts consistently, if somewhat unsystematically, con-
dense the earlier ones (Kalinke 58–63). There is, however, no instance in
which the paper manuscripts interpolate narrative material not found in
the fifteenth-century fragments. Hence, the cautious use of *Tristrams Saga*
to supplement the missing portions of Thomas' narrative represents a
sound methodological procedure.

I make the further assumption in this study that the episode of the intertwining trees given by *Tristrams Saga* (Ch. 101) was the invention of
Thomas, in whose romance it originally figured. I have presented elsewhere (*'Mouvance'*) the evidence in favor of this supposition, which may
be summarized as follows. The discrepancy between the two manuscripts
that contain the extant conclusion to Thomas' poem (Douce and Sneyd[2])
permits the assumption that neither preserves the canonical form of
Thomas' romance. The presence of an episode of the miraculous plants in
Tristrams Saga and MS. B.N.fr. 103 strongly suggests that a similar episode
in *T* was their common source. With the exceptions detailed above, it was
inconsistent with the practice of the Old Norse translator of Thomas'
romance and with that of the Icelandic copyists of that translation to interpolate non-canonical narrative material in *Tristrams Saga*. It would appear
that the perception that *T* was subversive was responsible for the suppres-
sion of the episode of the intertwining trees in the Douce and Sneyd[2]
manuscripts, a specific instance of a generalized effort to suppress the
French Tristan poems. Taken together, these conclusions suggest that
the episode in the Old Norse *Tristrams Saga* was composed by the poet
Thomas.

Every complete primary version of the Tristan narrative (i.e. Eilhart, the
reconstructed Thomas, and the French prose *Tristan*) contains four major
parts and divides naturally into two halves, which I propose to call the
'roman de Tristan' and the 'roman de Tristan et Iseut': the account of the
birth and childhood of the hero (N^1), the account of the hero's deeds until
the marriage of Iseut and Mark (N^2), the account of the lovers' adulterous
relationship before Tristan's definitive banishment from Mark's court
(N^3), and the account of the lovers' relationship from the moment of
Tristan's exile until their death (N^4).[11] These four parts are framed by a

---

[11] The following discussion is taken from Blakeslee, 'Structure', in which the object of study
was *T*. However, in the more generalized form in which they are presented below, the
conclusions apply to all of the primary versions of the Tristan legend.

genealogical forematter and by an account of the miraculous plants.[12] However, while the structure of the narrative is symmetrical, its parts are not proportional in length.[13] The 'roman de Tristan' (N^1 and N^2) incorporates three traditional narrative patterns that are widely distributed in world literature: (1) that portion of the heroic biography detailing the birth and childhood of the hero (Raglan), (2) the expulsion and return formula (Rank), and, most prominently, (3) the bride-quest motif (Propp). In the primary versions of the Tristan matter, the 'roman de Tristan' demonstrates the greatest stability of any portion of the narrative. However, the non-canonical conclusion to the bride-quest narrative (i.e. the non-marriage of hero and heroine) serves to initiate the Mark-Iseut-Tristan love triangle and to set in motion the events of the second portion of the romance, the 'roman de Tristan et Iseut' (N^3 and N^4).

In the 'roman de Tristan et Iseut', the narratives given by each of the primary versions of the legend (including Beroul's poem, which gives a divergent narrative of N^3) differ markedly from one another. As Thomas, Beroul, Eilhart, and Gottfried all remind us, competing versions of the legend were in circulation.[14] In composing his version of the 'roman de Tristan et Iseut', each poet utilized to his own ends the narrative freedom afforded him by this rich and diverse tradition and by the non-canonical character of this portion of the Tristan narrative.

In particular, there existed an established tradition of composing episodic Tristan poems recounting the clandestine returns of the hero from exile to tryst with Iseut. That this is a very old tradition in the Tristan matter is demonstrated by the existence of a Welsh return episode entitled 'Three Mighty Swineherds' that is perhaps as old as the eleventh century (Bromwich, 'Remarks' 33–35). Three of the French return episodes were independent compositions (Marie's 'Chevrefoil' and the *Folies Tristan*, as was the German *Tristan als Mönch*), two were inserted in non-Tristanian texts (*Tros* in the *Donnei des amanz* and *Tmen* in Gerbert de Montreuil's *Continuation de Perceval*), and many were incorporated in the full versions of Eilhart, Thomas, Beroul, and the French prose *Tristan*. The majority of these return episodes belongs to the narrative of N^4, although in *Ch*, which, it has been suggested, derives from an early version of the legend in which the other Iseut does not figure (Adams-Hemming '"Chèvrefeuille"'), there is no mention of Tristan's marriage, and his exile is passed in South Wales, said to be his birthplace, and not in Brittany.

---

[12] The latter episode is found in Eilhart's poem, in the *Saga* (and, hence, presumably in *T*), and in the variant version of the French prose *Tristan* contained in MS. B.N.fr. 103. Only *R* is lacking such an episode.

[13] It was Eugène Vinaver who first noted the symmetrical structure of the archetypal Tristan narrative (*Etudes* 7–10). On symmetrical composition in *B*, see Ribard (242). On *O*, see Buschinger, 'Composition', 'Structure'.

[14] Thomas, D 835–84; Beroul 1265–70, 1787–92; Eilhart 9446–57; Gottfried 131–54.

It is a basic premise of Tristan scholarship that the first generation of extant Tristan texts (*O*, *B*, *T*, and perhaps *R*) shared a common source, although opinion has long been divided on its precise nature. One school of thought, believing that by their very nature literary cycles are fluid and that this instability was particularly pronounced in the twelfth-century Tristan matter, has held that the source of the extant Tristan poems was a diverse body of oral and written tales and motifs (Vàrvaro, 'Teoria'; Adams-Hemming, '"Chèvrefeuille"'). Another school has maintained that the archetype was a complete, written version of the romance composed in mid-twelfth-century France by a single poet who adopted and unified earlier source material (Bédier, *Thomas* 2: 186–87).[15] Proponents of both theories agree, however, that the three texts of the so-called *version commune* hewed more closely to their common source(s) that Thomas also knew but substantially altered (Fourrier 35–36; Delbouille, 'Premier Roman' 275; Frappier, 'Structure et sens' 259).[16]

I believe the source for the French Tristan poems to have been a unified, canonical narrative that was freely expanded by the adaptation of independent narrative material and extensively modified, within the limitations imposed by the canonical episodes, in light of an individual poet's artistic bent and ideological concerns. This core narrative recounted Tristan's early life and the passion and death of the lovers. It was most detailed and most firmly fixed for N[1] and N[2], although independent narrative additions and embellishments even to this portion were possible. The account of Rivalen and Blancheflor in *T* is clearly one such embellishment, for it liberally expands the much shorter narrative that existed in its source and that is preserved in *O*. N[3] and N[4], on the other hand, were the most malleable portions of the legend, although the death of lovers and, perhaps at a somewhat later date, the marriage to Iseut aux Blanches Mains, came to be considered as obligatory parts of N[4]. It is in N[3] and particularly in N[4] that the return episodes are situated and, hence, here that the most prolific expansion of the narrative takes place. It would appear that independent,

---

[15] Delbouille, who has argued most recently in favor of this thesis, maintains that Eilhart's poem is a close and reliable translation of this lost archetype ('Premier Roman'). Le Gentil ('Légende' 117) and Jonin (*Personnages* 33) have stressed the differences between *B* and *O*. Yet, even the staunchest proponents of the theory of a single archetype admit the possibility of the later interpolation by the first-generation texts of material not found in the archetype. Delbouille, for example, contends that the episodes of the Irish harper and the ambiguous oath, traces of which are found in all of the first-generation texts save Eilhart, are not canonical ('Premier Roman' 277–82, 419–23).

[16] Most scholars who have treated the question of the genesis and evolution of the Tristan matter in the twelfth century have failed to give proper weight to the wide divergences within the *version commune*, prominently those dividing Eilhart from Beroul and those separating the dominant French prose *Tristan* and MS. B.N.fr. 103 from one another and from Eilhart and Beroul.

episodic material was also in circulation and might be incorporated or adapted by a given poet. The majority of these independent episodes recounted the clandestine returns of Tristan to Iseut, but other self-contained episodes, like the *Luite Tristrant* mentioned by Gerbert de Montreuil (*Continuation* 7018–19), also existed. The return episodes represent a special type of independent material; for, once given, the form was self-generating; and the poets were at liberty to ring the changes on this single narrative premise, each selecting a different disguise and elaborating the narrative and metaphoric possibilities inherent in it.

I

TRISTAN'S SOCIAL IDENTITIES

Tristan's Personae

While the protagonist of the French Tristan poems manifests the obligatory conventional attributes of the valorous knight, the cultivated courtier,
and the dutiful lover of twelfth-century chivalric romance, Tristan differs
markedly from other romance protagonists of the period in the multiplicity and complexity of his persona, which anticipates the protean hero of
the Renart cycle, and in his persistent uncourtliness: his renunciation of
the chivalric ideal of armed combat in favor of guile, deceit, and trickery,
and his failure to keep faith with Iseut. Although his chivalric prowess is a
given of his persona, it plays a decidedly secondary role to his anti-
chivalric *engin* (see below, 'Tristan the Trickster'). Unlike that of Yvain or
Lancelot, essentially courtly figures who are immediately chastized and
instantly repentant for any show of uncourtly behavior towards their
ladies, Tristan's more radical uncourtliness, which Thomas links to his
trickery, results from his inability to satisfy the obligations of the courtly
love ethic, chief among which is fidelity to his beloved. While he is inter-
mittently chastized and repentant for his lapses, which are concretized in a
series of grotesque, degrading disguises, in Thomas' romance these lapses
persist until his death. Barber's observation that the Tristan texts lie outside of the ethos of *fin' amor* that was current in the other courtly romances
of the twelfth century points the way to a partial explanation of these
differences. However, while it is broadly true to assert, as Barber has done,
that in the Tristan poems the 'idea of love as an overwhelming, dark,
supernatural and tragic force is at loggerheads with the troubadours' concepts' (95), the representation of Tristan the lover as a poet and musician,
an anachronism for a romance protagonist of the twelfth century, links
Tristan to the figure of the lover/poet of the troubadour lyric and to the
motifs of love sickness and love death that characterize that tradition.

This study investigates first Tristan's parentage and antecedents, the
circumstances of his birth and naming, his education and special skills,
and his physical appearance. It then considers his social identities –
knight, musician, and hunter – and analyses the narrative function and
metaphoric significance of each of the disguises that he adopts: leper, fool,

minstrel, 'nightingale', and pilgrim, as well as the facetious depiction of the hero as a wild man. Finally, it discusses the hero as victim and savior figure, identities that bring together in a single, unifying metaphorical complex the varied and often contradictory elements of the protagonist's persona.

Tristan's persona is initially defined by the identities of knight, musician, and hunter that pertain to the court society to which, as Mark's kinsman and favorite, he belongs. Tristan has mastered those complex bodies of military, musical, and cynegetic knowledge whose first function in twelfth-century society was to distinguish the aristocrat from the villein. Not only do these identities serve as the basis of his social persona in the first half of the narrative but they are the point of departure for the inversions and metaphorical embellishments of the disguise identities of the second half. The opposition in the Tristan narrative between the 'roman de Tristan' and the 'roman de Tristan et Iseut' reflects the fundamental opposition between Tristan's social identities and those covert, anti-social identities that he later adopts. Each of his social identities is, moreover, linked metaphorically to the figure of the lover; for Tristan's skill as knight, musician, and hunter is the means by which the hero merits his lady, winning, preserving, or regaining her according to the shifting circumstances of their lives. In fact, the entire narrative may be considered as an exercise in working out the effects of Tristan's actions – as determined by his three social identities – in varying sets of circumstances. In the 'roman de Tristan' each plays a role in Tristan's winning of Iseut and in his integration into the social Order of Mark's kingdom; in the 'roman de Tristan et Iseut' each is utilized by the outlawed hero in his efforts to save, to regain, or to be reunited with Iseut and in his defense of a Counter-Order of love.

Tristan's Antecedents

Only *T* (as given by *S*) preserves an account of Tristan's parentage, birth, naming, and *enfances*, although its general lines are confirmed by the similar account in *O*, and *B* presumably contained a roughly analogous narrative. In composing this portion of his poem, which functions as an explicative prologue to the narrative of Tristan and Iseut, Thomas was guided by the philosophical principle that events are explained by their origins, specifically, by the genealogical principle that *probitas* is transmitted through the blood (Duby, *Knight* 37) and by the etymological principle that the significance of words, and hence of the objects they designate, may be found in their origins. The story of Rivalen and Blancheflor and the circumstances of Tristan's birth and naming fore-shadow subsequent events in the romance: Tristan's prowess as a knight, the ill-fated love of Tristan and Iseut, and their tragic deaths. Tristan's childhood, and especially his education, like his name and his heredity, contain in germ the essential elements of his subsequent biography and the key to its meaning.

Tristan is the son of Rivalen, lord of the kingdom of Ermenie, and of Blancheflor, sister of King Mark of Cornwall.[1] Rivalen wages war against his liege-lord, Duke Morgan, forcing the latter to sue for peace (*S* Ch. 1). Then, confiding his domains to the keeping of his retainer, Roald le Foite-nant, Rivalen sets sail for the court of King Mark (*S* Ch. 2), where he receives an apparently mortal wound in a tournament (*S* Ch. 11). As he lies dying, Blancheflor, who has loved him from afar since his arrival in the kingdom, slips into his chamber and lies with him, thereby restoring him to health (*S* Ch. 12). Having gotten Blancheflor with child, Rivalen carries the king's sister back to Ermenie where he weds her (*S* Ch. 13-14).

In his absence, Duke Morgan has renewed his attacks on Rivalen's lands, and, upon his return, Rivalen is obliged to lead an army against his enemy. In the battle, Rivalen is killed (*S* Ch. 15). At the news of the death of her husband, Blancheflor grieves so bitterly that she gives birth to the child she is carrying and then dies of sorrow (*S* Ch. 15). Roald, who receives the babe, names him Tristan in memory of the sorrowful circumstances attending his conception and birth:

> He was ... given the name Tristram, and he received this name because he was conceived in sorrow, carried in distress, and born in the afflictions of grief. All his life was filled with sadness. He well deserved his name, for he was sad when awake, sad when he slept, and sad when he died, as those will learn who continue to listen to this story. (*S* Ch. 16)

Roald le Foitenant keeps secret the birth of Tristan, whose life the duke would certainly have sought, had he known of the child's existence. Roald orders his wife to keep to her bed and, a short while later, announces the birth of a son. He raises Tristan with his other sons, and no one save husband and wife knows the secret of the child's identity (*S* Ch. 16).

Because the pun on *triste/Tristan* is comprehensible only in Latin and the Romance languages, it presumably originated in a French text, per-haps in *T*, where the priest who baptises the orphaned child counsels:

---

[1] Although, as I have stated above, I rely solely on the narrative of *S* in my discussion of the lost content of *T*, for the purposes of the present discussion I follow Bédier in using the names *Rivalen* and *Blancheflor* for Tristan's parents, names preserved by *G* that are certainly closer to those used by Thomas than *Kanelangres* and *Blensinbil*, the names given in *S*.

'It seems advisable to me that in view of the grief and affliction, the care and torments, the anxiety and unrest, the sore and many sorrows, and the distressing event which has befallen us through his birth that the boy be named Tristram.' For in this tongue *trist* means *sorrow* and *hum* means *man*. (*S* Ch. 16)

The motif of Tristan's symbolic naming becomes a commonplace in subsequent versions of the legend. The explanation given in *S* is repeated in *G* (1988–2022),[2] in *R* (Curtis 1: §229), in MS. B.N.fr. 103 (Bédier, *Thomas* 2: 321–22), and in *Tristan de Nanteuil* (8431–33, 9461–67). In *Fo*, Tristan puns on his name:

> ... 'Ja sui je *Tristran*,
> Ki en *tristour* vif e haan.'   (615–16)

a practice continued in contemporary allusions to the Tristan narrative:

> Quis ille *Tristanus* qui me *tristia* plura tulit?[3]

> Vostre amors me fait endurer
> Tant *tristre* moys et tant *tristre* an
> Que plus sui *tristres* de *Tristran*.[4]

> Or as ton pere fait *Tristrant*,
> Car *tristes* sui quant je te voi
> Mal bailli par malvaise loy.[5]

---

[2] Gottfried proposes to his reader:
Sehen wie trureclich ein leben
Ime ze lebene wart gegeben;
Sehen an den trureclichen tot,
Der alle sine herzenot
Mit einem ende besloz,
Daz alles todes übergenoz
Und aller triure ein galle was.   (2011–17)

[3] Arrigo da Settimello, *De Diversitate Fortunae et Philosophiae Consolatione* p. 458, vv. 97–98.

[4] Gautier de Coinci, 'De l'empeeris qui garda sa chasteé contre mout de temptations' 3: 314, vv. 298–300.

[5] Gui de Cambrai, *Barlaam et Josaphat* 158, 12–14. See also *Le Roman de la Poire* 101–02. Chrétien's identification of Tristan as he 'qui onques ne rist' (*Erec et Enide* 1687) is echoed in Peire Cardenal's 'Sel que fes tot cant es' (PC 335, 14) 89, the Long Redaction of the First *Continuation of the Perceval* (2: 5447), *Durmart le Galois* (8512), Raoul de Houdenc's *Vengeance Raguidel* (263), and the *Atre Périlleux* (5392 ff.). (In fact, only the second half of the *Vengeance Raguidel* is attributed to Raoul de Houdenc, and the allusion to Tristan is the work of the anonymous author of the first half.) In the twelfth-century texts, it appears that the Tristan so designated is Iseut's beloved. In the thirteenth, 'Tristan qui onques ne rist' comes to designate an entirely different personnage, whose story is elaborated in inceasing detail with each new romance in which he figures.

The motif passes into the reality of thirteenth-century daily life with the naming of Jehan Tristan, the son of Louis IX of France, so named to commemorate the anguish suffered in the last stages of her pregnancy by his mother, who learned only three days before the child's birth that her husband's forces had been encircled by the Sarrasins outside of Cairo (A. Foulet).

Thomas, who cultivates a classical symmetry in the structure of his romance, opens each half of his poem with a pun that serves as guide to its meaning. To the *triste/Tristan* pun that opens the account of Tristan's youth correspond the puns on *amare* ('aimer'), *amarum* ('amer'), and *mare* ('la mer') in the account of the consumption of the potion that begins the story of the lovers (see below, 'Tristan's Infirmities and Suffering'). Walter ('Mélancholie' 649) has suggested that Tristan's *tristesse* is to be associated on one hand with the sin of Adam, 'hominem tristem et desperantem' (Hildegard von Bingen 73), and on the other with the erotic melancholia that characterizes one of the three categories of lovers to which Thomas alludes in his *envoi* (Sn² 822), the 'pensis' and 'amerus'. In keeping with Isidore of Seville's assertion that 'nomina sunt consequentia rerum', it is understood that the child whose birth was marked by suffering for love will, in his turn, suffer deeply and die for love (as did his mother), of a wound received in battle (as did his father).

The story of Tristan's parents is an example of Thomas' extensive use of doubling.[6] Each double is a projection of aspects of the character or the life of one of his protagonists. As Iseut is doubled by the two women who share her name, her mother and Tristan's wife, by her compatriot and confidante Brengvein, and by her statue in the *salle aux images*, so is she by Blancheflor, who, like her, dies of sorrow at the death of her beloved. As Tristan is doubled by the second Tristan, by his friend and confidant Kaherdin, and by that other slayer of giants, Arthur, so is he by his father Rivalen, whose heroic qualities and tragic destiny are mirrored in his son.

Tristan is of noble but irregular birth, conceived out of wedlock, orphaned, dispossessed, and raised under a false identity; and his irregular heredity and early life provide the model for the irregularities of his later life. He belongs by merit and birth to the innermost circle of Mark's court; yet, because of his love for Iseut, he forfeits that right and is finally proclaimed an outlaw. Like his father, Tristan will defend Mark's kingdom and, in so doing, will be grievously wounded. Like Rivalen, he will be healed of his wound by his lady's love (see below, 'The Sexual Wound and its Healing in *T*'). Like that of his parents, whose deaths prefigure those of

---

6 On Thomas' obsession with doubling, see Dannenbaum; Bruckner; and Trindade, 'Time' 391. The symmetry referred to above is yet another example of doubling.

the lovers, his love will be a source of sorrow, hardship, and death. *T* is framed by symmetrically disposed death scenes, each containing a vegetative motif – Blancheflor's name and the intertwining trees that grow from the graves of the lovers. These motifs mirror another arboreal image that stands at the center of the poem, the single tree that grows above the subterranean grotto where the lovers lie as though in death, entwined in one another's arms (*S* Ch. 64; cf. *T* Sn² 809–12).

Tristan's Person and Education

The physical descriptions of Tristan in the poems stress his strength and superlative physical beauty, essential elements of his persona as peerless knight and archetypal lover.[7] In *T* the Norwegian merchants admire his 'skill, handsomeness, and ability' (*S* Ch. 18), and Iseut, upon seeing him in his bath, is struck by his handsome face and imposing stature (*S* Ch. 43).[8] In *Fo* she observes of the ill-favored fool:

> '... cist est laiz,
> E hideus e mult conterfait
> E Tristran est tant aliniez,
> Bels hom, ben fait, mult ensenez.'   (575–78)

Tristan's hair, like that of his beloved, is blond (*bloi*: *Fb* 132, 283; *B* 212). He is large and strong (*Fo* 243; *B* 3623, 3929), and possesses well-formed limbs (*Fb* 293–95, *B* 4425); in *T* his remarkable stature allows Iseut to recognize him under his leper's disguise (D 552–54).

In the poems, Tristan is repeatedly disfigured and weakened as a result of an injury or of a disguise. These episodes, which depict Tristan as grotesque and powerless, invert his fundamental attributes of physical beauty and strength. The *Fo* poet insists on the contrast between his extraordinary beauty and his disfigurement (e.g. 577–80, 707–10, 835–38).[9]

---

[7] In *R* it is said:

Et sachiez quant [Tristan] fu en aage de doze anz, adonc fu il tant preuz et tant biax, et tant faisoit a loer de totes choses que nus ne le veoit qu'il ne se merveillast de li. Il n'i avoit ne dame ne demoisele qui ne se tenist a beneüree se Tristanz la vosist amer.

(Curtis 1: §263)

[8] Cf. Curtis 1: §229. Analogies may be drawn with the beauty of Orpheus, of David, and of Absalom, with Diarmaid's love spot that caused women to fall in love with him, and with the beauty of Baile (Eisner 91, 96).

[9] Cf. MS. B.N.fr. 103 (Bédier, *Thomas* 2: 334, 365).

When Tristan announces to Iseut that he is that same Tantris whom she had once healed, drawing a parallel between the effects of his earlier injury and the disfigurement that mirrors the disorder of his spirit, Iseut's shocked protest emphasizes the distance that separates his previous and his present appearance:

> Isolt respunt: 'Par certes, nun!
> Kar cil est beus e gentils hum,
> E tu es gros, hidus e laiz,
> Ke pur Trantris numer te faitz.'   (365–68)

The Chertsey tiles confirm the evidence of the texts. The haggard, wasted features of the dying Tristan in 'Tristram Drifts in the Rudderless Boat' (Tile 20) stand in stark contrast to the youthful, well-formed features of the hero in 'Tristram Harps before Mark' (Tile 4), 'Tristram Teaches Isolt to Harp' (Tile 21) and 'Tristram Presents the Potion to Isolt' (Tile 27).

Perhaps the most intriguing paradox of the Tristan romance is the depiction of the hero as a trickster (see below, 'Tristan the Trickster'); for the traditional, but by the twelfth century increasingly archaic, conception of knighthood was founded on physical prowess rather than on mental agility. If Tristan's prowess nominally identifies him as a literary descendent of Roland and Guillaume d'Orange, his trickery makes of him a literary ancestor of Renart and Pathelin. While the extensive description of Tristan's education follows the traditional *enfances* narrative of twelfth-century romance, his extra-military skills, which surpass the obligatory attributes of the conventional protagonist of courtly romance, serve as the basis for a number of episodes in which Tristan obtains his ends through *engin*. Even his extraordinary physical qualities are utilized as frequently for trickery as for overt confrontation with his enemies.

The account of Tristan's education given in *T* stresses his extraordinary intellectual qualities: his literacy, his mastery of the seven arts, his fluency in languages, and his proficiency in music (*S* Ch. 17).[10] Descriptions of his qualities found elsewhere complete the list of Tristan's special skills, all of which will play a role in subsequent episodes of his life. In *Tros* it is said that Tristan:

> Apris l'aveit en tendres anz;
> Chascun oisel sout contrefere
> Ki en forest vent ou repeire.   (476–78)

---

[10] The account given in *R* places less emphasis on his intellectual accomplishments:
Si crut [Tristan] et amenda tant que chascuns se merveilloit de son amendement et sa croissance. Il sot tant des eschés et des tables que nus ne l'en pooit aprendre un sol point. De l'escremie fu il si mestres en po de tens qu'il ne pooit trover en nule maniere son per. De bel chevauchier et de sagement faire ce que il faisoit ne se pooit nus jovenciax aparegier a li.   (Curtis 1: §263)

The description of Tristan's skills in *Tmen* not only repeats certain of the details given in *S* and *Tros* but adds considerable detail concerning his skill at games, both the parlor variety (chess, checkers, and dice) and those quasi-military exercises in which he excels: the hunt, throwing the lance, and wrestling (3703–18). In *T*, the description of the games that precede the jousting at Mark's tourney during Tristan's first return to England furnishes the pretext for another enumeration of his skills:

> E plusurs jus comencer funt
> D'eskermies e de palestres.
> De tuz i fud Tristran mestres.
> E puis firent uns sauz waleis
> E uns qu'apelent waveleis,
> E puis si porterent cembeals
> E lancerent od roseals,
> Od gavelos e od espiez:
> Sur tuz i fud Tristran preisez.   (D 798–806)

In the *Folies* Tristan repeats similar enumerations of his qualities in a burlesque mode (*Fb* 184–87 and *Fo* 502–25), although certain of his declarations veer abruptly towards the literal truth (*Fo* 519–24). Tristan's expertise as an archer, mentioned nowhere else in the poems, plays an important role in two episodes of *B*: the life in the forest and the deaths of Denolaen and Godoïne.

Tristan's skill at chess is apparently a detail that originates with Thomas, who alone among the French Tristan poets gives the episode of the Norwegian merchants.[11] He portrays the young Tristan playing chess on board the merchants' ship at the moment of his kidnapping (*S* Ch. 18), a detail reproduced in Chertsey Tile 2. Thomas treats this skill as a sign of his hero's courtly sophistication; for, in juxtaposing the episodes of the chess game, the breaking of the stag (*S* Ch. 21–22), and Tristan harping before Mark's court (*S* Ch. 22), he equates Tristan's skill at chess with his mastery of the no less esoteric vocabulary and techniques of the hunt and the musical arts.[12] This detail is seized on by Thomas' epigones, each of whom associates it with another of Tristan's fundamental attributes: his linguistic ability, his skill at arms, and his passion. In recounting the same scene, Gottfried emphasizes Tristan's command of the arcane vocabulary of chess:

[11] In the Irish saga *The Wooing of Etain*, an analogue and possible source of the episode of the Irish harper (Newstead, 'Harp' 465), Midir wins Etain, wife of Eochaid, at chess.

[12] On the importance of the mastery of esoteric knowledge, particularly of chess, to the sense of identity of the aristocratic classes, see Blakeslee, 'Partie' 220. Brault makes a similar point about the hunt ('Rituel' 114).

Der höfsche hovebære
Lie siniu hovemære
Und vremediu zabelwortelin
Under wilen vliegen in:
Diu sprach er wol und kunde ir vil,
Da mite so zierter in sin spil.   (2287–92)

The metaphorical association of chess and military strategy is undoubtedly responsible for the linking of Tristan's skill at chess and at arms in G,
Tmen, R, and the Lai de l'ombre. In the latter text, Jean Renart declares of his
protagonist:

Il sot d'eschés et d'escremie
Et d'autres geus plus que Tristans.   (104–05)[13]

In Sir Tristrem the hero carries with him on his healing voyage not only his
musical instruments but his chess game (1226–27), and it is his skill at this
game as much as his musical ability that wins the admiration and sym-
pathy of the queen (1244–52).

The association of chess and love becomes a literary commonplace in
northern France only after the twelfth century (Blakeslee, 'Partie'). It
would appear that the seagoing chess game of T suggested to the redactor
of R, who was perhaps aware of the association of chess and love in the
troubadour lyric, the transposition of that game to a more symbolically
charged sea journey. In R (Curtis 2: 445) and in MS. B.N.fr. 103 (Bédier,
Thomas 2: 341), the lovers are portrayed playing chess together during the
return voyage from Ireland at the moment at which they are served the
potion, a scene depicted in a miniature from MS. B.N.fr. 112 (fo 239, reproduced in Payen, Les Tristan en vers, plate 7), whose iconography is
remarkably similar to that of Chertsey Tile 2, which depicts Tristan playing chess with the Norse merchants; in a ceiling painting in Palermo
(reproduced in Loomis, Arthurian Legends, plate 115); and in the Burghley
Nef, a table ornament presently in the Victoria and Albert Museum
(Tristan 1489 iii).

The skills that Tristan acquires during his education and that he refines
thereafter may be grouped as follows:

(1) training in the arts of refinement and learning that will fit him for the
role of courtier: literature, music, and the courtly games of chess, tric-trac
(a kind of backgammon), and dice;

(2) training for the role of statesman and future leader of a people: law,
customs, and languages;

13 Cf. R, Curtis 1: §263 (quoted above) and Löseth §481. Likewise, in G the episode of the
Norwegian merchants follows immediately the description of Tristan's education, in which
Gottfried mentions his skill at arms (2113).

(3) training in the arts of the hunt, the 'deduit' *par excellence* of the nobility of the twelfth century, as well as a rehearsal for war; and

(4) training in the arts of war and physical exercise: horsemanship, jousting, the mastery of weapons, and physical gamesmanship.[14]

The portrait of Tristan that emerges from the foregoing enumeration is that of a sophisticated courtier and superlative knight, an individual mentally agile and physically redoubtable, eminently qualified to assume the position of leadership for which his education has prepared him and equally qualified to lead the life of exile and outlaw that will be his portion.

Tristan the Knight

> 'J'ere chevaler mervilus,
> Mult enpernant e curajus:
> Ne dutai par mun cors nul home
> Ki fust d'Escoce tresk'a Rume.'
> (Fo 403–06)

Tristan is, first and foremost, a knight, the strongest in Mark's kingdom, a quality without which his other attributes would be of little moment. The early episodes of *T* recount his chivalric education, and his prowess is publically and irrevocably established by his victory over Le Morholt (*S* Ch. 27–28).[15] Even Mark, at a time when his nephew is in open rebellion against him, concedes:

> 'Je ne quit mais q'en nostre tens,
> En la terre de Cornoualle,
> Ait chevalier qui Tristran valle.' (B 1470–72)

Yet, because of the peculiar circumstances of Tristan's dilemma, his prowess avails him little in his conflict with Mark for Iseut; for his allegiance to his overlord and uncle prevents him from seizing Iseut by force, as he is eminently capable of doing. Nevertheless, his uncontested merit in this domain allows the poets the liberty of repeatedly portraying the protagonist in the most unheroic of circumstances – disguised as a leper or fool or

---

[14] For example, his extraordinary ability in jumping, referred to in *T D* 801–02, will serve as the basis of two important episodes, the leap between the beds in *B* in which Tristan, in spite of being wounded, jumps 'le lonc d'une lance' (695) and the 'saut mortel' (909–64).

[15] This episode, perhaps the most frequently alluded to in the poems, is also evoked in *B* 27–28, 50–53, 135–42, 848–57, 2038; *Fb* 77, 97–103; and *Fo* 327–40.

hunted as an outlaw. Were Tristan of any other station save that of heroic knight, many episodes of the Tristan poems could only have been written as *fabliaux*, a fact borne out by a comparison of the poems with the *Roman de Renart*, certain portions of which exhibit a close similarity of narrative detail and a radical dissimilarity of tone (Tregenza; Regalado; Sargent-Baur).

In *T*, during the period of his early manhood at Mark's court, Tristan successively conquers or preserves three realms: his father's kingdom of Ermenie, which he liberates from the dominion of Duke Morgan (*S* Ch. 24); Mark's kingdom of England, which he frees from the subjugation of the Irish (*S* Ch. 26–28); and finally Ireland itself, which he preserves from the ravages of a dragon (*S* Ch. 35–36). Moreover, he negotiates a peace treaty between Ireland and England, the chief article of which is the marriage of Mark and Iseut. In exile in Wales, Tristan vanquishes the giant Urgan le Velu, thus saving that kingdom (*S* Ch. 62). Exiled again from England, Tristan serves the king of Rome and later the king of Spain, preserving the latter's kingdom from a giant (Sn[1] 729–52). He then journeys to Brittany where he serves the Duke Hoël, defending that kingdom against an aggressor (*S* Ch. 69). He vanquishes and subjugates Moldagog, a giant who has presented a long-standing threat to the borders of the Duke's domains (*S* Ch. 73–76). His prowess is equally impressive when turned to personal ends. Accused of cowardice, Tristan and Kaherdin return to England disguised as pilgrims, where, in order to obtain revenge for the false allegation leveled against them by Cariado, Kaherdin slays Cariado and Tristan another baron (D 785–834). Following their return to Brittany, Tristan and Kaherdin pass their time riding abroad to joust:

> Il orent le los e le pris
> Sur trestuz ceus del païs
> De chevalerie e de honur. (D 891–93)

Finally, Tristan champions the cause of Tristan le Nain, his namesake and double, and is mortally wounded in unequal combat against the abductors of the knight's lady, Estult l'Orgillius and his brothers (D 885–1050).

In *B*, Tristan's prowess is also a central element in the unfolding of the narrative. In the episode of the 'Tryst at the Tree', Tristan recalls his feats of arms on behalf of his uncle (133–42) and, since no member of Mark's court will consent to meet him in an ordeal by combat, announces his readiness to demonstrate his innocence through an ordeal by fire (149–56). He later rescues Iseut from the lepers to whom Mark has delivered her, although he does so without recourse to arms (1233–70). In his letter to Mark proposing restitution of Iseut (2556–618), he reminds the king that his marriage to Iseut was accomplished by his prowess:

'Rois, tu sez bien le mariage
De la fille le roi d'Irlande.
Par mer en fui jusque en Horlande.
Par ma proece la conquis,
Le grant serpent cresté ocis,
Par qoi ele me fu donee.' (2556–61)

Having made this point, Tristan offers both to continue in the service of the king and to defend the queen's good name against any challenger in armed combat. Following the scene at the Gué du Mal Pas, Tristan and Governal, incognito, enter a tourney at the Blanche Lande where Tristan wounds Andret and Governal slays the forester who denounced the sleeping couple to Mark (3985–4074).

In *Tmen* Tristan arrives incognito at Arthur's court at Carlion where he challenges and unhorses the king's best knights. Upon learning Tristan's identity, Arthur welcomes him into his court. During his stay, Tristan also demonstrates his extraordinary skill as a wrestler. Finally, with twelve companions chosen from among Arthur's best knights, Tristan sets out for Mark's court at Lancien in search of Iseut. The companions arrive at Lancien just as a great tournament is about to begin, and in the midst of the tourney Tristan and his companions come to the aid of Mark's forces and turn the tide in their favor. In the first day of the tourney, 'ot Tristrans de touz le pris' (4290). Only with the arrival of Perceval, in quest of the grail and the bleeding lance, is Tristan finally struck down and taken prisoner, a detail that reflects the revised hierarchy of Arthurian knights in the thirteehth-century Grail romances.[16]

The valorous knight of courtly romance is conventionally an object of erotic desire; and Tristan's prowess is a necessary, if banal, proof that he is worthy of Iseut's love. So trite is this commonplace that, although it is fundamental to Tristan's literary character, it is evoked explicitly in only two episodes (*T S* Ch. 4–6; *Tmen*). Perhaps for this reason, Tristan's identity as knight is, of all his identities, that which is the object of the least metaphorical development in the poems, although it is repeatedly inverted in the disguise episodes. His feats of arms are set in implicit opposition to his degradation as outlaw, exile, and disguised interloper in the disguise episodes, which require that he substitute guile for physical prowess and wear garments that conceal his strength and belie his station. In only two episodes is his physical prowess the object of explicit concep-

---

[16] The episode of *Tmen* is found in Gerbert de Montreuil's continuation of Chrétien de Troyes' *Perceval*. Composed between 1226 and 1230, Gerbert's work is an interpolation that figures between the continuations of Wauchier and Manessier of Chrétien's unfinished romance. *Tmen*, which is complete and unbroken, comprises lines 3309–4832 of Gerbert's 17,000-line work.

tual play: in the scene in *Fo* in which he burlesques his skill at arms and in the episode in *T* in which he and Kaherdin are accused of cowardice. Nevertheless, the theme of Tristan's skill as knight and jouster runs as an undercurrent throughout the narrative; and in *T* the 'roman de Tristan et Iseut' is framed by Tristan's two most important combat's, those against Le Morholt (and its doublet, the combat against the Irish dragon)[17] and against Estult l'Orgillius.

In the 'roman de Tristan', which recounts Tristan's parentage, his education, his early life, and his first and most important combats, Tristan's role is that of epic hero; for the 'epic deals with insertion of persons (actors) into societal conflicts, not with the personal conflicts with society (this latter being part of the structural characterization of romance)' (Crist 6). Tristan's victories over Le Morholt and the Irish dragon, and his quest for a bride for his uncle, the king, constitute societal struggles that Tristan resolves through his prowess. In the 'roman de Tristan et Iseut', which recounts his love for Iseut, his role shifts to that of a romance hero in conflict with his society, irreconcilably at odds with the very social Order whose champion he had previously been. In spite of his superior prowess, Tristan never openly contests the status quo by virtue of which Mark possesses Iseut.[18] Instead, he tacitly accepts the validity of the social and legal proscriptions against his passion for Iseut, circumventing them through clandestine or anti-courtly means.[19] In *B*, when Tristan and Iseut flee Mark's court for the forest, 'le lieu où se brisent ... les mailles de la hiérarchie féodale' (Le Goff and Vidal-Naquet 545), Tristan's actions there demonstrate his alienation from the values of the court. He and Governal, his *alter ego*, each ambush and decapitate an enemy, unchivalric actions that reveal their rejection of the codes of courtliness and the day in favor of those of wildness and the night (1656–712, 4369–89). Later, Tristan employs his bow, 'une arme qui est celle de chasseur, non du chevalier guerroyant et tournoyant' (Le Goff and Vidal-Naquet 546), to slay the traitor Godoïne, who seeks to spy upon the lovers' pleasure (4410–85).

Possessed by his passion and, in consequence, outlawed by the representatives of the social Order, Tristan serves the Counter-Order with his

[17] For the double structure of N[2], in which the combat against Le Morholt in England is paralleled by the combat against the dragon in Ireland, see Blakeslee, 'Structure and Sense' 378, 386–88.
[18] Even in the three episodes in which Tristan takes revenge on his persecutors, the felonious barons, he never directly challenges Mark (*B* 3985–4074, 4267–485; *T* D 785–834). Moreover, each of these episodes contains an element of concealment that suggests their association with the disguise episodes.
[19] His combats on behalf of other kingdoms and particularly his participation in tournaments (*Tmen*, *T* D 885–93), are incidental to this portion of the narrative, whose key episodes recount his trickery and disguises.

craftiness rather than with his prowess.[20] Only when Mark, his uncle and surrogate father, is no longer his adversary can Tristan lay aside his trickery and resort to the same force of arms with which he served the Order. Thus, in the episode of Tristan le Nain in *T*, which symmetrically mirrors the combat against Le Morholt of the first portion of the romance,[21] Tristan takes up arms for another Order, although that entity is defined differently than it was previously when he served the moral and social Order represented by Mark's kingdom. Tristan le Nain seeks out 'Tristran l'Amerus' and pours forth the sorrowful story of the abduction of his lady by Estult before pleading for Tristan's aid. When Tristan temporizes, his suppliant's angry outburst, in making clear what Tristan's role as defender of those who suffer for love ought to be, succinctly defines the ideology of this newly constituted Counter-Order:

> ... 'Par fei, amis,
> N'estes cil que tant a pris!
> Jo sai que, si Tristran fuissét,
> La dolur qu'ai sentissét,
> Car Tristran si ad amé tant
> Qu'il set ben quel mal unt amant.
> Si Tristran oïst ma dolur,
> Il m'aidast a icest amur.'   (D 977–84)

Once Tristan consents unconditionally to aid the persecuted lover, his allegiance to the Counter-Order is sealed, a new hierarchy of values consciously embraced, and his fate willingly assumed. As in the climactic combat against Le Morholt in the 'roman de Tristan' his prowess as a knight once again becomes central to the narrative in the 'roman de Tristan et Iseut'. Yet, this time it is the prowess not of an epic hero but of a romance hero whose allegiance is no longer to societal values but to that personal set of values incarnated by the Counter-Order.

Tristan the Musician

Throughout the poems, Tristan, in whose education the study of music figured prominently, is portrayed as an accomplished musician whose skill as a harper, a singer, and a composer of lays plays an important role in

---

[20] The concept of the Order and the Counter-Order in the Tristan poems has been formulated by Françoise Barteau (53–82).
[21] As in the combat against Le Morholt, he is mortally wounded with a wound that only a queen in a foreign land holds the power to heal.

shaping the events of his life and gives rise to important metaphoric resonances. In the episode of the Irish harper in *T* (*S* Ch. 49–50), Mark is compelled to deliver Iseut to an Irish baron who has obtained Mark's promise of an unspecified recompense for his song. Tristan, who has been absent from the court, returns and, upon learning what has transpired, sets off in pursuit of the pair. He finds them on the shore about to embark on the baron's ship. With his music, Tristan diverts the baron for so long that the rising tide prevents the latter from conveying Iseut to his ship. Tristan then volunteers the services of his mount in transporting the queen through the sea. When the baron agrees, Tristan, whose words make explicit the connection between his music and his trickery, sets Iseut on his horse and rides away, declaring to his rival:

> 'Listen . . . you heedless and foolish fellow. You won Ísönd with your harp, and now you have lost her because of a fiddle. You deserved to be deprived of her since you won her with deception. . . . You took her from the king with deception, and I took her from you with deceit' (*S* Ch. 50).

Cluzel links this episode to that of the combat against Le Morholt and to that of the life in the forest, observing: 'Tristan avait incontestablement mérité Iseut trois fois, par l'épée, l'arc et la rote' ('Harpeur' 96). Each of Tristan's three major social identities – knight, hunter, and musician – plays a role in Tristan's love for Iseut; for he must win her, save her, or regain her by the successive exercise of each of his heroic attributes. Moreover, this episode weakens Mark's moral right to Iseut, for, as Tristan remarks to the king upon his return: '"Sire . . . by my faith, it is not very befitting for a woman to love a man who gives her away for a performance on the harp"' (*S* Ch. 50). Finally, Tristan's music, a metaphor for his passion, gives him access to the *élan vital* that resides in the natural world, a power on which he draws in his roles as hunter, as warrior, as lover, and as trickster.

A passage from the *De Proprietatibus Rerum* of Bartholomaeus Anglicus, composed toward the middle of the thirteenth century, summarizes certain of the metaphoric associations attaching to music, which stirs erotic desire and possesses curative powers over mental and physical disorders:

> For musike meueþ affecciouns and exciteþ þe wittes to dyuers disposiciouns. (Lib. 19, Cap. 131)

Specifically, music is said to alleviate sorrow and relieve melancholy:

> And conforte of voice pleseþ and conforteth þe herte and wittes in alle

disese and trauayle of workes and werynesse. And musik abateþ
maystry of yuel spirites in mankynde, as we redeþ of Dauid þat
delyuerede Saul of an vnclene spirit by craft of melody.

(Lib. 19, Cap. 131)[22]

These qualities are commanded by Tristan the musician, who can change
the hearts of his hearers, move men to favor and women to love, and relieve
pain and suffering.

Following his abduction by the Norwegian merchants and his subsequent
abandonment on the shores of Cornwall in *T* (*S* Ch. 18–19), Tristan is
brought to Mark's court where his acceptance is assured by the knowledge
of the arts of the hunt that he has demonstrated before Mark's huntsmen (*S*
Ch. 21). One evening, a Welsh minstrel performs before the court. In his
turn Tristan requests the opportunity to perform. Accompanying himself
upon the harp, he sings a lay from his native land of Brittany:

> He played such a lovely lay for the king and his men that the king and
> all who heard it marveled. All expressed praise at how well he had
> learned and what a well-educated man he was, endowed with mani-
> fold mildness and goodness of heart and many kinds of entertaining
> talents. He displayed splendid virtuosity. Never in their lives had
> they heard the harp played more beautifully.   (*S* Ch. 22)

Mark is so moved by Tristan's playing that he decrees that the youth is to
sleep in his chambers, where, on those evenings when Mark is unable to
find repose, he will harp to calm the king's disordered spirit.[23] Tristan's
skill in the musical arts confirms him as Mark's favorite, a process that his
expertise in the arts of the hunt had begun; for these courtly attributes are
in this perspective complementary.

---

[22] A similar sentiment is expressed in Shakespeare's *Richard II* by the king who muses:
'[Music] have holp madmen to their wits' (V, v, 62). See also Doob 39–40 and Neaman
25–26.

[23] The parallels with the David legend, here and elsewhere in the Tristan legend, are striking.
In addition to the points made by Denomy in this regard, there are similarities between
David's relationship with Saul and Tristan's with Mark, including the persecution by the
king of his former favorite. Tristan, like David, is an adulterer, and, like David, who composed the Psalms, a harper and composer of lays. In the Welsh triad 'Three Mighty Herds-
men', Tristan serves as Mark's swineherd, while David, in his youth, was a shepherd. In
Cerveri de Girona's proverbs (§§997, 1001) and in *La Mort le Roi Artu* §59) David and Tristan
are both said to be men undone by a woman. The depiction of Tristan as harper (in both the
literary texts and the iconography) is manifestly patterned on the David-Orpheus model.
Finally, perhaps inevitably, Tristan is said by one of the redactors of the *Compilation de
Rusticien de Pise* (Löseth §631a), a variant version of *R*, and by the author of *Giron le Courtois*
(§181) to be a descendant of David.

Tristan's skill with voice and instrument also gains him entry into the court of Ireland following his *navigation à l'aventure* (*T S* Ch. 30), and into Mark's court at Lancien (*Tmen*). The description of the effect of Tristan's music on its hearers in *Tmen*, where Tristan and his companions play before Mark's court, echoes similar passages in *T* (*S* Ch. 22) and in *Tros* (479–82):

> Sonent et acordent si bien
> Que nus n'i set a dire rien,
> Tant est dolce la melodie,
> Car n'i a chevalier ne die
> C'ainc mais n'oïrent si dols son.   (3913–17; cf. 4071–72)

At critical junctures in his life, Tristan is able to draw on the special power residing in his music to influence others and to order events to his will.

The association of music and love is an ancient one, and the conceit of music as the food of love was a commonplace in the twelfth century, when Heloise wrote to Abelard:

> Duo autem, fateor, tibi specialiter inerant quibus feminarum quarumlibet animos statim allicere poteras, dictandi videlicet et cantandi gratia. ... atque hinc maxime in amorem tui femine suspirabant.
>   (115)

It is not by chance then that, in enumerating his qualities before Mark and his court in *Fo*, Tristan evokes in successive verses his accomplishments as musician and lover:

> 'Ben sai temprer harpë e rote
> E chanter après à la note.
> Riche raïne sai amer:
> Si n'at sus cel amand mon per.'   (519–22)

As he reminds Iseut in *Fo*, when he arrived for the first time in Ireland, his repute as a harper came to her ears and at her insistence he was brought to her father's court:

> 'Ben tost en oïstes parler
> Ke mult savoie ben harper.
> Je fu sempres a curt mandez,
> Tut issi cum ere navrez.'   (353–56)

Once healed of his wound, he became Iseut's tutor, instructing her in the musical arts:

'Bons lais de harpe vus apris,
Lais bretuns de nostre païs.' (359–60)

In both *T* (*S* Ch. 30) and *Fo* (353–60) the first meeting of Tristan and Iseut occurs when he undertakes to instruct her in the arts of music, a moment depicted by Chertsey Tile 21. Jean Marx has postulated that in the *version courtoise* the love of the couple is awakened before the drinking of the potion, citing to this effect the account of *T* ('Naissance'). When Tristan sends Kaherdin to seek Iseut in England, he charges his friend with a message:

'Dites li qu'ore li suvenge
Des emveisures, des deduiz
Qu'eümes jadis jors e nuiz,
Des granz peines, des tristurs
E des joies e des dusurs
De nostre amur fine e veraie
Quant ele jadis guari ma plaie.' (D 1214–20)

Since the wound in question is that inflicted by Le Morholt, Tristan affirms in this passage that the couple's love dates not from the consumption of the potion but from the period of his first sojourn in Ireland. However, it is more likely that in the lost portions of *T* the suggestion that the couple's love is born in that moment, called up by the power of Tristan's music, is merely implicit and is made explicit by Thomas only in the final episodes of the romance (see below 'The Sexual Wound and its Healing in *T*'). In their urgent need to obtain Iseut's compliance with their designs, the Tristan of D 1214–20 finds it to his advantage to assert that the couple's love dates from his first voyage to Ireland and the Tristan of *Fo* finds it to his to link their love with his instruction of Iseut in the musical arts on the same occasion.

The Tristan poems also develop the poetic conceit that music has the power to relieve the pain of physical suffering and even, on occasion, to effect the cure of a physical ailment.[24] The scene in *T* in which Mark ordains that Tristan will harp for him when the king is unable to find repose has numerous analogues in medieval literature, all deriving ultimately from the biblical episode referred to by Bartholomaeus in which David harps in order to soothe Saul (1 Samuel 14) and all predicated on a belief in the

---

[24] For example, Christine de Pisan writes that Orpheus 'tant melodieusement faisoit sons a la harpe que par les proporcions des accors tant a point ordenez il garissoit de pluseurs maladies et les tristes faisoit estre ioyeux' (*Lavision Christine* 120).

capacity of music to alleviate mental turmoil.[25] In the episode of 'Harpe contre Rote' in *T*, Tristan discovers the Irish baron fruitlessly attempting to comfort Iseut who, is overcome with sorrow at her abduction. The baron addresses Tristan in the following terms: '"Churl", he said, "give us some good entertainment with your fiddle, and I shall give you a cloak and good robe if you can cheer up my lady"' (*S* Ch. 50). Later in *T* Tristan's music, like his hunting, provides him solace in his sorrow during his separation from Iseut (*S* Ch. 69) At the same period, Iseut, left without word of Tristan since his flight from Cornwall, 'fait un lai pitus d'amur' (*T* Sn[1] 782) in order to console herself in Tristan's absence.

The harp figures again in Tristan's first voyage to Ireland, although there is wide divergence among the various versions as to the precise role that it plays.[26] Aitken has argued persuasively that the version of the episode given by *Fo* and seconded by the iconographic tradition of the Chertsey tiles[27] reproduces substantially that of the lost portion of *T* on a number of critical points that the shortened translation of *S* and the expanded version of *G* are incapable of elucidating. Specifically, *Fo* retains the motif of the *navigation à l'aventure*, rejected by Gottfried, in which Tristan sets to sea in a small boat, fully expecting to die before reaching land. As Tristan tells Iseut:

> 'En mer me mis, la voil murir,
> Tant par m'ennuat le languir.

---

[25] For example, in Gerbert de Montreuil's *Continuation de Perceval*, when the hero retires to rest in the castle of Gorneman, a minstrel comes to his chamber:
> A estive de Cornoaille
> Li note uns menestreus sanz faille
> Le lai Gorron molt dolcement;
> Endormis est is nelement.   (6117–20)

See also F. Michel, *Recueil* 3: 95–96, who cites two additional analogues from *Anséis de Carthage*, in one of which a lay telling of Tristan and Iseut is performed:
> Li rois seoit sour .j. lit à argent;
> Pour oublier son desconfortement
> Faisoit chanter le lai de Graelent.

> Li rois s'asist sor .j. palis d'orient;
> Por oblier som desconfortament
> Faisoit soner .j. de Tristam vorament
> Quant se parti de Isole oltre son talent.

[26] In *O* on his voyage to Ireland following his wounding in the combat against Le Morholt, Tristan gives himself as a minstrel, Pro of Iemsetir, and the harp he carries seems to be but an extension of his disguise. In *G* Tristan embarks on a well-provisioned ship in search of Queen Iseut, who alone (Le Morholt has revealed) is capable of healing Tristan's wound. Having arrived off the coast of Ireland, the hero is set adrift in a small boat where the Irish discover him playing his harp and bring him to the court. The account of *E* is elliptical and says only that Tristan asked to be put in a ship with his harp. In *S* Tristan harps after his arrival at the court of Ireland and subsequently teaches Iseut to play the harp.

[27] In Chertsey Tile 20, 'Tristan Afloat to Ireland', Tristan, horribly disfigured by the effects of the poisoned wound, is shown alone in a tiny boat playing his harp. In Tile 21, 'Iseut taught by Tristan to Harp', the couple is shown seated together with a harp.

> Le vent levat, turment out grant,
> E chaça ma nef en Irlant.
> Al païs m'estut ariver
> Ke jo deveie plus duter,
> Kar j'aveie ocis le Morhout.   (341–47)

The lost account of B probably contained the same motif, which is preserved in O:

> Trÿstrand gedaucht do,
> Er wölt varen uff daß mer.
>
> Er en rûchte, daß er also ser
> Númer zû land käm.
> Er batt, daß man in näm
> Und trüg in in ain schiffelin:
> Dar inn wölt er allain sin
> Und uff dem sterben.   (1092–99)

In every extant version of the account of the first voyage to Ireland (S Ch. 30, Fb 397, Fo 351, O 1135–36, G 7359–61, R Curtis 1: §308), Tristan carries with him a harp that serves as a magical guide for the wounded hero, preserving him against the perils of the voyage and seeing him safely to his destination where Iseut awaits him and where he will be healed of his mortal wound. In Fo, the motif of the healing power of music is made explicit; as Tristan reminds Iseut:

> 'Mais jo fu naufrez e chitifs.
> Od ma harpe me delitoie:
> J'en oi confort, ki tant amoie.'   (350–52)[28]

Implicit in the account of Fo is the suggestion that music plays an active role in the twin processes of healing Tristan's wound and of conjoining the future lovers. The healing process initiated by Tristan's music will be completed by Iseut's double, her mother the queen, when that music brings Iseut together with Tristan, 'ki tant amoi[t]'. The medicinal herbs with which the queen treats Tristan's wound prefigure the potion, also prepared by the queen, that will complete the process of conjoining the lovers.

---

[28] While Hoepffner and Payen both read, 'Je n'oi confort', the reading 'J'en oi confort', is required by the sense of the previous line. It is not clear whether the motif of the curative power of music in this scene is the invention of the Fo poet or of his source, Thomas. In O Tristrant carries his harp with him (1135–36), but no mention is made of its healing qualities.

One of the ironic inversions of values in the madness episodes is the representation of Tristan the musician as madman. Although Bartholmaeus ascribes to music the power to soothe the fury of the madman, who 'schal be gladed weþ instrumentis of musik and somdel be occupied' (Lib. 7, Cap. 6), Tristan is unable to heal himself with his music, which in these poems is only a grotesque pantomime,[29] and must seek another remedy, that of Iseut's love. However, the irony is compounded, for it is by adopting certain attributes of the minstrel that Tristan is finally enabled to regain Iseut's companionship and healing love (see below, 'Tristan the Minstrel').

Tristan the musician is also an artist who transforms the stuff of reality for his own ends. In *Ch* Tristan puts into verse and music the circumstances of his clandestine meeting with Iseut:

> Por la joie qu'il ot eüe
> De s'amie qu'il ot veüe,
> E pur ceo k'il aveit escrit
> Si cum la reïne l'ot dit,
> Pur les paroles remembrer,
> Tristram, ki bien saveit harper,
> En aveit fait un nuvel lai.   (107–13)

In *Tmen* Tristan, who by virtue of his musical talent has been taken into Mark's service, performs before Iseut the lay of the 'Chèvrefeuille', allowing her to recognize him beneath his minstrel's disguise:

> En sa main a pris en flagueil,
> Molt dolcement en flajola,
> Et par dedens le flaguel a
> Noté le lai de Chievrefueil,
> Et puis a mis jus le flagueil. ...
> Ensi est Yseus percheüe
> Par le lai que Tristrans nota.   (4066–70, 4094–95)

In the *Folies* it is in retelling the myth whose hero he is that Tristan seeks, in a strategy that fails, to persuade Iseut of his true identity (Haidu, 'Text'). Only by relinquishing the past and inventing the present, by divorcing himself from his myth, does Tristan succeed in regaining his lady.[30]

---

[29] In *Fo* after announcing himself as a minstrel and referring to his staff (525–26), it is probable that Tristan pretends to play upon the latter as upon a harp.
[30] In *R* Tristan is said to have composed four lays: 'le lai *de Plor*, quand il s'embarqua pour chercher un remède à la blessure que lui avait faite le Morhout, le lai du *Boivre amoureux* et le lai du *Deduit d'amour*, fait pendant son séjour avec Iseut dans le Morois ... et *le Lai mortel*',

In *The Consolation of Philosophy* Boethius writes of Orpheus and Eurydice: 'Quis legem det amantibus? / Maior lex amor est sibi' (Lib. 3, M. xii, 47–48), a sentiment that might aptly serve as an epigraph to the entire Tristan legend. The representation of Tristan throughout the poems exhibits certain analogies with the Orpheus myth in its classical form and in its medieval avatars, although the Christian allegorization of the myth in the later Middle Ages, which was posterior to the redaction of the Tristan poems, has left no traces. The existence of a twelfth-century French lay of Orpheus is scarcely in doubt, given the numerous allusions to it (Vàrvaro, 'Utilizzazione' 1067; *Sir Orfeo* xxxi–iii) and the widespread familiarity with the classical versions of the legend (Frappier, 'Orphée' 291–94, Friedman 164). As the Tristan and Orpheus cycles evolve throughout the Middle Ages, their development runs parallel. While the dissimilarities between the two cycles are legion, the similarities, though fewer in number and restricted to specific portions of the Tristan narrative, are striking. Due most frequently to the influence of fixed literary conventions in the ethos that they jointly inhabit and, more rarely, to direct, reciprocal influence, these similarities testify to a common filiation of influence in the two legends.[31]

Friedman has noted the tendency in the Middle Ages for the literary and iconographic representations of Orpheus and the biblical David to converge in a single set of attributes (147–55).[32] Each is of noble or divine descent. David with his harping soothes the mad Saul as Orpheus with his lyre charms the beasts of the woodland and Hades, King of Tartarus. Each is pre-eminent as a musician, playing a stringed instrument and composing songs, and the music of each possesses medicinal and tranquilizing powers. Tristan, who shares with David and Orpheus *topoi* that do not originate with a single literary or mythological figure but that attach in turn to many such figures, participates in this process of conflation.[33] With the biblical David and the classical Orpheus, the medieval Tristan completes a trinity of marvelous musicians. Each is a musician upon a stringed instrument and a maker of songs (psalms, poems, or lays) who exercises to a high degree the power vested in music and poetry to change the hearts of

---

composed on the occasion of his first access of madness (Löseth §80). These lays will serve not only to console Tristan but, like the figures in the *salle aux images*, to substitute artistic creation for reality, to erect a world of fantasy between himself and the real (Barteau 125–26; Ferrante, 'Artist Figure' 27).

[31] In a French *ars poeticae* of the XVth Century, for example, Orpheus is portrayed composing for the dead Eurydice a 'lay mortel que toute sa vie chanta pour s'amie' (Langlois, *Recueil* 39). Cf. Tristan's *lai mortel*, Fotitch 19–30.

[32] Examples of convergence in the iconographical conventions of representing each figure may be found in Friedman, plates 19–22.

[33] Orpheus and Tristan are also represented in a strikingly similar manner in the iconography. The miniature 'Orpheus and Eurydice Courting' from Lydgate's *Fall of Princes* (MS. B.M. Harley 1766, fo. 76r [c.1450], Friedman plate 24) is remarkably like Chertsey tile 21 that depicts 'Iseut taught by Tristan to harp'.

its hearers. However, because the legend of Tristan and, until the later Middle Ages, that of Orpheus are largely independent of Christianizing influences, the two heros share fundamental traits not found in the figure of David. Specifically, each derives the power that resides in his music from an affinity with the forces of nature, and each plays out a story of extraordinary and ultimately tragic love.

The classical Orpheus is a musician on the lyre and a poet as Tristan is a player of the harp and a composer of lays. Orpheus' voyage with the Argonauts in search of the golden fleece, for which he is chosen because of his skill with the lyre, recalls both Tristan's first voyage to Ireland, whence he sails in a rudderless boat bearing with him only his harp, and his second voyage, with a fully equipped ship and crew, in search of the golden-haired Iseut. The description of Tristan's grief at his separation from Iseut in the opening verses of *Fo* and *Fb* recalls the scene in Ovid's *Metamorphoses* in which Orpheus, grief-stricken at the loss of Eurydice, sits on the bank of a river in rags for seven days (Lib. X, 73–74). In search of Eurydice who had died from the bite of a serpent, Orpheus journeyed to the Underworld where he charmed Hades with his song, won his lady and then, through his own error, lost her again.[34] This central episode of the Orpheus legend has left its imprint on two specific episodes of the Tristan poems and offers a more general analogy with all of the return episodes. The episode of the Irish harper in *T*, in which, with the aid of his music, Tristan rescues Iseut from her abductor, is a clear echo of Orpheus' liberation of Eurydice from Tartarus,[35] while *Tros* contains a more detailed reminiscence of the same scene. Iseut is straitly guarded in a prison-like castle by the jealous Mark, who is explicitly identified with the forces of winter and death. His music metamorphosed to birdsong, Tristan sings so sweetly that her vigilant guards fall into a sound sleep[36] and the jealous Mark permits her to leave the castle.[37] In a more general sense, all of the return episodes in which Tristan trysts with Iseut constitute metaphorical journeys to the Underworld of Mark's kingdom where Iseut is imprisoned and

[34] There is an analogue of this episode in the twelfth-century *De Nugis Curialium* of Walter Map (Dist. iv, Cap. viii).

[35] Bédier regards as unfounded the assertion that the episode is imitated from a version of the Orpheus legend (*Thomas* 1: 168, n. 1), a conclusion that Cluzel contests ('La reine Iseut'). Newstead ('Harp' 469) and Lyle likewise assert the influence of a lost Breton lay of Orpheus on the episode of the Irish harper in *T* and on the Middle English *Sir Orfeo*.

[36] Cf. the commentary of one Adam of Fulda, writing in the thirteenth century: 'Orpheum per suam musicam mutasse corda principum de tristitia in lætitiam; nam excitat dormientes, dormitare facit vigilantes & sanat melancholiam' (3: 334).

[37] On three other occasions Tristan rescues Iseut from a would-be abductor or from the threat of death. He saves her from an abhorrent marriage to the treacherous *sénéchal* in *T* (*S* Ch. 41–45), from Yvain and his band of lepers in *B*, and from sentence of death in the episode of Iseut's *escondit* in *T* and *B*.

where Tristan comes on peril of death.[38] Each tryst is a small rescue from the loveless tyranny of Mark's dominion, and each, like Orpheus' rescue of Eurydice, is temporary, destined to ultimate failure.[39]

When Orpheus arrives at the gates of Tartarus, he charms the ferocious Cerberus with his music, a scene that may have furnished the germ of the recognition scene in *Fo* in which Tristan is welcomed by the savage Husdent, who, since his master's departure '... ert fel e de puite aire / E mordeit e saveit mal faire' (921–22). Two accounts of Orpheus' death in classical mythology (Graves 1: 112–3) present analogies with that of Tristan's death. The first recounts that Venus and Proserpine contended for possession of Adonis and asked Jove to decide who should have the youth. Jove appointed Orpheus' mother Calliope as judge, and she ruled that each goddess should possess Adonis for half of the year (a detail echoed in the *Ystori Trystan*, where Arthur makes the same provisions for Mark and Tristan). Angered at this decision, Venus stirred up the Thracian women to seek Orpheus' love, and in their jealousy they tore the poet limb from limb. In another account, Orpheus, who mourned Eurydice, spurned the Thracian women who loved him; and for this reason they killed him. In each, Orpheus is the victim of feminine jealousy and vengeance, like Tristan who dies at the hand of the jealous Iseut aux Blanches Mains. Likewise, a miracle is associated with the death of each. Following Orpheus' dismemberment, his head and lyre are thrown into the sea where they sing and play, signifying the continuity of Orpheus' love for Eurydice, a detail parallelled by the miracle of the intertwining plants in *T*, which signifies the continuity of the love of Tristan and Iseut.

Tristan's music, like Orpheus', draws its potency from the natural forces of the woodland and endows him with an enchanter's power over the hearts of men and women, over the denizens of the wild, and over certain natural phenomena.[40] Indeed, it gives Tristan, hunter, knight, and

[38] In *Sir Orfeo* Orfeo appears before the King of the Fairies in the disguise of a minstrel, as Tristan does before Mark in *Tmen* (and, implicitly, in *Fb* and *Fo*). Orfeo's playing so pleases the king that he grants Orfeo the reward of his choice, and Orfeo naturally chooses Heurodis as the Irish harper chooses Iseut in *T* (*S* Ch. 49). Indeed, at the reluctance of the King of the Fairies to grant his wish, Orfeo makes use of the same argument as the Irish harper before Mark, each contending that the king may not, in law, forswear himself.

[39] The following paradigm describes not only Orpheus' descent into Tartarus and Orfeo's trip to the Land of the Fairies but the return episodes of *Tmen*, *Fb*, and *Fo*. *Tros*, *Ch*, and *T* (Tristan the leper, D 492–736) omit #3.

1. Loss of lady.
2. Perilous journey and menace of death.
3. Confrontation with lady's captor and
4. Winning of lady.
5. Loss of lady.

[40] Campbell has argued eloquently for the mythic identity of the harper in the Tristan legend, the Orpheus legend, and Celtic mythology:

In the context of the Tristan legend, the symbolic forms and motifs through which the intimation is communicated of a moving destiny and alien power ... were derived – as

lover, access to the *élan vital* that resides in the natural world – in the wilderness, the forest, and the garden. *Tros* articulates most clearly the relationship between Tristan's music and the natural powers in which he clothes himself. In the *Donnei des amanz* the topos that associates love and music lies at the heart of the episode of *Tros*.[41] In the frame story an amorous poet walks early abroad in the countryside 'al tans d'esté, après Pascur' (1). The song of the nightingale evokes the erotic associations of spring when all the creatures of God's creation, save the monstrous *vilain* and the *gelus*, feel the pull of nature in their bloodstream. He comes to a garden where, his thoughts set in motion by the songs of the birds, he meditates on the place of music and love in the divine scheme:

> Tant cum j'oieie lur estorie,
> Si m'est venu [lors] en memorie,
> En memorie e en membrance,
> Cum par est grant la Deu pussance,
> Ki doune joie e enveisures
> Par si diverses creatures:
> D'omes, de bestes, de oiseaus
> Trove l'en pers e paringals. (17–24)

The birdsong that resounds in this garden of love, a trope for the poet's own amorous song, is an echo of:

> ... la celeste armonie
> [Des] angeles de paraïs
> Ki devant Deu chantent tut diz. (34–36)

we have seen – from the pagan Celtic lore of Ireland, Cornwall, and Wales. Inherent in them, consequently, was the old, generally pagan message of the immanent divinity of all things, and of the manifestation of this hidden Being of beings particularly in certain heroic individuals, who thus stand as epiphanies of that 'manifest-hidden' that moves and lives within us all and is the secret of the harmony of nature.... Such a figure was Orpheus with his lyre. The Celtic myths and legends are full of tales of the singers and harpers of the fairy hills whose music has the power to enchant and to move the world: to make men weep, to make men sleep, and to make men laugh. They appear mysteriously from the Land of Eternal Youth, the Land within the Fairy Hills, the Land below Waves; and though taken to be human beings ... they are not actually so, but open out behind, so to say, toward the universe. (*Creative Mythology* 200)

[41] The episode of *Tros* is an exemplary tale found in a twelfth-century didactic work, the *Donnei des amanz*. While the *Donnei* is incomplete, the episode of *Tros*, which comprises lines 453–662, is complete. The *Donnei* presents a conversation in the form of a debate between two lovers whom, in the fiction of the text, the poet overhears. The young knight or clerk (105–07) pleads for less rigor on the part of his lady, citing the examples of celebrated ladies who took great risks in order to satisfy their lovers. He then tells the story of 'Tristan rossignol' to prove by Iseut's example that the lady who loves 'de vere amor' (290) is prepared to risk greatly for her lover and to persuade his lady to do likewise.

In the *Donnei des amanz*, love is a manifestation of the *élan vital* of nature, and in *Tros* Tristan's music is the means to command that power. He imitates the song of the nightingale in order to summon Iseut from Mark's bedchamber to the garden where he awaits her, liberating her from the castle of death of the *gelus*, Mark, as the springtime liberates the running waters (Mod.Fr. *eaux vives*) from the icy thrall of the winter's *gelee*. This motif of death and rebirth echoes the metamorphosis of the lovers of *T* into intertwining trees (*S* Ch. 101), a metamorphosis that reveals their kinship with the natural world and that permits the continuation of their love in a domain secure from the interference of Mark and the constraints of the social Order.

Tristan the Hunter and Woodsman

The medieval Tristan corpus contains numerous references to the hero's skill in the arts of the hunt (Remigereau; Saly; Brault, 'Rituel'). Eilhart observes of Tristrant:

> Fúr wăr mir man sagt
> Und main, er wer der erst man,
> Der ie anglen began.
> Ouch hort ich sagen mer,
> Daß er der erst wer,
> Der daß erdächte,
> Daß bracken brächte
> Zŭ recht wildeß gefert. (4538–45)

Chrétien declares of Cligès:

> Si sot plus d'escremie et d'arc
> Que Tristanz li niés le roi Marc,
> Et plus d'oisiax, et plus de chiens. (2749–51)

Malory writes of Tristram:

> ... as he growed in myght and strength, he laboured in huntynge and in hawkynge – never jantylman more that ever we herde rede of. And as the booke seyth, he began good mesures of blowynge of beestes of venery and beestes of chaace and all maner of vermaynes, and all the tearmys we have yet of hawkynge and huntynge. And therefore the book of venery, of hawkynge and huntynge is called the booke of sir Trystrams. (1:375)

The French poems contain similar assertions. In *B*, Dinas reminds Mark, who has just learned of Tristan's escape from the chapel, of his nephew's ability to elude those who seek to recapture him:

> 'Les plains, les bois, les pas, les guez
> Set forment bien, et molt est fiers.' (1102–03)

Gerbert de Montreuil asserts that Tristan's knowledge of the woodland lies beyond that of ordinary, civilized mortals, be they courtiers or countrymen:

> Molt fu, ce sachiez vous, Tristrans
> De toz deduis entremetans. ...
> Il set de riviere et de bois
> Plus que vilains ne que cortois. (*Tmen* 3703–04, 3707–08)

The third of Tristan's overt identities is, then, a double one: hunter and woodsman. These two states represent the social and the asocial manifestations of the same competence in the natural world. On one hand, the skills of the hunt, the sport of nobility, are closely allied to those of war; and it is natural that Tristan the knight should excel as hunter. On the other, the art of the hunt is linked metaphorically with the art of love, and Tristan the hunter turns his skills to the ends of Tristan the lover. Finally, Tristan's identity as woodsman forms the basis for his 'disguise' as nightingale in *Tros* and for his characterization as a wild man in *Fo*.

The association of Tristan with the woodlands is constant in the Tristan poems. The hero conceals himself in a forest in *Ch* (29–30), in *B* (3010–27, 4267–485), and in *T* (Str[1] 1–68) in order to effect a meeting with Iseut, and, for the same purpose, in a garden (a doublet of the forest) in *Tros*. The *salle aux images* episode in *T*, a negative doublet of the episode of the life in the Morois, presents another forest sojourn in which Tristan dwells in a cave in the depths of a wood with (a facsimile of) his beloved. In *R*, whose author(s) apparently wished to reinforce this association, Tristan is born in a wood (Curtis 1: §§228–29). The motif of Tristan's skill as hunter is reflected in two key scenes in the Tristan poems. In *T*, abandoned on the uninhabited coast of Cornwall by his abductors, Tristan stumbles upon Mark's huntsmen in pursuit of a stag. Present at the kill, he instructs the hunters in the proper manner of breaking the stag according to the customs of his own country of Ermenie (*S* Ch. 21). So original are Tristan's instructions and so much does he impress his hearers by his courtliness that he is brought before King Mark. Soon after he is made a member of the king's household where his skill at harping will complete his elevation to the status of the king's favorite (*S* Ch. 22). The scene of the breaking of the stag in *T* foreshadows and prepares the capital episode of the life in the forest (given by both *T* and *B* and probably belonging to a very early version of the Tristan matter), where the lovers retreat to live on the fruit of Tristan's skill as a hunter. The hunting scenes in *B* are explicit and realistic (e.g., 1285–89), and Beroul also describes in detail Tristan's training of Husdent to hunt silently (1527–636). After restoring Iseut to Mark, Tristan returns to the Morois where he is still dwelling with the forester Orri when the *B* fragment breaks off.

By its very nature, the figure of the hunter allows more scope for conceptual play than do those of the musician or the knight; for the hunter is always in danger of becoming the hunted.[42] In a larger perspective, the Tristan poems may be understood as the narrative of a hunt whose quarry is Tristan. The hero is marked as victim from the first hour of his life, and his story is the working out of a destiny in which, though he sometimes appears to be behind the hounds, ultimately, he is their quarry. This metaphor is made explicit in *R*, where Tristan, punning on *la mors* and *l'amors*, sings:

> 'J'ai ja furnie mainte cache, (i.e. chasse)
> Or sui cachies, *la mors* me cache.'   (Fotitch 1, xxvi, 1–2).[43]

There is a deep disparity between the descriptions of the forest sojourn in *B* and *T*. Thomas (*S* Ch. 64) and the *Fo* poet present the forest sojourn as an unalloyedly tranquil idyll in a sylvan *locus amoenus* safe from intrusion.[44] While Beroul stresses the realistic details of survival in an inhospitable environment, the lovers of *T* pay little heed to practical questions of food and shelter:

> Tristram and Ísönd ... went out into the wide wilderness. They gave little thought to who would give them food and drink, for they felt certain that God would provide them with nourishment wherever they were. ... Of all that the world had to offer they desired no more than what they now had, for they now had that which pleased their hearts if they might thus always be together without blame and enjoy their love in bliss.   (*S* Ch. 64)

When the lovers of *T* do hunt, this activity is depicted not as a necessity for survival but as a gentle recreation with erotic overtones:

---

[42] See also Walter's different and highly original treatment of this theme ('Orion' 442–43).

[43] Palamède expresses a similar sentiment: 'Amours m'a pris, amours me lache, / Conme son serf me loie et lache' (Fotitch 9, iii, 1–2).

[44] It may be, as has been recently suggested, that the term *forest* in *Fo* (861) designates not a deep wood but a moor or heath (Legge, 'Problème' 375).

But when the weather was pleasant, they went to the spring to enjoy
themselves and to those places in the forest that were best for strolling because they were level and beautiful, or else they hunted game
for food, for Tristram had his favorite dog with him. First of all he
trained the dog to catch roe deer, and then he hunted as many of them
as he wished. This afforded them joy and entertainment, for they had
their pleasure and solace night and day.   (S Ch. 64)

In contrast, the description in *B* of the lovers' forest sojourn is ambiguous. Although it contains early, fleeting echos of the pastoral idyll of *T*, in
general it follows the poet's affirmation that, in spite of their love, the
lovers 'aspre vie meinent et dure' (1364). Beroul, who emphasizes the
concrete details of their arduous existence, stresses not only the vital
necessity of hunting but the mediocrity of the diet thus provided:

> Li pain lor faut, ce est grant deus.
> De cers, de biches, de chevreus
> Ocist asez par le boscage.   (1425–27)

> Molt sont el bois del pain destroit,
> De char vivent, el ne mengüent.
> Que püent il, se color müent?   (1644–46)

The first night that the lovers pass in the forest, however, is described in
terms that stress their joy and sense of security:

> Tristran s'en voit a la roïne;
> Lasent le plain, et la gaudine
> S'en vet Tristran et Governal.
> Yseut s'esjot, or ne sent mal.
> En la forest de Morrois sont,
> La nuit jurent desor un mont;
> Or est Tristran si a seür
> Con s'il fust en chastel o mur.   (1271–78)

Thereafter, their sense of security quickly dissipates, and to the physical
hardships of their sojourn in the Morois is added a constant anxiety.
Shortly after their arrival in the forest, they learn from Ogrin that Mark has
declared Tristan an outlaw and offered a reward for his capture (1371–76).
In *B*, unlike *Fo* and *T*, the lovers never remain in the same location for more
than a single night but are constantly on the move to avoid capture
(1360–61, 1430, 1639–40). Their sense of insecurity is increased by the
escape of Husdent (1431–605), for they erroneously believe that Mark has
set the hound on their scent in order to hunt them down. Their discovery
by Mark (1801–2132) terrifies them, for they misunderstand the meaning

of the king's actions and believe that he intends to return with reinforcements to capture them.

At the same time, the lovers of B are portrayed as the lords of the forest, whose presence there strikes fear into the hearts of Mark's courtiers and retainers. In this sense, the lovers are equated metaphorically with dangerous wild beasts who threaten all who trespass upon their domain. The fear that they inspire in Mark's courtiers and that is alluded to time and again (1524–26, 1661–67, 1712–28, 1748–50, 1845–48, 1894) reaches its apogee following Governal's killing of one of the three felonious barons. Completely given over to the passion of the hunt, the baron, who has outdistanced his companions, comes too near the boundaries of the Morois, where he is ambushed by Governal. The latter hacks his unfortunate victim to pieces, cuts off his head, ties it to a forked stick – a sinister echo of Tristan's instructions to Mark's huntsmen for the preparation of the *fourchiée* in *T* – and brings it before his master. When Governal arrives at the shelter, Tristan is asleep; and the first object that he sees upon awakening is the contorted, leering face of his archenemy swaying gently before his own. While his fright lasts only a moment, it emblematizes the fear that continually haunts the fugitives.

Ironically, at the very moment when Tristan feels the situation of the fugitives to be most hazardous and experiences a profound and anguished sense of their continuing danger (a fear not unjustified, as their discovery by the forester will prove), the entire countryside is filled with terror as a result of Governal's action:

> Poor ont tuit par la contree;
> La forest est si esfreee
> Que nus n'i ose ester dedenz.　　　　　　　　　　　(1747–49)

The irony of the feared and fearful fugitives is developed in the episode of Husdent and in that the discovery of the lovers. In each case, the lovers, who fail to understand the power of the fear that they inspire, are themselves in mortal dread of pursuit by the king's forces. Beroul plays on the twin themes of the hunter hunted (the episodes of Husdent and the discovery of the lovers) and that of the hunted hunting (the episode of the killing of the baron). The fact that in each case the danger is past before the lovers become aware of its presence and take fright compounds the irony. In the Husdent episode, the pursuing courtiers have already turned back, afraid to venture further into the forest, when Husdent rejoins the lovers. In the episode of the killing of the baron, his enemy is already dead when Tristan awakes to find the grotesque face dangling before him like a symbol of his own mortality. In the discovery episode, Mark has already pardoned and spared the sleeping lovers when, upon awaking, they realize their discovery and take flight.

Georges Duby's sensitive commentary on marriage, abduction, and relations of power between the *juventus* and the established class of knights in eleventh and twelfth-century France offers another perspective for understanding Tristan the hunter:

> [In the twelfth century] one of two models [for taking a wife] was available to male members of the aristocracy, according to whether they were 'old' or 'young', as long as one understands that the distinction then referred *not* to two different age groups but to the impact on social behavior of two different sets of values, one prizing order and good behavior and the other boldness and energy.... In the high society of Europe in the eleventh century ... the most important split was probably that between the younger and the older males, and the code of conduct followed by the 'younger generation' may be supposed to have grown out of this conflict. The code required them to seize women by violence in the teeth of husbands and matchmaking families. There is an obvious parallel here with hunting.
>
> (*Knight* 39–40)

This practice, a legacy of the Carolingian period, is accurately reflected in the Tristan poems of the twelfth and early thirteenth centuries. Tristan the hunter is a *juvenis*, a member of the class of unestablished or dispossessed knights who were, for that reason, unfitted for marriage and constrained to take their women in violation of established marital practices (Duby, '"Jeunes"' 842–43).[50] Ironically, Tristan, who is the guarantor of Mark's power and the maker of his uncle's marriage, is unable, save by stealth and finally by abduction, to secure a mate for himself.

Following the diminution of the effects of the potion and the restitution of Iseut to Mark in *B*, Tristan continues to tryst with Iseut, proof that their love is no longer 'un amour contraint et subi, mais un amour volontaire et construit' (Poirion 201). Silhouetted against the night sky, the nocturnal hunter is observed stealthily entering the queen's chambers, his bow in one hand, two arrows in the other. (4288–93). The hunt as a metaphor for the amorous pursuit had become a literary commonplace by the later Middle Ages, and in its evocation Iseut and her lover, Tristan the hunter, were not forgotten.[45] In his *Paradis d'amour*, Jean Froissart includes the

---

[50] See in this regard the excursus in the *Donnei des amanz* (173–208) on the 'gevene gent' whose youthful joy will come to an end when they are obliged 'a garder e a tenir terre' (197).

[45] The most frequent formulation of the metaphor, in which an ardent lover pursues a coy, chaste maiden, does not, for the most part, fit the circumstances of the Tristan poems, where Tristan and Iseut are lovers almost from the beginning and where, therefore, with the exception described below, the metaphor is rendered in other terms.

couple among those who follow the hunt of the god of love (*Méliador* 1:
L–LI). In the early evolution of the Tristan matter, it is Gottfried who
exploits most fully the possibilities of this metaphor. His version of the
forest scene is a masterpiece of allegorical symbolism that owes little but
its narrative premises to his predecessors (Thiébaux 128–43; Anson
594–607; Ferrante, *Conflict* 129–30). Yet certain of the associations that
Gottfried develops in his poem are implicit in the French poems, notably
in *T*, Gottfried's immediate source, where they lie just below the surface of
the work.

A linguistic anomaly of Old French, the ambiguity of the terms *deduit*
and *(se) deduire*, reinforces the metaphoric equation of the hunt and the
amorous pursuit in the Tristan poems. Within the general sense of 'diver-
tissement', 'plaisir' (*T* D 619) and '(se) divertir', '(s') amuser' (*T* D 707, 887),
the terms conveyed two more specific meanings: on one hand, 'divertisse-
ment amoureux' (*B* 4269; *T* Sn[1] 19, T[1] 138; *Tros* 653), and 'faire l'amour' (*B*
4301, *T* D 723); on the other, 'les plaisirs de la chasse' (*B* 1660) and 'chasser',
'aller à la chasse' (*Fo* 535).[46] Following the fool's appearance before the
court in the *Folies*, the king orders his servants to prepare his horse and
departs for the hunt (*Fb* 252–55, *Fo* 533–36), leaving Tristan alone to prose-
cute his liaison with Iseut. Similarly, in *B* the spy who denounces the
lovers' to the three barons says:

> 'Tristran set molt de Malpertis;
> Qant li rois vait a ses *deduis*,
> En la chanbre vet congié prendre.'   (4285–87)[47]

Fb concludes with Brengvein's wish, echoed by the lovers, that Mark find
such a plenty of game at the hunt that he not return for eight days (569–70).
In these three texts the ambiguity of *deduit* makes explicit the irony of Mark
at his pleasure and Tristan at his.

While the conceit of the ardent lover as huntsman pursuing his quarry
does not, in general, fit the circumstances of the Tristan poems, the notable
exception is to be found in the return episodes, where Tristan must once
again win an often resisting Iseut, either by overcoming obstacles to their
meeting (*T* D 492–73), by performing feats of arms (*T* D 785–834), by per-

[46] The hunting manual of Henri de Ferrières, written between 1354 and 1377, is entitled *Le
Livre des Deduis du Roi Modus et de la Royne Ratio*. MS. B.N.fr. 103 contains a passage that, in
recounting the lovers' sojourn in the Morois, simultaneously incorporates both senses of *se
deduire*: 'Ainsi se deduit Tristan en la cache et en la compagnie d'Yseult, et use sa vie en telle
maniere qu'il ne lui souvint mais de nulli' (Bédier, *Thomas* 2: 362). In the passage from *S*
quoted above, in which Robert asserts that the lovers 'had their pleasure and solace night and
day' (Ch. 64), the original pun on *deduit* is still faintly perceptible across the double translation.
[47] Payen understands *prendre congié* as an ironically euphemistic equivalent of 'faire
l'amour' (*Les Tristan en vers* 135 and n. 163, p. 341).

suading Iseut of his true identity (*Fb, Fo, Tmen*), or by luring her from her refuge (*Tros*). Indeed, the whole of N⁴, that portion of the romance that follows Tristan's exile from Cornwall, may be seen as a circular hunt in which Tristan, outlawed and pursued by the king (*Fb* 1–8; *Fo* 161–64), returns by stealth time and again to poach on the monarch's preserves.

The most systematic exploitation in the Tristan poems of the semantic ambiguity of *deduit* occurs in *Fo*, which incorporates a series of references to the hunt that serves as an extended metaphor for the lovers' attempts to be reconciled in love. The *chasse à l'envers* (487–512) is at once a veiled allusion to the sojourn in the forest and a play on the metaphorical equation of hunting and love:

> Li fols li dit: 'Reis, quant me plest
> Chacer en bois u en forest,
> Od mes leures prendrai mes grues
> Ki volent la sus par ses nues;
> Od mes limers les cingnes preng,
> Owes blanches, bises, de reng.
> Quant vois od mun pel berser hors,
> Mainz prend jo plunjuns e butors.' (489–96)

The flight of fancy in which Tristan successively evokes his skill at the hunt, at arms (513–16), and in music (519–20) concludes with his declaration that: '"Riche raïne sai amer: / Si n'at sus cel amand mon per"' (521–22), a scarcely veiled reminder that while Mark hunts *à l'endroit* in the forests and the marshes, so does Tristan *à l'envers* in Iseut's bedchamber.[48] There is another dimension to the hunting metaphor in *Fo*. Husdent, who in *B* hunted down the lovers in the Morois, causing them moments of anxiety as keen as any that they knew during the forest sojourn, is again allowed to 'hunt down' Tristan in Iseut's presence. Husdent's recognition of his master leads Iseut towards her own recognition of the fool. This scene constitutes a double *chasse à l'envers*, for Tristan the hunter is hunted down by Husdent, allowing him to obtain his quarry, Iseut.

Another literary conceit concerning the hunt is integrated into the depiction of Tristan the hunter: the hunt is a diversion that assuages the suffering occasioned by unhappy or unrequited love. This remedy for love melancholy is recommended in Xenophon's *Cynegeticus* and again in Ovid's *Remedia Amoris*, whence it passes into the medieval consciousness (Thiébaux 98). Thus in *T*, both in the earlier and in the later periods of his

---

[48] It may be that there is implicit in this motif an irreverent play on a homelectic commonplace of the medieval hunting manuals that held that the hunt was an antidote to idleness (Thiébaux 77–78), a notion alluded to at *Fo* 537–38.

exile from Mark's court and separation from Iseut, Tristan hunts avidly.
Shortly after Tristan's arrival in Brittany at the court of Kaherdin, Thomas
remarks:

> Tristram's situation was a grievous one. And yet he tried to appear
> cheerful and happy, and never to let people notice that something
> caused him hurt and harm. He concealed his grief by seeking distrac-
> tion on hunting expeditions with the duke and his most powerful
> friends.   (S Ch. 73)

Nor is it surprising, then, to read in R that Mark himself, the cuckolded,
dishonored husband, is also an avid hunter 'qi a celui tens se delitoit plus
en chace qe nul home del monde' (Löseth §168).[49] It is this depiction of
Mark as a melancholic cuckold that explains his sudden departure for the
hunt in both Fb and Fo, leaving the field to Tristan, who loses no time in
pursuing his own quarry. Beneath his boisterous good humour during the
audience with the disguised Tristan, Mark, who appears to have failed to
measure the import of the fool's allusions, has in reality been touched by
them and turns to the hunt to assuage his old sorrow, newly awakened by
the fool's pointed allusions.

Another significance attaches to the hunt in the Tristan poems. A hunting
expedition frequently serves as the preliminary to another adventure, as
though the regions of the hunt, the forests and marshes, constituted a
mythical zone of transition, a border march between the real and the
marvelous, the natural and the supernatural.[51] The medieval forest, 'l'horizon inquiétant du monde médiéval', in Jacques Le Goff's felicitous phrase,

---

[49] Similarly in G, where the poet writes:
>   Under diu do diz geschach,
>   So hæte ie michel ungemach
>   Der trurige Marke:
>   Er trurete starke
>   Umbe sin ere und umb sin wip.
>   Im begunde muot unde lip
>   Von tage ze tage swæren,
>   Ere unde guot unmæren.
>   Sus gereit er in den selben tagen
>   In disen selben walt jagen
>   Und me durch sine triure
>   Dan durch kein aventiure.   (17275–86)
Mark's love of the hunt is also alluded to in Jean Renart's Guillaume de Dole 170–72.
[51] 'Metaphorically and symbolically, therefore, the chase becomes an imperative Journey by
which a mortal is transported to a condition charged with experience: a preternatural region
where he may be tested or placed under an enchantment; a transcendent universe; or the
menacing reaches of the self. The act of the chase may reflect not only the compulsion arising
from within his own nature to undergo change, but also an external force that imposes this
necessity on him: that is, the god.'   (Thiébaux 57)

is the domain of the mysterious and the fearsome, the seat of the dark forces of nature; and the hunter who ventures into those regions exposes himself to their powers. The account of Tristan's conquest of Moldagog's land in *T* begins with a hunt that leads Tristan to pass beyond the boundaries prescribed for ordinary mortals (*S* Ch. 75). The episode of the last wound in *T*, in which Tristan must (through his proxy, Kaherdin) again seek Iseut beyond the sea, begins with a hunt over the Blanche Lande, a domain lying beside the sea. Tristan and Kaherdin:

> Un jur erent alé chacer
> Tant qu'il furent al repeirer,
> Avant furent lur compaingnun:
> Nen i aveit se eus deus nun.
> La Blanche Lande traverserunt,
> Sur destre vers la mer garderent:
> Veient venir un chevaler
> Les walos sur un vair destrer. (D 901–08)

It is not difficult to discern in the name 'la Blanche Lande' and in the figure of the rider who seems to emerge from the sea, a symbol of Tristan's impending death, for the *lande*, like the forest and the sea, is an antechamber to the Other World.[52]

On three occasions in the Tristan poems, the pursuit of a stag, a familiar literary device whose purpose is to lead the unheeding hunter from the realm of the familiar to a sudden, unexpected discovery that has no connection with the chase itself (Thiébaux 56), introduces a major peripeteia in the narrative. In *T*, the young Tristan, present at the death of a hunted stag in Cornwall, is, as a result of this chance encounter, enabled to enter the court of Mark. In *T* and *B*, the critical moment at which the lovers' decision to return from the forest is determined occurs under widely differing circumstances. While in *T* the discovery by the king of the lovers in circumstances that would seem to absolve them of any wrongdoing permits their return to the court, in *B* their return is determined by the diminution of the force of the potion. Yet, in each case, the episode begins with a huntsman following a stag.[53] In *T*, Mark's chief huntsman is led to the lovers' grotto by his quarry. In *B*, Tristan is in pursuit of a wounded stag when the fateful hour revolves:

---

[52] The name *la Blanche Lande* also occurs in *B* (2653, 3268, 3298, 4009, 4085) where it designates the area separating the Morois from the Croix Rouge. The Gué du Mal Pas lies on its edge and Iseut's *escondit* takes place there.

[53] Similarly in *R*, Mark, following a stag in the Morois, happens upon the mad Tristan (Löseth §104).

Tristran, sachiez, une doitie
A un cerf traist, qu'il out visé,
Par les flans l'a outrebersé.
Fuit s'en li cerf, Tristran l'aqeut;
Que soirs fu plains tant le porseut.
La ou il cort aprés la beste,
L'ore revient, et il s'areste,
Qu'il ot beü le lovendrant;
A lui seus senpres se repent.   (2152–60)

Tristan abandons the hunt from fatigue, a failure that marks the end of the lovers' forest sojourn and signals their impending separation. There is in both episodes the implicit association of Tristan (or perhaps of both lovers) with the hunted stag. In *B*, however, where the metaphor is extended beyond the more conventional symbolism of Thomas' poem to equate the wounding of the stag with the drinking of the potion, Tristan's life during the three-year period of the potion's greatest efficacy is likened to the travail of the wounded, tracked stag who is spared when the effects of the potion suddenly diminish. This detail forms a single facet of the larger metaphorical mosaic that alternately associates the consumption of the potion with intoxication, with poisoning, and with wounding (see below, 'The Ailing Hero').

The Garden, the Forest, and the Cave

Linked to the depiction of Tristan *l'Amerus* as hunter and woodsman is another complex of images portraying a *locus amoenus* where the lovers enjoy a brief period of happiness, for it is Tristan's woodcraft that permits the lovers to inhabit this domain. The term *amoenus*, 'pleasant or lovely' was early associated with *amor* (cf. Eng. *lovely/love*); Petronius calls it: 'Dignus amore locus' (Curtius 192, 196). The term as I shall use it designates not a formal rhetorical figure describing in pre-ordained terms an idealized landscape but rather a sub-category of that figure, become motif and metaphor – the idealized natural setting to which the lovers flee to enjoy an idyllic *séjour amoureux* and, by extension, any of the settings in which the lovers take refuge and pleasure. As such, the *locus amoenus*, in its most common manifestation as garden, pleasance, or forest glade, stands in contrast to Mark's city and residence, the seat of a repressive social Order and the metaphorical prison of Iseut. While it too is a closed space 'séparé du reste du monde, où tout lien avec une vie sociale normale et les

responsabilitiés qui en découlent est brisé' (Haidu, *Lion* 38), unlike the
prison its closure is protective and nurturing, not repressive and punitive.
In the Tristan poems, these *loci amoeni* are, implicitly, avatars of the Other
World, particularly of that portrayed in Celtic mythology, although there
are distant echos of the Classical, the Christian, and even the Oriental
Other Worlds. Since the Other World is a distant land difficult of access
and protected by barriers of various sorts (most often by a water barrier),
the motif of the journey, and specifically of the sea voyage, is closely linked
to that of the *locus amoenus*. Finally, the *locus amoenus* represents only one
sort of Other World, the idyllic Upper World in contrast to which stands
the demonic Lower World.

The first of the *loci amoeni* in the Tristan poems – and that corresponding
most closely to the classical figure of the grove or mixed forest – is the
lovers' abode in the forest of the Morois in *T* and *Fo*. Its chief feature, which
provides security and intimacy to the fugitives, is a grotto where the lovers
dwell:

> ... they found a secluded place by a certain river in that cliff that
> heathen men had had hewn out and adorned in ancient times with
> great skill and beautiful art. It was vaulted above, and it had been
> sunk deep into the earth. The entrance was underground, and a
> concealed path deep down led to it.   (*S* Ch. 64)

> 'A la forest puis en alames
> E un mult bel liu i truvames.
> En une roche fu cavee;
> Devant ert estraite l'entree;
> Dedenz fu voltisse e ben faite,
> Tant bele cum se fust putrait;
> L'entaileüre de la pere
> Esteit bele de grant manere:
> En cele volte cunversames,
> Tant cum en bois nus surjurnames.'   (*Fo* 861–70)

Yet this secret refuge is depicted not as a place of darkness but as the most
intimate recess of a secure sylvan Upper World bathed in a golden summer
sunlight, a trope for the lovers' bliss:

> There was much earth on top of the structure, and on it stood the most
> beautiful tree in the forest, and the shade of the tree spread and
> provided protection from the heat and burning of the sun. Beside the
> structure was a spring with wholesome water, and around the spring
> grew the sweetest herbs with lovely flowers that one could wish for,

and a brook flowed eastward from the spring. When the sun shone upon the herbs, they gave forth the sweetest fragrance, and then it seemed as though the sweetness of the herbs mingled like honey with the water. Whenever it rained or was cold, Tristram and Ísönd remained in the dwelling beneath the cliff. But when the weather was pleasant, they went to the spring to enjoy themselves and to those places in the forest that were best for strolling because they were level and beautiful. (S Ch. 64)

The minimum ingredients of the *locus amoenus* are all present: 'a beautiful, shaded natural site ... a tree ... a meadow, and a spring or brook ... bird-song and flowers' (Curtius 195), here lying within a wild wood.[54]

The description of the life in the forest in *B*, which stresses both the pleasurable and arduous aspects of that sojourn, is, as I have noted above, more ambiguous and complex than that of *T*. The forest in *B* is difficult of access, a conventional attribute of the Other World, a domain that in Celtic mythology is sometimes called the 'foret sanz retor' (Paton 40, n. 2). Before entering it, Tristan must make a metaphorical descent into the Lower World (his 'saut mortel') to rescue Iseut, who is held captive by its hideous denizens, the lepers of Yvain's band. Then the couple, accompanied by Governal, must make their way across the Blanche Lande, whose very name suggests the state of unconsciousness (sleep or forgetfulness) that they are about to enter.[55] Initially, the forest is depicted as a secure natural fortress (*B* 1275–78). Only after that security is shown to be illusory does the forest episode change from an idyllic sojourn to one of hardship and suffering. Yet even after the fragile sense of security is shattered by the intrusion of their enemies and in spite of the privations that the couple undergoes, a vestige of that idyllic quality persists:

> Aspre vie meinent et dure;
> Tant s'entraiment de bone amor,
> L'un por l'autre ne sent dolor. (*B* 1364–66)[56]

---

[54] Such an idealized landscape presents the essential features of the archetypal Other World garden: a tree, often the Tree of Life or the Tree of Good and Evil, a fountain, stream, or four-fold river, and a plethora of fragrant flowers. The detail of the grotto in *T* and *Fo* indicates the influence of the Celtic *sid* or fairy mound, the Other World within a hill (Patch 46–51). In *B* the Other World retreat is initially located upon, rather than within, a hill (1276). The Other World tradition is divided, perhaps in consequence of the ambiguity of the Latin *in montem*, '*in* or *on* a mountain', between the two sorts of Other World retreats. The lovers' retreat in the *Tavola Ritonda* is 'in cima d'una grande montagna' (Bédier, *Thomas* 1: 238).
[55] The Blanche Lande is an analogue of the mist barrier that in some Celtic texts hides the Other World from mortal eyes (Patch 44–46).
[56] See also *B* 1649–50.

Their love attenuates their suffering, an idea rendered metaphorically by the motif of sleep, often induced by the heat of the summer sun, which produces a forgetfulness of the world beyond the wood.[57] Indeed, the lovers' sojourn in the Morois is a descent into an Other World of beneficent unconsciousness, and Iseut's first action upon their arrival in the forest is to fall into a deep, healing sleep:[58]

> La roïne ert forment lassee
> Por la poor qu'el ot passee;
> Somel li prist, dormir se vot,
> Sor son ami dormir se vot.
> Seignors, eisi font longuement
> En la forest *parfondement*.
> Longuement sont en cel desert.   (*B* 1299–1305)

In *B*, the heat of the sun during the forest sojourn (1730, 2034–42), which is linked to the motif of the lovers' somnolence, is a metaphor for their passion. In the episode of Mark's discovery of the lovers, who are again asleep, the ray of sunlight that Mark seeks to prevent from falling on Iseut's face, threatening its delicate skin 'que plus reluist que glace' (*B* 1828), associates their passion with the natural forces of the woodland. To Mark, the wintery *gelus* of *Tros*, the summer sunlight that reddens Iseut's pale, emaciated features symbolizes the lovers' unseemly, uncourtly, and untempered passion, which contrasts with the pallor of conventional feminine beauty and with the paleness of his own marital passion. More importantly, the ray of sunlight evokes the drinking of the potion; for every account of that scene in the French poems says or suggests that it was the heat of the day that prompted Tristan and Iseut to request a refreshing drink and so, inadvertently, to consume the potion.[59] In *Fb*, whose author knew *B* or his source, the association of sunlight, sleep, and the potion is particularly emphatic. Echoing his earlier evocation of the unseasonable heat in the forest on the day of the lovers' discovery (*Fb* 202), Tristan

---

[57] E.g. *B* 1276, 1673–77, 1729–33, 1793–830. See in this regard the remarkable study of Ribard, esp. 236–41.

[58] Sleep as a means to entry into the Other World is a commonplace of Western dream literature from the *Somnium Scipionis* to the *Divina Commedia* and beyond.

[59] *S* Ch. 46, *Fb* 429–32, *Fo* 465–69, 641–45. See also MS. B.N.fr. 103 (Bédier, *Thomas* 2: 341). While lines 2156–59 of *B* confirm that the potion was consumed at the end of the day, Beroul lays stress on the fact that the potion was consumed at the summer solstice, on the longest, and presumably the hottest, day of the year (2147–49, see below). It would seem that the reference to evening alludes metonymically to the waning of the effects of the potion; for the association of the passion and sunlight is otherwise extensively developed in *B*, and the two texts most closely associated with *B*, *O* (2332–41) and *Fb* (428–32), contain the motif of the potion consumed in the heat of the day.

remembers the day on which the potion was drunk: 'Granz fu li chauz, s'aümes soif' (Fb 432) and employs the image of a dream to describe its effects:

> 'Moi et Ysiaut, que je voi ci,
> En beümes: demandez li,
> Et si lo tient or a mançonge,
> Don di je bien que ce fu songe,
> Car jo lo songé tote nuit.'   (Fb 176–80)[60]

In B, the lovers consume the potion on the Feast of Saint John (2147–49), which is celebrated at the summer solstice, a detail that opens a long vista of metaphorical associations.[61] The potion is drunk on the day on which the sun reaches its highest point in the sky, the longest day of the year and the juncture between spring and summer. Beroul also prefaces the description of Iseut's escondit, in which the lovers reaffirm their love and once more evade detection, with a similar solar reference: 'Li soleuz fu chauz sor la prime' (4119). The motif of the summer sun and the heat of the summer's day, the cause of the consumption of the potion and the symbol of the great ardor (thirst/passion) that it engenders, is linked to the motifs of the leper's grant ardor (see below, 'Tristan the Leper') and the healing draught of water (see below, 'The Ailing Hero'). The motif of the summer sun is a particularized aspect of the larger seasonal metaphor that associates the lovers' union with spring/summer and their separation (and death) with fall/winter (see below, 'Tristan the Nightingale'). The seasonal metaphor is paralleled by the opposing images of castle and wood, by the arboreal metaphors of Ch and T, and by the complex of images describing the potion as poison and/or healing draught (see below, 'The Ailing Hero').

---

[60] The Fo poet, who stresses Tristan's suffering for love, inverts the image of healing sleep to one of a drunken nightmare (455–60).

[61] 'The Nativity of Saint John the Baptist ... in the West since the fifth century has been kept on June 24th, thereby coinciding with the summer solstice. ... This date is the turning-point in the sun's course on the horizon, when after climbing higher and higher in the sky it begins, at first almost imperceptibly, to retrace its path until on Christmas Day it reaches its lowest place. ... As the lighting respectively of bonfires and Yule logs on these two occasions is a very ancient and widespread custom in solar ritual and long antedates the Christian observances at the summer and winter solstice, only a very thin veneer of Christianity has been given to them on these two occasions. Thus, the midsummer ceremonies include, in addition to the fires on eminences, processions with torches round the fields ... presumably to drive away evil influences at a very critical juncture in the annual cycle, as well as to stimulate the life and energy of the sun at the beginning of its downward course.'   (E. O. James 225–26)
'La nuit des amants fut celle de la Saint-Jean. Or, toutes les traditions populaires rapportent que cette "midsummer night" est celle du feu, de la célébration des forces vives, de Cérès. ... Le bouillonnement imprévisible de la vie ébranle les "parapets culturels" qui s'effondrent sous la vague.'   (Cahné 17–18)
See also Walter ('Solstice').

The most evocative of the *loci amoeni* presented in the romance is that conjured up by the mad Tristan, a mansion or crystalline palace suspended in the empyrean:

> 'Entre les nues et lo ciel,
> De flors et de roses, sans giel,
> Iluec ferai une maison
> O moi et li nos deduison.'   (Fb 166–69)

> 'Reis', fet li fol, 'la sus en l'air
> Ai une sale u je repair.
> De veire est faite, bele e grant;
> Li solail vait par mi raiant;
> En l'air est e par nuez pent,
> Ne berce, ne crolle pur vent.
> Delez la sale ad une chambre
> Faite de cristal e de lambre.
> Li solail, quant par main levrat,
> Leenz mult grant clarté rendrat.'   (Fo 299–308)

This aerial palace presents three features common to descriptions of the Other World: the negative formula ('sans giel', 'Ne berce, ne crolle pur vent') that describes the domain as one sheltered from the more unpleasant natural elements (Patch 142), the motif of a world suspended in the heavens, and the presence of crystal.[62] The celestial dwellings that Tristan evokes in *Fb* and *Fo* are idealized, metaphorical descriptions of the lovers' dwellings in the Morois. The celestial mansion of *Fb*, set within a flowered garden where it is always summer, abstracts and idealizes the chief characteristics of the sun-shot bower of *B*, while the crystalline chamber of *Fo* mirrors the sylvan grotto of *T*. Moreover, the crystalline chamber of *Fo* evokes an image common to the forest scenes of *B* and *T*, the ray of sunlight that falls on the face of the sleeping Iseut. As crystal may be imagined to distill and capture the essence of sunlight, the crystalline chamber, which Barteau considers one of the 'symboles totalisants' of the legend (307–09), distills into a single image the multiple associations linking the summer sunlight and the lovers' passion.[63]

[62] Crystal figures extensively in the description of the new Jerusalem in the *Book of Revelation* and, in a manner that approximates very closely the description of *Fo*, in the eleventh-century Irish vision of Saint Adamnán (*Fis Adamnáin*, found in the *Book of the Dun Cow*), which describes a heavenly city composed entirely of crystal and flooded with the sun's light. For other examples of heavenly Other Worlds, see Patch 14–15, 107–08 and especially the description of the palace of the sun in Ovid's *Metamorphoses* Lib. II, 1–23.

[63] Gottfried's description of the lovers' grotto contains the detail of light streaming down from small windows set in the ceiling and converging on a crystal bed (16716–27). The bed symbolizes love (16977–84), and the light from the windows is said to send its rays into the poet's heart (17133–35).

The image of the celestial dwelling also evokes another *locus amoenus*, Iseut's chamber, whence the lovers retire to take their pleasure (cf. *Fb* 259 and *Fo* 306). In *B*, (2179–84), Tristan contrasts the bower in the Morois, the symbol of their life of hardship and deprivation, with Iseut's apartments 'portendues de dras de soie' (2183). In *T*, Tristan the leper is taken by Brengvein to her mistress' chamber where the couple passes the night:

> Suz en une chambre marbrine;
> Acordent sei par grant amur,
> E puis confortent lur dolur.
> Tristran a Ysolt se deduit.
> Apres grant pose de la nuit
> Prent le congé a le enjurnee.   (D 720–25)

Fo concludes with a similar detail:

> Ysolt entre ses bras le tint.
> Tel joie en ad de sun ami
> K'ele ad e tent dejuste li
> Ke ne set cument contenir;
> Ne le lerat anuit partir
> E dit k'i avrat bon ostel
> E baus lit e ben fait et bel.
> Tristran autre chose ne quert
> Fors la raïne Ysolt, u ert.
> Tristran en est joius e lez:
> Mult set ben k'il est herbigez.   (986–96)

In each case the description stresses two elements: the repose that Tristan will be afforded ('grant pose', 'bon ostel e baus lit') and the richness of the furnishings ('chambre marbrine', 'baus lit e ben fait et bel'). Tristan's fatigue, occasioned by the hardships that he endures in the return episodes, constitutes an infirmity motif, and the repose and pleasure afforded him by the night spent with his lady 'heal' him both of his fatigue and of his metaphorical malady (leprosy or madness). In addition, of course, sleep is a trope for the lovers' passion. Finally, the image of Iseut's chamber, where Tristan the hunter pursues his *deduit*, is, like the celestial palace and dwelling in the Morois in *T*, a *locus amoenus* that combines the most pleasing elements of the natural and man-made worlds.

The chamber as *locus amoenus* is an apocalyptic image that stands in opposition to the demonic image of Mark's castle. In this perspective, even Tintagel, conceived of not as Mark's but as Iseut's palace, within which lies her 'chambre marbrine', takes on the characteristics of a beneficent, apocalyptic city in *Fo*:

> De marbre sunt tut li quarel
> Asis e junt mult ben e bel.
> Eschekerez esteit le mur
> Si cum de sinopre e d'azur.   (105–08)

This splendid jewel, another referent of the mad Tristan's *salle de cristal*, is set within a landscape of unsurpassed natural beauty:

> Plentet i out de praerie,
> Plentet de bois, de venerie,
> D'euves duces, de pescheries
> E des belles guaaineries. . . .
> Li lius ert beus e delitables,
> Li païs bons e profitables.   (117–20, 127–28)

It is an Other World castle that lies under an enchantment:

> E si fu jadis apelez
> Tintagel li chastel faez.
> Chastel faë fu dit a dreit
> Kar douz faiz lë an se perdeit . . .
> Une en ibern, autre en esté.
> So dient la gent del vingné.   (129–32, 137–38)

The Tintagel of *Fo* is not the city of night of a vengeful Mark, whose wish to put Tristan to death is stressed in *Fb* (1–8, etc.) but hardly mentioned in *Fo*, but a *locus amoenus* gained by a sea voyage and holding the princess who is the object of the hero's desires.

Set in opposition to the images of the Other World as a beneficent *locus amoenus* are a group of images that paint the natural world in darker colors. The first of these is the *salle aux images* of *T*, a counterfeit *locus amoenus* that reproduces the form of the forest grotto of the Morois while inverting its content. When Tristan proposes to take Kaherdin there, the latter expostulates: ' "If we cross the river, we shall never return alive" ' (*S* Ch. 85). Set in a deep forest in a forbidden and dangerous region, it lies within a Land of the Dead that may only be gained by a descent beneath a river-barrier (*S* Ch. 75). The river-barrier, a familiar motif in Other World literature, is often a deep, swift cascade of inky, boiling water. Usually it is crossed by a perilous bridge, as in Chrétien's *Lancelot*, less often in a boat or by supernatural means. Tristan's crossing, which suggests a descent to the Lower World, stands in contrast to the sea voyage, the crossing of the Blanche Lande, or the ascent to the empyrean that characterize his journeys to a beneficent *locus amoenus*.

The *salle aux images*, like the grotto in the Morois, duplicates certain features of the Celtic *sid*, the Other World within a hill, and of the Germanic

Other World within a barrow or mound.[64] What distinguishes it most radically from the grotto and the *feuillée* in the Morois is the lack of sunlight. While it is said that 'the hall was decorated with gold all around so that it was as bright inside as it was outside' (*S* Ch. 79), the lighting is not that of the sunshine that bathed the grotto and suffused the *feuillée* but rather an eerie, unearthly light, a Miltonic 'darkness visible'. Associated with the *salle aux images* are claustrophobic images of confinement and suffocation. The *salle*, which is guarded by Moldagog, is a locked chamber within a cave built by a giant, who long before had abducted the daughter of the Duke Hoël:

> Because she was a very beautiful woman, he desired to have carnal relations with her. But he was unable to accomplish his purpose because of his huge size and weight, and she suffocated and burst beneath him. (*S* Ch. 78)

This demonic image stands in contrast to the innocence and pleasure of the lovers' sexual union in the other *loci amoeni*. The cave is, moreover, a place of frenzy, jealousy, and *fole irur* (T¹ 44) where Tristan:

> Corrusce soi, quant est irez,
> Que par penser, que par songes,
> Que par craire en son cuer mençoignes,
> Que ele mette lui en obli
> Ou que ele ait acun autre ami.   (T¹ 6–10)

The chamber, 'le tombeau d'une Iseut perdue' (Brusegan 53), whose inhabitants are but counterfeit artifacts and lifeless automata, transforms the image of vitality and beatitude of the grotto of the lovers into a metaphorical Land of the Dead where Tristan must reside in isolation before returning to the Upper World to seek his lady. It is an objective correlative for the unfounded jealousy and angry suspicions whose prisoner he is.

A second image of the Lower World is that which Iseut, in despair of ever again seeing her dying lover, evokes during the storm-wracked voyage from England to Brittany:

> 'Amis, jo fail a mun desir,
> Car en voz bras quidai murrir,
> En un sarcu enseveiliz,
> Mais nus l'avum ore failliz.
> Uncore puet il avenir si:

---

64 For the Germanic barrow, see Patch 78; for submersion in a river, see Patch 101 and the lay of *Graelent*, in which the hero traverses a dangerous river that closes over his head (Patch 247).

Car, se jo dei neier ici,
E vus, ço crei, devez neier,
Uns peissuns poüst nus dous mangier;
Eissi avrum par aventure,
Bels amis, une sepulture.'   (D 1649–58)

The descent into the belly of the whale is a literary motif of considerable antiquity that in the archetypal quest narrative represents one of the trials to be undergone before the hero finally achieves the object of his journey (Frye, *Anatomy* 189–90; Campbell, *Hero* 90–95). In *T*, the watery grave, like the cave of images, is a demonic counterpart of the *salle de cristal*, Iseut's chamber, and the forest grotto. Like the *salle de cristal*, the belly of the whale is a mental image evoked by one of the lovers to render metaphorically an understanding concerning their union. The evocation of the Upper World of the empyrean, made radiant by the sunlight that symbolizes their ideal union, contrasts radically with the image of the cold, watery Lower World of the whale's belly, a world of pain and death where, like the statues in the *salle aux images*, the lovers are become lifeless figures whose union is only apparent, whose forms alone are in contact.

The intertwining trees, the final image of Thomas' romance, inverts those of the *salle aux images*, the whale's belly, and the dark grave:

> It is said that Ísodd, Tristram's wife, had Tristram and Ísönd buried on opposite sides of the church so that they would not be close to each other in death. But it came to pass that an oak tree or other tree grew up from each of their graves, so high that their branches intertwined above the gablehead of the church. And from this it could be seen how great had been the love between them.   (*S* Ch. 101)

The lovers, metamorphosed into twin oaks, leave the isolation of their separate graves in the dark Lower World to rise together toward the sunlight. The final image of the conjoined tree-tops bathed in sunlight anticipates – in a vegetable rather than a mineral image – the celestial dwelling of *Fo* and *Fb*. The intertwining trees recall the love of Tristan's parents, Rivalen and *Blancheflor* and the single tree standing above the lovers' grotto in *T* in the Morois, and echo or anticipate the intertwining honeysuckle and hazel of *Ch*, the lovers' *feuillée* of *B*, the garden landscape of Tintagel in *Fo*, and the nocturnal garden of *Tros*.[65]

---

[65] Moreover, they recall all of the trees standing within Other World gardens – the Tree of Life, the Virgilian golden bough, the Yggdrasil of Germanic mythology, and the evergreen, holly and yew of the *Ystori Trystan*. The trees are the One Tree, the World Tree, the Tree of Life standing, in permanent springtime, within the One Garden – Eden, the Elysian Fields or any of the innumerable avatars of the garden of the Earthly Paradise.

II

TRISTAN'S DISGUISES

Narrative Functions of the Disguises

The tragic dimension of the Tristan legend results, as Vinaver has observed, from the fact that the hero accepts the validity of the social and legal proscriptions against his love for Iseut and, therefore, in spite of his superior strength, never *openly* contests the *status quo* by virtue of which Mark possesses Iseut (*Etudes* 13–14), although he does take revenge on his enemies, the felonious barons. Instead, in the period following his banishment from Mark's court, he conducts his love affair in secret, utilizing the device of the disguise in order to be reunited with his beloved. Tristan's disguises must be considered in several different perspectives. Each disguise has a narrative function in the economy of the romance. The disguise identities also frequently play on and invert the content of the overt identities, thereby adding new dimensions to the latter. Several of the disguises elaborate a metaphoric conceit. Finally, each disguise represents an aspect of Tristan's larger identity as a trickster figure.

The disguise episodes, reduplicated variants of a single paradigm, include the following: Tristan disguises himself as a merchant on the second voyage to Ireland in *T* (*S* Ch. 34–35; *Fo* 393–98) and appears at Iseut's *escondit* disguised as a pilgrim in *T* (*S* Ch. 58) and as a leper in *B* (3563–984). In *T* Tristan returns to Cornwall three times, disguised successively as a pilgrim (Str¹ 1–68), as a leper (D 492–736), and again as a penitent pilgrim (D 785–834). The independent episodes recount Tristan's disguises as madman/fool (*Fo*, *Fb*) and minstrel (*Tmen*) and his 'disguise' as nightingale in *Tros*. On other occasions he dissembles or conceals his identity. Upon his arrival in Cornwall in *T*, he gives himself as a lost hunter (*S* Ch. 20), while on the first voyage to Ireland, he presents himself as a castaway named Tantris (*S* Ch. 30, *Fo* 363) and a student of astronomy (*S* Ch. 31). On three occasions, he adopts an incognito by appearing as an anonymous knight, displaying no device on his arms (*B* 3985–4074, *T* D 795–834, *Tmen*). Finally, at Tristan's behest, Kaherdin, his friend, agent, and metaphorical double, journeys to England disguised as a merchant to carry Iseut back to Brittany (*T* D 1304–530).[1]

---

[1] *O* gives four disguise episodes in which Tristan successively disguises himself as leper,

On the most explicit narrative level, the choice of a given disguise is dictated by its efficacy in allowing Tristan to travel undetected through the kingdom of Cornwall, to appear at Iseut's *escondit*, or to enter Mark's very court, there to appear unrecognized before the king and his courtiers. Certain of the disguises represent an especially natural choice for one who would undertake a clandestine journey. The movement of pilgrims and minstrels in the twelfth century was constant and unremarkable; and Tristan's decision to disguise himself as a member of those estates in *T* and *Tmen* is hardly extraordinary.[2] In general, the low social station implied by the disguises of leper, minstrel, madman, and penniless pilgrim offers a guarantee of anonymity and freedom of movement. As the *Fo* poet observes:

> ... de povre home k'a pé vait
> Nen est tenu gueres de plait,
> De povre messagë e nu
> Est poi de plait en curt tenu.   (37–40)

Furthermore, Tristan's disguises as leper in *B* and *T* and as a violent madman with a ready club in *Fb* and *Fo* are proof against close scrutiny by the overly curious.[3] Only in *Fb*, however, is one of these latter two disguises utilized to allow travel over long distances; otherwise they serve only to permit Tristan's appearance at Iseut's *escondit* or in Mark's court. While Tristan's disguise as an anonymous knight represents a higher social station than those discussed above, it serves the same function of discouraging scrutiny and permitting freedom of movement. As an anonymous knight, Tristan can preserve the secret of his identity from all save those who, by force of arms, are capable of forcing him to reveal it, hardly a threat to the most redoubtable knight in Mark's kingdom. Yet, the usefulness of this disguise is limited, and Tristan utilizes it only in two episodes, where it enables him to take revenge on his persecutors in a joust (*B* 3985–4074, *T* D 795–834).

---

pilgrim, minstrel and fool. Additionally, on the first voyage to Ireland, he gives himself as a minstrel named Pro of Iemsetir and, on the second voyage, as a merchant named Tantris. In *G* Tristan calls himself Tantris and claims to be a minstrel on the first voyage to Ireland, while on the second, he pretends to be a merchant. An episodic German poem, *Tristan als Mönch*, recounts Tristan's false death and his disguise as a physician-monk. Finally, a Welsh triad, 'The Three Mighty Swineherds', recounts Tristan's disguise as a swineherd.

[2] In *T* the lovers make use of minstrels to carry messages to one another on two occasions. Tristan enlists a fiddler to convey Petit-Crû to Iseut (*S* Ch. 63), and Iseut commissions a *vielur* to carry word of her plight to Tristan (D 772–76).

[3] Despite legal restrictions against the movement of lepers in the Middle Ages, it is clear that, at least during certain periods, lepers enjoyed a considerable freedom of movement (Jonin, *Personnages* 129; Brody 93–94). Thus, Tristan's disguise as leper is not *ipso facto* without versimilitude.

All of the above disguises presuppose that one travel alone or at most with a small body of companions. In two episodes, however, circumstances dictate the more elaborate disguise of merchant, which requires the presence of a ship, rich goods, and a substantial retinue, in order to gain *entrée* to a royal court. On Tristan's second voyage to Ireland in *T*, where he has come in quest of Iseut, he fits himself out as a wealthy merchant (*S* Ch. 34). Later the wounded Tristan instructs Kaherdin to adopt the same disguise in order to sail to England to seek Iseut, another example of Thomas' cultivation of structural symmetry. Kaherdin's disguise provides a plausible excuse for entering Mark's court, a pretext for producing the ring that serves as a recognition device, and an explanation for the presence of the ship that will transport Iseut to Brittany.

With the exception of those of merchant, anonymous knight, and 'nightingale', all of the disguises that Tristan adopts in order to be reunited with Iseut or to be present at her *escondit* reflect, as has been noted, a humble social station. Tristan is by turns a penniless pilgrim, a mendicant leper, a wandering fool, and a lowborn *jongleur*. The first knight of the courts of Cornwall and Brittany and nephew to King Mark, the disguised Tristan is at best a villein and at worst a social pariah, the bearer of a loathsome disease indicative of an even more odious state of spiritual health. In every instance, his disguise emphasizes the opposition between his courtly persona and those anti-courtly identities that, willingly or unwillingly, he assumes. Clothed in garments of *povre atur*, his behavior extravagant, his features disfigured, his wits apparently disordered, he presents every possible contrast with the courtly, handsome, intelligent knight of the earlier portions of the narrative.

The Disguise as Metaphor

Each of Tristan's attributes is travestied in the disguises. The noble harper and knight gives himself in *Tmen* for a minstrel of such low birth and station that he would bring dishonor to any knight who engaged him in combat (4440–44). His skill at the royal sport of the hunt is parodied in his account in *Fo* of the *chasse à l'envers*. The knight who vanquished Le Morholt and sundry giants receives blows from youths and squires in *Fo* (246–56) and insults and blows from menials and messengers in *B* (3642–49). When the fool proclaims to the queen, ' "J'ere chevaler mervilus",' she protests in horror: ' "A chevalers faites vus hunte!" ' (*Fo* 403, 408). His disfigurement is extreme: his head is shaven, his voice altered, and he is apparently missing an eye. In the *Folies* his crudely tonsured head implies the loss not only of his wits and beauty but of his physical strength (Ménard, 'Fous' 439–40). *Fb*, *Fo*, and *Tmen* abound in Iseut's protestations against this individual who proclaims himself her lover. Tristan, she affirms, is nothing like this vile creature – minstrel or madman – capering before her.[4]

The inversion of values and the distortion of reality suggested by the disguises have several implications. They signify Tristan's involuntary exclusion from the society of the court as a penalty for his lawless passion. They further suggest his voluntary abasement in the service of his lady in conformity with a personal code of honor that differs radically from that of the collectivity, either as a means of reaffirming his love or as a penance for real or imagined wrongs committed against his lady's love. Finally, the disguise episodes hold up to the narrative a mirror that inverts or distorts – for comic, ironic, or dramatic effect – the values set forth therein.

Before embarking on a discussion of these implications, it is well to explore the concepts implicit in the term *vilain* and its derivatives. From its original, neutral sense of 'peasant' (<V.L. *villanus*, 'habitant de la campagne' <S.L. *villa*), the term quickly evolved to incorporate in its adjectival derivative, *vil*, the concepts of 'méprisable', 'déshonorant', 'méchant', 'laid', and 'mauvais'.[5] In addition to those associations listed by Ménard, *vil* is an antonym of *courtois*, especially as the latter figures in the term *courtoisie* and in the concept of a code of behavior appropriate to the courtly lover and cultivated aristocrat. The *Donnei des amanz* contains a long diatribe against the *vilain* (25–84) who, like the *gelus* with whom he is associated, seeks to thwart the conjunction of true lovers in opposition to God's will and celestial design (34):

---

[4] *Fb* 368–75, 384–85, 468–69; *Fo* 365–70, 407–10, 575–82, 833–46; *Tmen* 3894–99, 4074–85.

[5] '... par sa hideur, ses vétements grossiers et sa massue le *vilain* paraît un être inférieur, primitif et comique. ... Le paysan, appuyé sur sa massue, a traditionnellement les cheveux hérissés, le teint noir, le visage sale, la mine patibulaire et porte de méchants habits et de mauvais souliers. Comique de la rusticité, de la saleté et de la sauvagerie pour la société courtoise qui prise les étoffes délicates, les tenues propres et soignées, les manières raffinées. La noirceur même du vilain, tanné par soleil, a quelque chose de ridicule et d'inquiétant en un temps où il n'est point de mode de paraître bronzé et où l'on admire la blancheur du teint. Le *vilain* est noir comme les méchants qui noircissent de colère, comme les païens, comme le diable. ... Alors que les chevaliers font montre d'un courage à toute épreuve, les *vilains* se signalent par leur couardise. Pour un noble chevalier endosser l'habit d'un *vilain*, passer pour un être de bas étage, contrefaire le fou a sinon quelque chose de déshonorant, du moins un je ne sais quoi de dégradant. Dans la société médiévale où la classe chevaleresque a une haute conscience d'elle-même et un superbe dédain pour le populaire, où chacun porte les habits et partage les sentiments de son état, il est piquant de voir des êtres de haute condition renoncer aux signes extérieurs de leur rang et prendre, fût-ce provisoirement, un habit modeste et une humble contenance.'   (Ménard, *Rire* 169–70, 343)
Cf. the portraits of the grotesque *vilain* found in Chrétien's *Yvain* (288–313) and *Perceval* (6986–97), in *Aucassin et Nicolette* (XXIV, 12–22), and in Marie's 'Guigemar' (488–92).

Se me suvint pus al derein
Ke mut est fel quer de *vilein*,
E la sue vie est maudite,
Quant en joie ne se delite.
Li suens deliz n'est fors grucer,
Pendre surcilz, batre e tencer,
Aver tuz jorz morne semblant,
Haïr deduiz, joie e chant.
Contrairie est mut la sue vie
A la celeste armonie
E as angeles de paraïs
Ki devant Deu chantent tut diz.   (25–36)

The figure of the *vilain*, whose condition Tristan adopts in the disguise episodes, assembles all of those vices most antithetical to the system of courtly values that Tristan initially exemplifies: cowardice, ill breeding, ugliness, ridiculousness, poverty, and stupidity.[6] An instructive example of the horror that these vices inspired in the members of the courtly class is found in the episode of the *eau hardie* in *T*, where Kaherdin, misunderstanding the motive for his sister's laughter, fears that he has unwittingly covered himself with ridicule:

Caerdins la voit issi rire,
Quid lui ait oï dire
Chose ou ele note *folie*
Ou *mauvaisté* ou *vilannie*,
Car il ert chevaler hontus
E bon e frans e amerus.
De *folie* a por ce poür
El ris qu'il vait de sa sorur;
Honte li fait poür doter.   (T¹ 228–36)

This fear of dishonor (*honte*), of foolishness (*folie*), of dispicableness (*mauvaisté*), and of the behavior associated with low breeding (*vilannie*) is the conscience of an entire class; and Tristan's adoption of personae that exemplify these highly disturbing vices is at once an index of the strength of his passion and of the disorder of his spirit.

The theme of Tristan's disguises as a divesting of his social identities is linked to that of his disinheritance (not only of goods but of name) and orphaning in *T*. Following his exile from Mark's court, Tristan is again dispossessed; and his status becomes that of *marginal*, of one who is and is

---

[6] In this respect, the Tristan poets portray a far more humiliating degradation of the hero than that visited upon Lancelot in Chrétien's *Chevalier de la Charrete*.

not of the society on whose fringes he dwells. As *marginal*, Tristan is ready
at any moment to cross the line that separates his social identity from his
interior self, subjugating the former to the latter. His situation following
his exile is similar to that of the forest sojourn in *B*, where Tristan summarizes his dilemma by declaring: '"Oublïé ai chevalerie"' (2165). His choice
(or compulsion) to love Iseut is punished by the stripping from the hero of
those honors that the society had bestowed on him while he remained
ostensibly one of them.

Mendicancy was a normal practice for the leper, the madman, and the
pilgrim, and Tristan is depicted begging in *T* and in *B*. Underlying these
episodes, which metaphorically portray the lover as supplicant abjectly
soliciting the favor and favors of his lady or as a penitent begging for her
forgiveness, is the notion that without his beloved the lover has nothing of
value. This implies a radical redefinition of social values with passion
replacing birth, wealth, and status as the highest value in the new
Counter-Order (see above, 'Tristan the Knight'). The conceit of the penitent lover as mendicant is developed most fully in *T* (D 492–736) where the
poet ironically underlines the hidden intentions of the begging leper by
remarking that those who witness his begging at the church 'ne sevent
cum [i.e. de quoi] est besuignus' (D 544).

A second, closely related aspect of the *vilité* of the hero's disguises is
Tristan's voluntary abasement in the service of his lady. In the message
that he transmits to Iseut, Kaherdin says of Tristan: '"Liges hum vus est e
amis"' (*T*D 1441). The transfer of the hero's allegiance from the social to the
personal order could hardly be more clear. As he declares to Ogrin in *B*:

> 'Mex aim o li [i.e. Iseut] estre mendis
> Et vivre d'erbes et de glan
> Q'avoir le reigne au roi Otran.'   (1404–06)[7]

It is consistent with this transposition that Tristan should lay aside the
visible signs of his social persona to adopt in their stead those that reveal to
the knowing observer the hero's secret allegiance. Indeed, the more
debasing the disguise, the greater the lover's merit in the eyes of his
beloved, for the apparent *vilité* of the disguise conceals an essential *courtoisie*. Thus in *T*, Tristan dons the *vil abit* (D 503) of a leper in order not to act
ignobly (*vileinement* D 493) towards Iseut by quitting England before having ascertained how his beloved fares. Iseut's observation in *Tmen* makes
the same point:

> 'Je ne le doi pas tenir *vil*:
> En tel abit est por moi mis;

---

[7] Tristan expresses a similar sentiment, albeit in more conventional terms, in *Tmen*
3780–84.

Il ovre c'un *loiaus* amis,
Mainte paine a por moi eüe.'   (4090–93)[8]

In addition, Tristan's self-abasement becomes one aspect of his suffering for love, for which Iseut will ultimately reward him with the *guerredon* traditionally reserved to the faithful lover (*Fb* 223–33, 285–90, 476–79, 555–58).

There is a third dimension to the disguise as an aspect of Tristan's love service to his lady. Following his exile, Tristan commits two grave sins against his beloved, each of which must be expiated. The first and permanent offense against the love, and most particularly against the *covenance* made at the lovers' parting (*TC* 31–52, *B* 2777–803), is Tristan's marriage to Iseut aux Blanches Mains.[9] In the broadest sense, all of Tristan's mental and physical anguish following his exile represents his attempt to atone for this transgression. The most degrading episodes of the latter part of the narrative, the madness episodes of the *Folies* and the leper episode in *T*, owe their brutality to the depth of Tristan's betrayal of Iseut, a betrayal ascribed by Thomas to the most pernicious vices in the hierarchy of values of the Counter-Order, smallness of faith and *novelerie*.

In describing the disguising of Tristan and his companions, the poet of *Tmen* employs the term *bestorner*, 'tourner à l'envers' (3802). The phrase is felicitious, for Tristan is *bestorné* in each disguise that he adopts. In large measure, the content of the disguise episodes is determined by the verbal and conceptual play on the oppositions between Tristan's former, essential *être* and the *paraître* of the disguises, which frequently illuminate truths hitherto concealed by the mask of his courtly persona. The disguise episodes constitute a series of *adynata* that depict, through inverted images of reality, a world upside down.[10] The use of the *adynaton* was traditionally associated in classical and late Latin literature with two thematic contexts: the first, the lament for a lost golden age by a denizen of a corrupt present in which all seems upside down; the second, the lament of an unhappy lover who proclaims that, if love can play him false, as well can the *impossibilia* that he evokes come to pass.[11] The disguise episodes as *adynata* represent a distant echo of this dual tradition. The contrast be-

---

[8] Cf. Brengvein's declaration to her mistress, upon learning Tristan's identity and the suffering that he has endured, that he is '"[le] plus loial amant / Qui onques fust ne ja mais soit"'' (*Fb* 361–62).

[9] While *B* breaks off before the marriage, the romance, if it was completed, undoubtedly followed either the narrative of *O*, or, more probably, that of *R* (Adams and Hemming, 'Fin'), in both of which Tristan marries.

[10] On this theme in Old French literature, see Ménard, *Rire* 379–89.

[11] Curtius, 'The World Upside Down' 94–98. The *locus classicus* of the complaining lover's *adynata* is Virgil's Eighth *Ecologue* 52–56.

tween the lost union of the lovers in Cornwall and the separation of the lovers following Tristan's exile is rendered by the grotesque metamorphoses of the hero. In T, the disguises render the mutability not merely of the lovers' circumstances but also of Tristan's passion. Thomas' long dissertation (Sn[1] 1–364) on the instability of Tristan's love, contaminated as it is with jealousy and lust, serves to prepare Tristan's comings and goings, his sudden fits of anger, fear, and mistrust, and his kaleidoscopic changes of form in the disguise episodes (see below, 'Mutability, Shape-shifting, and Thomas' *Tristan*').

Robertson has commented on the 'increasing tendency [of the romance] to react upon itself as the story progresses, in the paradoxes and ironies which characterize its later development' (104). Nowhere is this tendency more apparent than in the disguise episodes, which turn on a seemingly endless series of binary oppositions. The noble courtier is become a *vilain*, the intelligent trickster a bumbling fool, the adulterous lover a pious pilgrim, the *fin amant* an uncouth, obscene mocker of the queen, and the paragon of courtly and chivalric virtue the Devil himself (*T* D 633). For the blond hair and surpassing beauty of the knight is substituted a shorn head and grotesque disfigurement, for his extraordinary strength the physical decrepitude of the leper, for the intellectual and carnal knowledge of the lover the incoherent and obscene maunderings of an ignorant fool. The valiant knight is cast in the role of coward (*S* Ch. 88–89 and *T* D 1–476), of craven, hunted outlaw, or of club-wielding buffoon. The slayer of giants is mockingly characterized as 'fis Urgan le Velu' (*Fo* 242).[12]

The disguise episodes are particularly rich in conceptual and verbal play. The *Folies* develop the oxymoron of the wise fool (*Fo* 179–86). *Tmen* embroiders the humourous conceit of the thief set to watch over that which he has come to steal. In *B* and in *T*, the couple's love is safeguarded and affirmed through a trick in which Iseut apparently swears that she and Tristan have never been lovers. In the *Folies* and in *B*, the random behavior of the fool or leper belies the purposefulness of the lover. The word play in the disguise episodes is likewise extensive. In *Fb*, Brengvein reproaches herself for her *vilenie* (325) for not having recognized Tristan under his *vil* disguise. In *Fo*, Iseut thinks to herself that it would be *folie* (843) to recognize Tristan in the *fou* who has almost driven her mad (593), while in *Fb* she laments that she is *fole* (545) for having failed to discern his true identity. In *B*, Tristan the leper declares of his malady: '"Cist maus me prist de la commune"' (3773), whose sense ('sexual intercourse' with a suggestion of

---

[12] As Robertson has remarked, 'A king's son and a king's nephew, whose place in society is established very near to the exact center of power ... is a grotesque marvel, a wandering outcast established nowhere, whose lot it is to be continually driven *out* of any given place' (42).

'promiscuous sexual activity') ironically emphasizes the exclusivity of the couple's love. The lover of the *Donnei des amanz* wittily summarizes the significance of the madness episodes by saying of the burlesque fool whose *gas* have so amused the king (*Fb* 191) and so distressed the queen (*Fb* 373): 'Apertement dunt [Tristran] mustra / Ke pas *en gabes* nen ama' (673–74). And when in *Fb*, having finally recognized Tristan beneath his disguise, Iseut appeals to Brengvein for counsel, her *suivante* insists that she take the fool's imposture seriously: '"Dame, nel tenez mie a *gas*"' (560). Ultimately, the disguise episodes, with the madness episodes going to the greatest extremes, contest every verity of the narrative and, in holding up to reality a distorting mirror, impart to the lovers' story its greatest resonance.

Tristan the Leper

Tristan's debasement in the leper episodes was the more shocking to its twelfth-century audience because of the horror that leprosy inspired at the period, a horror reflected in the legal and spiritual procedures invoked in dealing with the afflicted. The medieval leper was ordered sequestered, although, as Tristan's peregrinations show, the regulation was unevenly enforced. This banishment was accompanied at certain times by a religious ceremony of separation that 'differed little from the office for the dead, for in principle the leper was no longer one of the living' (Brody 65). During one such ceremony, the leper, his face covered with a black veil, knelt before the altar while the priest threw a spadeful of earth from the cemetery on him, explaining that the ritual symbolized the death of the leper to the world. Following the mass, the priest read in the vernacular the prohibitions that would apply to the leper (Brody 66–67). Moreover, lepers were stripped of their legal rights and their property (as were the insane) and were declared legally dead (Brody 81). In *B*, Tristan the leper, who earlier lamented the alienation of his rank and privileges (2160–2222), declares to Mark at the Mal Pas that he has been 'fors de gent' (3759), figuratively for the three years since he drank the potion and literally since the couple fled the court to take refuge in the forest. Tristan appears disguised as a leper in two episodes of the French poems. In *T* he adopts a leper's garb in order to communicate with Iseut and to repair the damage done by Cariado's false accusation of cowardice (*D* 492–736). In *B* he adopts the disguise of a leper in order to be present at Iseut's *escondit* and to perpetrate the trick that permits the queen to swear in truth the oath that apparently exculpates her (3563–984).

In the Middle Ages a pilgrimage to a holy shrine was often undertaken by the afflicted in the hope of obtaining a cure – particularly of an affliction visited by God in punishment for a sin – through the intervention of a special providence at the place of pilgrimage. In *T* Tristan's leprosy is depicted as a punishment for his real or imagined sins against his lady's love, and his journeys to England to seek her forgiveness are, metaphorically, penitential pilgrimages undertaken to seek a cure for this malady. In Thomas the clerk's poem, the pilgrimage motif takes on an obsessive quality, for on three of the four occasions that Tristan adopts a disguise in order to rejoin Iseut, he choses that of a pilgrim. The significance of this disguise varies from episode to episode. It is, of course, a natural disguise for one who would undertake a clandestine journey, a fact that undoubtedly explains its use for the first time in the episode of Iseut's *escondit* where, at her bidding, Tristan carries the queen across the ford. When he stumbles with his burden, the king's men rush forth to punish them, but Iseut restrains them, saying that 'he was weak and weary from walking – "for he is a pilgrim and has come from a long journey"' (*S* Ch. 58).

On the second and third occasions that it is used, however, its significance becomes entwined with that of the leper disguise. In *T* the entire narrative of N⁴ is dominated by the themes of transgression and punishment, of repentance and expiation; for Tristan's infidelity to Iseut in his marriage to Iseut aux Blanches Mains is a sin that must be expiated. When Iseut aux Blanches Mains reveals to her brother that Tristan has never consummated his marriage to her, Kaherdin angrily demands an explanation of his friend. Tristan describes his misfortunes and his lady, asserting that Iseut la Blonde is so beautiful that her very *meschine* surpasses Kaherdin's sister. As proof of this assertion, Tristan takes Kaherdin to the *salle aux images* where he shows the two statues to his friend, who falls in love with the image of Brengvein. Tristan and Kaherdin disguise themselves as pilgrims and set out for England to find the queen and her maid (*S* Ch. 86). They lie in hiding in a forest and witness the passing of the queen's retinue. Kaherdin's wonder increases as each group of ladies proves more beautiful than that which has gone before, until at last Brengvein and Iseut ride into view. The linked episodes of the 'Salle aux Images' and the 'Cortège de la Reine' are depicted according to the conventions of religious adoration, which are imitated in the rhetoric of *fin'amor*.[13] In this context, the choice of pilgrim's garb by the two friends who have come to pay homage to the beauty of Tristan's mistress and her maid is appropriate, even necessary.

---

[13] Cf. Lazar's observation in reference to the episode of the *salle aux images* that 'la Dame aimée est une idole, et le culte dont elle est l'objet est une véritable idolâtrie' (166).

This episode, which culminates with a false accusation of cowardice leveled against Tristan and Kaherdin, motivates the two subsequent episodes, in which Tristan successively adopts the disguises of leper and penitent pilgrim. Brengvein, who has believed the accusation directed against Tristan and her lover, Kaherdin, flies into a rage against Iseut and threatens to denounce her adultery to Mark. Instead, she informs Mark that it is Cariado and not Tristan who has attracted Iseut's affection, a false accusation that mirrors that of Cariado; and Mark, who takes her at her word, places his wife under Brengvein's authority. Reluctant to abandon Iseut in her predicament, Tristan returns to Mark's castle disguised as a leper. On Brengvein's orders, he is beaten and turned away. In order to be reunited with Iseut, he must persuade Brengvein of his true identity as courageous knight, a situation that recalls the *Folies*, where he must persuade Iseut that he is the 'chevaler mervilus' (*Fo* 403) he claims to be. In part a prisoner of his source and in part bound by the conventions of the *fin'amor*, Thomas presents a leper scene containing profound ambiguities. The scene in *O*, which, in all probability, reproduces the version that served as Thomas' model, recounts Tristrant the leper's humiliation at the hands of Isolde in punishment for his alleged cowardice (7026–48). However, apparently in order to preserve the courtly tone of his version of the episode, Thomas causes Brengvein rather than Iseut to humiliate the hero. He portrays Tristan as a penitent expiating a sin that he has not committed in order to seek the pardon of one who does not believe that he is guilty. In Thomas' version of the episode, Tristan's disguise suggests his self-abasing penitence not for the cowardice of which Cariado has accused him but for his marriage, of which Cariado has also informed the queen (Sn[1] 856–63). Thomas implies that Tristan's infidelity, a sin against the ethic of faithfulness demanded by *fin'amor*, is an act of moral cowardice, a failure to remain steadfast in the face of adversity. Hence, his leprosy is at once a punishment and a penance for his transgression. In the following episode, Tristan, upon learning that Iseut is mortifying her flesh in penance for the suffering that she has caused her lover, clothes himself as pilgrim making an act of penance and returns to England (D 789–94). The double penance of the lovers atones for their transgressions against one another and against the ideal of *fin'amor*.

The identification of Tristan's metaphorical leprosy with the passion induced by the consumption of the *beivre* is made explicit in *B* by the choice of the *hanap* as one of the accoutrements of the disguised Tristan and by his allusion to the *arson* within his body. In begging money for drink, he announces that he suffers from an intense burning sensation:

> Il lor dit que il a toz boit:
> Si grant *arson* a en son cors

A poine l'en puet geter fors.   (3656–58)

While the *hanap* was a normal part of the equipment prescribed by law for the medieval leper (Jonin, *Personnages* 117), its use by Tristan as one of the elements of the disguise commanded by Iseut in *B* consciously alludes to the use of a similar vessel in the episode of the drinking of the potion. Two details are constant in the accounts given in *Fb*, *Fo*, and *S* of that latter episode: the heat of the day that provoked the lovers' thirst and prompted them to request refreshment and the use of an *hanap* or similar vessel in serving the potion. The *botele* and the *henap de madre* of the disguised Tristan in *B* (3300–01) appear to refer to similar vessels that figured in the potion episode in the lost portion of *B*, details preserved in *Fb*, which mentions the *tresseroil* in which the potion was stored and the *cope* in which is was served (309, 434–36).[14]

In *B* the potion was drunk on the feast of Saint John, the day of the summer solstice (2147–49). The sensation of a terrible, internal burning that the disguised Tristan describes as a great thirst (3656–58) and that Yvain the leper describes as a great lust is an explicit allusion to the lovers' thirst, which was provoked by the excessive heat of that day (*O* 2332, *Fb* 432; cf. *Fo* 467–69):

> 'Sire, en nos a si grant *ardor*
> Soz ciel n'a dame qui un jor
> Peüst soufrir nostre convers.'   (1195–97)

The word *ardor/arson* is deliberately equivocal and refers at once to the internal burning sensation that was supposed to be characteristic of leprosy (Guy de Chauliac 404) and to the extraordinary sexual appetite that lepers were popularly held to possess (Remy 210; Jonin, *Personnages* 113; Brody 129–31). Tristan's 'leprosy' is a metaphor for his adulterous, excessive, even pathological passion for Iseut, a passion provoked by the drinking of the potion and symbolized by Tristan's terrible *ardor*.

The epithets with which Tristan is taxed while disguised as a leper suggest that he possesses unnatural sexual appetites: *mignon* (3644) 'un

---

[14] Likewise, the *hanap de mazre* of *T* (D 512) is an echo of a similar vessel that figured in the potion episode (*S* Ch. 46), a detail preserved in *Fo*, which mentions an *hanap* (471, 649, 651). The *hanap de mazre*, given to Tristan by Iseut 'le primer an qu'il l'amat' (D 514), is, if not the very cup from which the potion was drunk, at least a gift commemorating the beginnings of their love. Two hypotheses may be advanced to explain the presence of an *hanap* in each of the *Folies*. While it may be that the poets were referring consciously to the use of a similar vessel in the leper scenes of their respective models, *B* and *T*, it is more likely, given the presence of such a vessel in the account of the potion episode in *S*, that they were reproducing the details of the episode found in their models. Thus, the responsibility for linking the two scenes would lie with Thomas and Beroul. The latter possibility is strengthened by the fact that *O* makes no mention of the vessel in which the potion was stored or served, suggesting that the detail was not present in the common model of *B*, *O*, and *T*.

homme qui se prête à la lubricité d'un autre', and *herlot* (3644) 'débauché'. Several of Iseut's remarks to and about the disguised Tristan likewise contain an ambiguous or oblique sexual connotation: '"Ge vuel avoir a toi afere"' (3913), '"Quides tu que ton mal me prenge?"' (3924), '"Soz sa chape senti sa guige"' (3965),[15] and finally, the terms of her ambiguous oath:

> 'Or escoutez que je ci jure ...
> Q'entre mes cuises n'entra home,
> Fors le ladre qui fist soi some,
> Qui me porta outre les guez,
> Et li rois Marc mes esposez.'   (4199, 4205–08)

In all of these passages, Tristan's leprosy, which, he asserts, resulted from his intercourse with Iseut (3763, 3773), is implicitly equated with disordered sexual desire.

The association of leprosy and illicit carnality, reflected in the formula of Adam Scot: 'Lepra corporis, luxuriae imago', was universal in the twelfth century (Jonin, *Personnages* 365; Brody 143). As Tristan's assertion indicates, leprosy was considered not only as a punishment for sexual misconduct but as its direct consequence, a venereal disease. Like *Fb*, *Fo*, and *Tmen*, the leper episode in *B* contains a scene in which the disguised Tristan sharply and bitterly mocks the king (3740–77). In *B*, however, where Tristan's disguise as a leper supposedly consumed by a terrible burning sensation permits him to rescue Iseut from the stake as he has rescued her previously from the *grant ardor* of Yvain's lepers, the irony is especially biting. Through the collusion of her adulterous lover, who flaunts before Mark the signs of that passion, Iseut, who is guilty of that of which she stands accused, is made to appear innocent. Tristan's statement that Mark himself is a leper ('"Dans rois, ses sires ert meseaus."' [3771])[16] implies that the jealous, vengeful Mark has also been corrupted by his lust for Iseut and that the selfish squabbling of the repugnant lepers for the possession of their prize has tainted Mark as well (Barteau 165, n. 64). The association of leprosy and carnality also explains Mark's decision to hand Iseut over to Yvain's band of lepers, who will provide for her a far more horrible fate than the penalty traditionally reserved for the convicted adulteress – burning. Not only will she share their miserable existence, but she whose passion was too great will become the object of their monstrous

---

[15] For 3913, see Reid, *Textual Commentary* 128.
[16] This assertion is analogous to the fool's statement in *Fb* that it is Mark who is the fool ('"Plus fol de moi vait a cheval"' [279]), a statement that, in the context of *Fb* 252, can refer only to the king.

lust.[17] Presumably, she will become infected in her turn and will contract
the *grant ardor* that, in replacing her death at the stake, will appropriately
and continuously punish her incontinent lust.[18]

Tristan Fou

In his infinite manifestations and metamorphoses, the fool invariably
retains one characteristic: 'He appears from some point of view erring and
irresponsible. He transgresses or ignores the code of reasoned self-
restraint under which society attempts to exist' (Swain 1). It is fitting, then,
that Tristan the adulterer should repeatedly be portrayed in the Tristan
corpus in the guise of the traditional fool, a depiction that renders metaphorically the distance that separates him from society, be it the society of
the non-amorous or that of the non-adulterous. The episodes of Tristan's
madness are the most frequently retold of the disguise episodes in the
medieval Tristan corpus,[19] and those found in the French Tristan poems,
Fb and *Fo*, represent the most complex and allusive portions of this body of
texts. In these two poems, elements of Tristan's garb, speech, and behavior
point successively or simultaneously to the stereotyped attributes of the
madman, the court fool, the seer, the *ménestrel*, the *jongleur*, the poet, and
the wild man.

The term *fol* that is applied to Tristan (*Fb* 125, 137, 155, 157, 214, etc.; *Fo*
178, 208, 227, 245, 247, etc.) is ambiguous in the twelfth century, designat-
ing indifferently 'les "fous de cour" dont les saillies égaient rois et barons
[et] les aliénés errant librement à travers villes et campagnes' (Ménard, *Rire*
179).[20] To the extent that Tristan's passion is portrayed as being within the

---

[17] The appellation applied by Yvain to Iseut, whom he calls 'la givre' (1214), is a reference to
her illicit passion; for the serpent was a popular emblem of lust in theological and didactic
literature (cf. Hildegard von Bingen 73–74). In the 'Lai mortel' in *R*, Tristan compares love
(and by implication Iseut) to a serpent that he has clasped to his breast (Fotitch 1, xii).
[18] While the other legal procedures applied to Tristan and Iseut in *B* accurately reflect contemporary judicial practices, burning at the stake was not a punishment meted out in cases of
adultery in the twelfth century (Jonin, *Personnages* 71). Hence, if Beroul retained this trait
from his model, which in all other respects he brought into conformity with contemporary
practice, he clearly did so because of the metaphorical link between burning and the symp-
toms of leprosy.
[19] Besides the accounts of *Fb* and *Fo*, there are madness episodes in *O* (8658–9032), in the MS.
B.N.fr. 103 variant of *R* (Bédier, *Thomas* 2: 374–79), and in the versions of Gottfried's contin-
uers, Ulrich von Türheim and Heinrich von Freiberg, while the *Donnei des amanz* alludes to
yet another madness episode no longer extant (667–74).
[20] See also Ménard, *Rire* 179, n.164. Swain adds a third category of fool, the 'particularly
unworldly spirit who bears his worldly burdens with gentle amiability' (3).

control of his will, the role of court fool as witty entertainer and manipulative trickster is an appropriate metaphor. To the extent that his passion is considered to lie beyond the exercise of his will, making him incapable of choosing freely to love or not to love his lady, the role of madman is a suitable metaphor. Finally, to the extent that his passion is represented as a force of nature, the role of court fool as oracle is a fitting metaphor. The question of Tristan's free will is central to the *Folies*, and each poet treats the question differently. While in the two poems descriptions of his disordered spirit alternate with descriptions of his cleverness, the *Fb* poet stresses Tristan's *folor* and the *Fo* poet, who refers to his choice of a disguise as 'sen e grant veisdie' (180), his wit.[21] In *Fo* Tristan's decision to adopt a disguise in order to effect his return to Cornwall is arrived at more or less lucidly, but the details of his mental anguish are also described at greater length than in *Fb*, and it is clear that the impulse to journey to Cornwall is closely allied to an obsession.

It is natural for Tristan, who says in *Fb* ' "Quant ne la voi, a po ne deve" ' (93) and in *Fo* ' "Pur vostre amur sui afolez" ' (173),[22] to choose the disguise of a madman, a choice of desperation that renders his desperate state of mind.[23] The representation of Tristan as madman in the *Folies* incorporates three metaphoric conceits concerning madness. First, madness is seen as a punishment visited upon the hero for a sin committed against his beloved. Second, madness is portrayed as a consequence of the jealousy and sorrow arising from unhappy love. Finally, the conceit of Tristan's madness, which turns on the accessory idea that the madman was sexually incontinent, is a metaphoric rendering of *aimer par folie* and its derivatives, terms referring to adulterous love.

To the twelfth-century mind, madness was frequently viewed as a punishment visited by God upon a sinner guilty of a transgression of divine law.[24] While the universe of the lovers is remote from that of Christian orthodoxy, and while, on the infrequent occasions when He

---

21 For Tristan's disordered mind, see *Fb* 90–93, 123–25, 283–84, 315, 482–83; *Fo* 13–14; for his cleverness, see *Fo* 47–48; 179–86.

22 Cf. Tristan's declaration in *O*: 'So ward ich durch sie tore' (8835, 'Thus it is that I became a fool because of her [love]'). See also *Fb* 123–25, 482–83. There is a pun on *afoler*, which may mean either 'to make mad' or 'to kill' (Tobler-Lommatzsch 1: cols. 194–95). In its second sense, *afolez* continues the series of references to death that characterize the opening lines of *Fo* (e.g. 'Ore est [Tristran] dunc de la mort cert' [17]).

23 As Lutoslawski felicitously puts it, 'Comme il est déjà presque fou d'amour ... il a l'idée de feindre la folie' (511).

24 Ménard, 'Fous' 452. As Doob observes: 'Insanity ... deprives men of reason – the image of God. Moreover, in that sin typically involves the overthrow or, worse, the perversion of reason by will and passion, there is an especially close resemblance between sin and madness, a resemblance that frequently becomes identity. ... In some ways, then, madness is the most appropriate punishment for sin as well as its most fitting emblem' (10).

manifests Himself, the Deity accords his approbation rather than his opprobrium to the lovers, the notion of transgression and punishment nevertheless colors the depiction of Tristan as a madman in the *Folies*. Implicit in those texts is the suggestion that Tristan's madness is a punishment for his infidelity to Iseut in marrying another and, more particularly, for the lack of faith that led to his marriage, a theme developed at length in *T*, where Tristan, who blames his dilemma upon his '*fol* corage' (Sn¹ 417), speaks of his marriage as 'ceste *derverie*' (Sn¹ 422) and of the act of consummating the marriage as 'fare *folie*' (Sn¹ 428). Like the leper scene in *T*, the madness scenes contain the suggestion that Tristan's affliction is the expiation of a crime against his beloved, who will, when his sin has been purged, pardon him and, through her renewed love, restore him to physical and emotional health.

An examination of madness scenes from two other works, MS. B.N.fr. 103 and Chrétien's *Yvain*, makes clearer the equation between madness and punishment. As is so often the case, a corresponding scene from the prose *Tristan* makes explicit what is merely implicit in the poems. In MS. B.N.fr. 103, Tristan, who has received a grievous wound to the head in battle, is carried home to be cared for:

> Grant peine mistrent les mires tant qu'il fu gari. Ung jour se jesoit en son lit et estoit presque gari, si lui print volenté de gesir avec sa femme, si just avec elle et en fist sa volenté; et, quant il ot fait son desir, si chay emprès elle tout pasmé aussi comme tout mort.
>
> (Bédier, *Thomas* 2: 374–75)

This is the first (and last) occasion in MS. B.N.fr. 103 on which Tristan consummates his marriage. Iseut aux Blanches Mains summons a physician who, with great difficulty, heals her husband; and Tristan at once departs for Cornwall in search of Iseut. The episode concludes: 'Et commencent cy endroit les soties de Tristan' (375). Tristan's physical infidelity, albeit ostensibly involuntary, resulting from the loss of his wits brought about by his wound, parallels and concretizes his spiritual infidelity. The 'madness' that led to his marriage is mirrored in the madness that, in depriving him of the image of beloved, is responsible for his physical infidelity; and the trials that he undergoes while his wits are disordered represent the penance through which his double infidelity must be expiated.

The episode of Yvain's madness in Chrétien's *Chevalier au Lion* also illuminates the depiction of Tristan's madness.[25] Following his marriage to Laudine, Yvain takes leave of his new spouse and departs in the com-

---

[25] See the penetrating analysis of this episode by Le Goff and Vidal-Naquet.

pany of Gauvain to fight in a series of tourneys in order to avoid the fate of those knights '"qui por lor fames valent mains"' (2486).[26] Laudine reluctantly grants his request but stipulates that he must remain absent for no longer than one year, '"Jusqu'a la feste saint Jehan"' (2750), failing which he should forfeit her love.[27] Before he leaves, she places on his finger a ring conferring extraordinary powers on the wearer:

> 'Prison ne tient ne sanc ne pert
> Nus amanz verais et leaus,
> Ne avenir ne li puet maus,
> Mes qu'il le port et chier le taingne
> Et de s'amie li sovaingne,
> Einçois devient plus durs que fers.
> Cil vos iert escuz et haubers.'   (2604–10)

The year passes swiftly and Yvain, caught up in his successes, forgets the condition set by Laudine. At Chester, Laudine's servant Lunete appears before him and berates him for his faithlessness. Snatching Laudine's ring from the knight's finger, she announces that he is never again to appear in the presence of his mistress. Stricken with grief and remorse at his mistress's ultimatum, Yvain loses his senses and lives as a mad man in a wood where a hermit cares for him. Like Tristan's, Yvain's lunacy, a punishment for his faithlessness towards his lady, is love madness, resulting from his sorrow at the separation from his beloved. When that punishment has been exacted and his sin purged, he regains both his reason and his lady.

In spite of obvious differences in the two episodes, the account of Yvain's madness presents important similarities with the account of Tristan's marriage in *T*, the episode in the Tristan poems that develops most fully the theme of Tristan's infidelity. There is a striking similarity in the circumstances surrounding the moment at which each knight realizes the consequences of his transgression. In *T*, as Tristan is disrobing to enter the nuptial bed, the ring given him by Iseut at their parting (C 51–52) falls from his finger, reminding him of the promise that he made at the moment when he received the ring and rendering him incapable of consummating his marriage with Iseut aux Blanches Mains. The psychology of Thomas' romance is remarkably modern, and the contemporary reader has little

---

[26] Yvain's marriage to Laudine, whose husband he has slain, recalls Tristan's liaison with Iseut, whose uncle he has slain.

[27] In *B*, the potion was drunk on the feast of Saint John and its effects diminished three years later, 'l'endemain de la saint Jehan' (2147). As I have noted above, *B* contains what may be an explicit reference to Chrétien's *Yvain* in the name of the leader of the band of lepers to whom Mark gives Iseut (1155–270). These two points of similarity raise the possibility that Beroul, and perhaps other of the Tristan poets, knew Chrétien's romance.

trouble identifying Tristan's impotence as a reaction to a situation producing guilt and stress. For Thomas, however, the central significance of the episode lies elsewhere: the healing power of Iseut's love has been lost with the loss of the ring that is its symbol, allowing the effects of an old wound, whose origin is described in the following episode, to rob him of his potency. Likewise, in *Yvain* Lunete's action in removing Laudine's ring from the knight's finger removes the protection afforded by Laudine's love and precipitates his madness. In each work, the idea of love as a protection against harm, one aspect of the theme of love's healing power, is linked to the notion of the punishment visited on the knight who forfeits that love.

Tristan's madness was also understood by the poems' twelfth-century audience to be the product of the pain and travail of unhappy love. In twelfth-century secular literature, unhappy or unconsummated love was conventionally depicted as a wasting, mortal illness and as a cause of madness. Hyperbole frequently inflated each conceit, with death substituted for the second term, as in *Fo* 1–24.[28] In *Yvain* the maiden who discovers the mad Yvain asleep in the forest affirms ' "qu'an puet bien de duel forsener" ' (2928).[29] This belief, a literary commonplace, persists to our own day, and Lawrence Durrell's observation in *The Alexandria Quartet* that 'the etiology of love differs only in degree from that of madness' applies equally to the protagonist of the *Folies*. Tristan the lover is an especially fitting subject for depiction as a melancholic madman, for he is the child of *tristitia*, the bearer of a heredity that insures his unhappiness in love.

Physical deprivation and hardship, the counterparts of and objective correlatives for mental anguish, were also cited frequently as causative agents of madness (Doob 45). In the later portions of the narrative, Tristan refers constantly to the suffering, both physical and emotional, that he has undergone for Iseut's love. In *Fb*, he complains:

> 'Je sui a doble traveillié,
> Mais el n'en a nule pitié.

---

[28] 'Known as "amor heroicus" or erotic love, love madness was mentioned by Hippocrates, Galen and all of those later physicians who renewed their knowledge of it through Arab medical documents' (Neaman 22). Examples of medieval lovers driven mad by love include Lancelot (see Bernheimer 14–15), Mathun le Brun in *R* (Löseth §102), Amadas in *Amadas et Ydoine*, and Cuchulinn in 'Cuchulinn's Sick Bed' (see Paton 29–30); and Chaucer refers to 'the loveris maladye / of Hereos' (KT 1373–74).

[29] The Châtelain de Couci laments:
> Se j'avoie le sens qu'ot Salemons,
> Si me feroit amours pour fol tenir;
> Quar tant est fors et crueuz sa prisons
> (Qu'ele me fait assaier et sentir)!   (XI, 9–12)

> O fain, o soif et ou durs liz,
> Pansis, pansant, do cuer, do piz
> Ai soferte mainte destrece.'   (346–50)

When in *T* he sends Kaherdin to England to bring Iseut to his side, Tristan enumerates the suffering and hardships that he has undergone for the sake of his love:

> 'De mes dolurs li dei menbrer
> Que suffert ai pur li amer:
> Perdu en ai tuz mes parenz,
> Mun uncle le rei e ses genz;
> Vilment ai esté congeiez,
> En altres terres eissilliez;
> Tant ai suffert peine e travail
> Qu'a peine vif e petit vail.'   (D 1227–34)

The suffering that Tristan undergoes in his journeys to Cornwall and England – beatings, travel by foot, poverty, illness, hunger, and cold – are all understood to contribute to his disordered mental state.

Finally, in addition to the sorrow and the physical suffering occasioned by his separation from Iseut, there is another element that contributes to the disorder of Tristan's mind – jealousy, a great maker of madmen.[30] The narrator of *Tros*, referring to Mark rather than Tristan, comments:

> Kar dure vie unt li gelus:
> Ire, tençun o[n]t chescun jor,
> La nuit suspeciun e p[a]or.
> Tres ben veium que li dolent
> Turmenté sunt assez greffment.   (534–38)

In *Tmen* Perceval observes of Mark:

> ... 'Fols est qui gaite
> Gens qui s'entr'aiment loialment,
> Car on voit tout apertement
> Qu'il emprendent trop *fol usage*:
> *Fol* en devienent li plus sage,
> Mais ce fait faire jalousie.'   (4718–23)

With little alteration, these lines might describe the Tristan of *T* (Sn[1] 1–182, T[1] 41–66) whose jealousy leads him into 'fole irur' (T[1] 44) (see below,

---

[30] In *R*, believing Iseut to be in love with Kaherdin, Tristan loses his wits through jealousy and lives in the Morois as a wildman in an episode that recalls Yvain's madness in the *Chevalier au Lion* (Löseth §§76–80, 101–04).

'Mutability, Shape-shifting, and Thomas' *Tristan*'). It is evident that the *Fo* poet, whose poem is based closely on that of Thomas, had in mind during its redaction the vivid picture of Tristan's jealousy and disordered mental state presented by his model. In its opening lines, Tristan, who claims to see no issue from his constant suffering save death, asks only that the 'faithless' Iseut know of his end, in order to demonstrate to her his unswerving, tragic, and self-pitying love (*Fo* 20–22).

Tristan's love-madness is an affliction that can only be healed by the one who caused it, for the remedy for love-sickness is, of course, to be found in the favors (the *mecine*) of the beloved (the *mire*).[31] As Tristan says to Brengvein: ' "[Ysiaut] m'avroit tost gari" ' (*Fb* 342). She whose love (like the fallen ring in *T*) has been taken from him, stripping him of his mental and physical faculties, has the power to restore him through her love, rendering Tristan at the end of the *Folies* both lucid and potent.

Finally, Tristan's madness must be understood as a metaphor for foolish or ungoverned passion. Passionate love (or lust) was often conceived as a moral disorder, an unbalancing of the reason in which the heart (or loins) governed the head, obscuring the image of right actions. The unlawful, adulterous passion of Tristan and Iseut is repeatedly characterized in *B* and *T* by the terms *folie, aimer par folie, aimer follement*.[32] To this abstract, moralistic metaphor is attached, in the *Folies*, the suggestion that the madman was an immoral being who, having lost his social conscience with his wits, was prone to extravagant sexual excesses (as was, for a different reason, the leper).[33] The metaphor of lust as a form of moral insanity, for

---

[31] Cf. the following passage from *G*:

> Des nahtes, do diu schoene lac,
> Ir triure unde ir trahte pflac
> Nach ir trutamise,
> Nu kam geslichen lise
> Zuo der kemenaten in
> Ir amis under ir arzatin,
> Tristan und diu Minne:
> Minne diu arzatinne
> Si vuorte ze handen
> Ir siechen Tristanden;
> Ouch vants Isote ir siechen da.
> Die siechen beide nam si sa
> Und gab in ir, im sie
> Ein ander zarzatie.   (12157–70)

[32] *B* 20–21, 301, 496, 661, 696, 801–02, 1655, 2007, 2013, 2297, 2323, 2536, 2838, 4155, 4193–94; *TD* 37, 213, 267, 310, 322, 363, 438, 677.

[33] 'Le fou peut incarner la licence sexuelle, la fécondité magique de la nature, la vie élémentaire et profonde' (Ménard 179). And again: 'To make up for his mental shortcomings, Nature was commonly believed to have endowed the Fool with an excess of virility, symbolized by his *bauble*. 'Fools please women best'. 'A fool's bauble is a lady's playfellow'. 'A foolish bed-mate, why, he hath no peer.' Priapus used to be described as *that foolish god*; and Mercutio's cynical notion of love is a *great natural* with his *bauble*' (Hotson 168–70). Hamlet's mad scene (III, ii, and especially ll. 107–113) is also grounded in this tradition.

which lunacy is a doubly appropriate punishment, is rendered in the *Folies* by the grossly suggestive speech and actions that Tristan's role as madman allows him to perpetrate with impunity. Like the explicitly obscene utterances of Tristan the leper in *B*, his speeches before Mark, Iseut, and the court, in which he announces that he seeks sexual relations with the queen, are shocking because of their public character.[34] Tristan, who in *Fo* has remarked to Mark: '"Bon est a asaer estrange"' (288), proposes in *Fb* to exchange a mythical sister for the queen whom he will carry away to a crystal dwelling in the empyrean, where, he says: '"O moi et li noś deduison"' (169). In *Fo* he cries: '"Je la sui venu doneier"' (378). The sexual aggressiveness of Tristan's speeches portrays covertly yet accurately his reason for coming to the court, and the *Folies* conclude, as do all of the return episodes (with the exception of 'Tristan the Pilgrim', *T D* 785–834), with the lovers reunited in bed.

In *Fo*, after enumerating before Mark his qualities of hunter, musician, and lover, Tristan asks of the king:

> 'Enne sui je bon menestrel?
> Ui vus ai servi de mun pel.'   (525–26)

This somewhat unexpected description of himself, seconded by Iseut's characterization of the fool as '"cist fol, cist fous jugleres"' (561), results from the fantastical juxtaposition of several ideas and, like all of Tristan's whimsical utterances before the king, contains a germ of truth.[35] One may imagine that as Tristan asks the question he pretends to play upon his staff as upon a harp; for he has made his staff the object of similar word play earlier in the scene when, before laying about himself with it, he declares:

> 'Dunc sai ben eskermir de pel:
> Nul ne se cuverat tant ben
> Ke il në ait aukes del men.'   (514–6)

The latter piece of bombast contains a covert allusion to his very real skill at arms, as the former alludes to his no less great skill, which he will evoke again in lines 519–20, as musician and performer of lays. The double role of

---

34 Tristan's suggestive speeches are as follows: *Fb* 161–69, 229–31, 244–46; *Fo* 280–92, 377–78, 521–22; *B* 3761–76. In the corresponding madness scene in MS. B.N.fr. 103, Tristan declares to the blushing Iseut before the assembled court: '"Mon pere m'envoya cha toy faire coup"' (Bédier, *Thomas* 2: 376). The word that Bédier reads as *coup* is corrupt in the manuscript. Löseth, who reads *cocu*, understands these lines to be addressed to Mark (§537a).
35 The choice of terms utilized by each conveys Tristan's oblique assertion that as a *ménestrel* he is a member of Mark's household and Iseut's angry contention that as a *jongleur* he is an outsider.

witty fool and furious madman provides Tristan the liberty of physical action and verbal expression necessary to tryst with Iseut. The ambiguity of his double role affords him the opportunity to play with impunity the most transparent of games and to employ in that game a variety of verbal styles from the coarsly obscene to the lyrically poetical.

In Old French *ménestrel* (<*ministerialem*, 'serviteur') originally designated a household official or an officer of the court (that is, the king's household or *maisnie*). In time, its meaning narrowed, and it came to designate a performer attached to the lord's person and household (Faral 104–06), a being socially superior to the itinerant *jongleur* (<*joculatorem*, 'homme qui plaisante'). While strictly speaking the two terms designated different estates, the itinerant and the domestic entertainer, in practice they come to be partially interchangeable. The distinction was further obscured because their spheres of activity overlapped. Both *ménestrel* and *jongleur* were competent in the oral performance of literary or musical works, often accompanying themselves on an instrument. In addition, their repertory might include acrobatics, legerdemain, and clownery, although these skills were more closely associated with the *jongleur* than with the more dignified *ménestrel*. Equally blurred was the distinction between performance and composition. However, while a member of either profession might exercise the talents and affect the literary pretentions that were more properly the province of the *trouvère*, this transition was perhaps easier for the theoretically more cultivated *ménestrel*.[36] The *fol* as court buffoon represents a specialized type of the *jongleur*/clown (Ménard, 'Fous' 453), while skills of the *fol* as oracle are an extension of those possessed by the *ménestrel*/poet.

The depiction of Tristan as fool in the *Folies* partakes of all of these elements. Alternating between physical and verbal humor, he plays the clown for the king and his court, maliciously mocking the monarch who has outlawed him and separated him from his beloved. He slips abruptly into the role of *ménestrel*, reciting a vivid account of his own life mixed with some gratuitous and highly entertaining flights of poetry. In contrast to the madness scene in O where Tristan wears a jester's motley and carries a jester's club and cheese, Tristan's tattered garb in the *Folies* suggests rather the deranged madman than the professional entertainer. Yet, it is precisely because he plays with such energy, cleverness, and versimilitude his role of madman that he amuses as fool. His hyperbolic language and extravagant behavior point to the *jongleur*/clown, whose stock in trade was prestidigitation and burlesque slapstick seasoned with low verbal humor. Tristan's burlesque description of his skills and attributes (*Fb*

---

[36] See Faral on the difficulties of definition and categorization (84–86, 106).

184–87, *Fo* 489–526) echoes the traditional *boniment* of the *jongleur*, a hyperbolic description of his diverse talents designed to insure his welcome and employment in noble houses. He alludes to his skills as a prestidigitator when in *Fb* he announces:

> 'Jë ai sailli et lanciez jons,
> Et sostenu dolez bastons.'   (184–85)[37]

In the broad, frequently obscene humour of his *gabs* and in chasing the courtiers from the great hall with his staff, he engages with great vigor in the ridiculous and outrageous behavior of the clown. Confined to *Fo* where they conveniently mark the transitions between scenes, the episodes of physical play consist in Tristan laying about him with his staff (*Fo* 246–56, 371–78, 513–16).[38]

While the province of the fool as clown is physical play and verbal extravagance, that of the fool as *ménestrel* is poetic recitation and, by extension, poetic invention. Hence, Tristan recounts, apparently for the king's amusement, a number of highly ingenious and occasionally ribald *contes* (a word he himself employs at *Fb* 171). *Fo* contains four scenes of verbal extravagance (the first occurring before the fool enters Mark's presence), while *Fb* presents shorter versions of the second and third:

(1) The marriage of the abbot of Mont-Saint-Michel (*Fo* 227–38).
(2) Tristan's account of his birth and suckling (*Fo* 269–79, *Fb* 158–60).
(3) His offer to exchange his own sister for Iseut (*Fo* 280–98, *Fb* 161–64) and the description of the crystal dwelling in the air (*Fo* 299–308, *Fb* 165–69).
(4) The *chasse à l'envers* (*Fo* 489–512).

Mark, who refers to these as *gas* (*Fb* 191), perceives them to be merely fantastical, a sort of improvised poetic creation designed to amuse and delight.[39] Indeed, Tristan's sallies mightily please both Mark and his courtiers, who laughingly declare:

> 'Cist est bon fol, mult par dit ben.
> Ben parole sur tute ren.'   (*Fo* 311–12, cf. 293, 497–98)

---

[37] Hoepffner understands 'sostenir dolez bastons' as a reference to Tristan's 'talent d'équilibriste' (*La Folie de Berne* 85). Both MS. B.N.fr. 103 (Bédier, *Thomas*, 2: 380–81) and O (6542–44, 9076–94) contain episodes recounting his skill in throwing reeds, said in the former to constitute one of the 'gieux Tristan' (Bédier, *Thomas*, 2: 381). See Schoepperle, *Sources* 292–96 for a discussion.

[38] In *R*, when the ship that has carried Tristan to Cornwall docks at Tintagel, the fool rushes from the vessel with such violence that Mark, who is at the port, flees and shuts himself up in his castle (Löseth §537a).

[39] Iseut uses the same, deprecatory term, reinforced by the adjective *vilains*, to dismiss the fool's allusions to her life with Tristan (*Fb* 373; *Fo* 370).

While appearing to play the role of court buffoon, Tristan has in fact imperceptibly assumed that of serious *ménestrel*; for these *contes*, the counterpart to his explicit allusions to his former life, refer in metaphorical terms to the past and present circumstances of Mark and the lovers. The first of these is perhaps a veiled reference to Tristan's own marriage, which has already been mentioned (*Fo* 49–50) and which, in the narrative of *T* that *Fo* follows, takes place a short time before the first of the return episodes. However, it is more likely that it is a deprecatory reference to the marriage ceremony of Mark and Iseut, whose ostentation, clearly an important detail of the narrative tradition, is alluded to in *B* (3004–06), in *O* (2807), in *G* (12544–55), in *S* (Ch. 46), in Jean Renart's *L'Escoufle* (1704–17), and, by means of a litotes, in *Sir Tristrem* (1706–07). The second reproduces in vague, figurative terms the circumstances of Tristan's own birth, orphaning, and adoption, while the mention of the whale is perhaps an echo of Iseut's despairing meditation in *T* (D 1654–56, Brusegan 55). The offer of the exchange of sisters is perhaps another allusion to T (T^1 51–183) where Thomas discusses the love quadrangle of the two ill-assorted couples, Mark and Iseut and Tristan and Iseut aux Blanches Mains; for the latter (and perhaps the former) live together more like brother and sister than husband and wife:

> Entre ces quatre ot estrange amor:
> Tut en ourent painne e dolur,
> E un e autre en tristur vit;
> E nuls d'aus nen i a deduit.   (T^1 71–74)[40]

Their predicament would, at least from the point of view of Tristan and Iseut, disappear were Mark to exchange his woman for the fool's. The celestial dwelling, the most explicit of these allusions, refers to the sojourn in the Morois. The *chasse à l'envers*, which continues the reference to the life in the forest, alludes covertly to Tristan's skill at the hunt while serving simultaneously as a metaphor for the inversion of reality represented by Tristan's disguise. Yet so oblique is the truth of these fantastical utterances that none who hears them fathoms their meaning.

Following his evocation of the crystalline dwelling, Tristan embarks on a series of explicit references to the events of his love, addressing these exclusively to Iseut in *Fo*, although in *Fb* he actually calls the king to witness the second of his evocations (196–97). The fantastical utterances were a necessary preliminary to the allusive speeches, which are perceived by the king to be of the same nature as the former. It is left to the

---

[40] Brusegan sees in this image a reference to the substitution of Brengvein for Iseut in the marriage bed (56).

reader to penetrate the extra dimension of truth implicit in Tristan's utterances, a dimension apparently invisible to Mark, although a glimmer of the truth appears to Iseut and the court.[41] Indeed, so explicit are these allusions and so completely does he leave off the role of fool that in *Fb* the last comment heard, chorus-like, from the courtiers before the end of the audience is:

> 'Mien escïant, tot avandroit
> Que mes sires cel fol crerroit.'   (250–51)

As *ménestrel*, Tristan recounts with great exactitude for the benefit of the queen (and the reader) incidents from their shared past. In this sense, he is a poet who treats of the entire matter of his life with Iseut as he has elsewhere treated of a single incident, first making of it a lay (*Ch* 107–16), then performing that lay before the queen (*Tmen* 4066–95). Yet, each of his roles conceals a hidden intent. As *jongleur* he vents his spleen on his unwitting persecutor and rival through his veiled but bitter mockery. As *ménestrel* he woos and wins his lady once more. The actions and speeches that he directs towards the king are those of a prating, capering clown who secretly mocks the person he is set to entertain, subtly calling attention to Mark's double credulity as dupe and cuckold. As he turns his attention to the queen, he slips into the role of *ménestrel*, evoking their past life and begging for her understanding and recognition. Adopting the persona of the poet/lover, he pleads eloquently for the favors of his lady. With Mark's departure, the second role entirely eclipses the first, and in the latter part of the *Folies* Tristan addresses himself exclusively to Brengvein and Iseut in an attempt to persuade the latter of his identity.

The depiction of the chivalric Tristan as court entertainer in the *Folies* (particularly in *Fo*) would appear to have been the inspiration for his disguise in *Tmen*. Tristan, who has proved himself against the best knights of Arthur's realm, begs the king's leave to depart from Carlion to seek Iseut, whom he has not seen for a year and a half. Arthur presses him courteously to remain,

> Mais Amors qui si le tient cort
> Li fait si son cuer esmovoir
> Que por mil mars de fin avoir
> Ne laira que ne voie Yseut
> Por cui amour sovent se deut.   (3780–84)

With the king's permission, Tristan selects Gauvain and twelve companions from among the most worthy of Arthur's knights and disguises them.

---

[41] As I suggest above, Mark may in fact have dimly grasped the import of the fool's utterances.

Dressed in ill-fitting garments and ridiculous hats they resemble nothing so much as quail hunters, remarks Gerbert. The fittings of their horses are of poor quality, and each carries a different musical instrument. Not surprisingly,

> ... Tristrans porte une vïele,
> Que nus mieus de lui ne vïele.   (3829–30)

His hair sticks through two holes in his hat, and he completes his disguise by closing one eye, the traditional grimace of the clown but also a sign of (semi-)divinity or divine inspiration.[42] When the band arrives in Lancien, so grotesque is Tristan's appearance that 'Par mi la vile maine esfroi' (3887).

Upon their arrival at Mark's court, the companions learn that a tournament is about to begin. They appear before the king asking employment and are given the post of guards. At dinner on the evening of the first day of the tournament Tristan plays the 'Lai du Chèvrefeuille' before the court. Iseut hesitates to recognize him because of his missing eye and his low station. She even thinks momentarily that Tristan has betrayed her in teaching another 'le lai que moi et lui feïsmes' (4085; cf. Fo 561–72, 957–65). Then, realizing the unworthiness of this thought, she is able to discern the minstrel's identity. The next day, Mark takes his pleasure at the tournament while Tristan and Iseut, left alone in the castle, take theirs in the queen's bedchamber. Meanwhile, on the tournament field the tide runs against Mark's forces. Gauvain, who has witnessed the reversal in his host's fortunes, seeks out Tristan and proposes that the companions come to the king's aid. Through Iseut's good offices they are fitted out with mounts and new armor. With their instruments slung from their necks, they ride into the fray where they show themselves to such brilliant effect that they return the advantage to Mark's forces. Their opponents consider themselves greatly dishonored ('en grand vielté' 4281) to have been defeated by minstrels.

At this moment, Perceval, who has been long abroad in quest of the Grail and the Lance Which Bleeds Ceaselessly, rides from the wood onto the field where the tournament is taking place. His armor and harness are in sad disrepair, his mount a 'noir ronchi bauchant / Maigre, pelu, redois et las' (4324–25). Wearing new armor but with his instrument still slung from his neck, Keu challenges the newcomer, mocking the sorry state of the

---

[42] In her notes to the Bédier edition of *Tmen*, Jessie Weston observes that in Scandinavian mythology, Odin adopts a similar disguise in his earthly wanderings (527), while Merlin appears as a *vilain* with one eye closed in the *Vulgate Merlin* (181, 8–10). The minstrel's closed eye also recalls the archetypal figures of the blind musician-poet (Homer) and the blind soothsayer (Teiresias), both vessels of divine inspiration.

other's equipment. Perceval declines the combat, saying that he would dishonor himself in fighting a minstrel:

> 'Mais, par cel Dieu qui fist le mont,
> Por mil mars, ce sachiez de voir,
> Ne volroie je mie avoir
> Mis main dedesus jogleor.
> Moi est vis, par le Salveor,
> J'en seroie trop *avilliez*.' (4440-44)

When Keu persists, Perceval defeats him and takes the side of Mark's opponents. He turns the tide in their favor and finally unhorses and captures Tristan. After the fighting has come to an end, Gauvain rides forward and addresses Perceval, asking his identity and proffering his own. Perceval refuses to believe him, saying:

> 'Je sai bien, toz en sui certains,
> Que onques me sire Gavains
> Ne fu menestreus en sa vie.' (4675–77)

Convinced at last of Gauvain's identity, he asks for and receives an explanation of the companions' disguises. Upon learning of Tristan's plight, he joins with Gauvain and Yvain in petitioning Mark to pardon his nephew. The king, who has no direct knowledge of the couple's adultery, consents, stipulating, however, that Tristan be prohibited the chambers of the queen.

In *Tmen*, the most chivalric of the disguise episodes, the greatest emphasis is placed on the *vilité* of the hero's disguise and, in consequence, on the courtliness underlying his actions. In fact, in causing Tristan's actions to mirror those of Perceval, Gerbert insists twice over on the contrast between essential worth and surface appearances. Like Perceval's garb and accoutrements, which fail to reveal his innate nobility and great prowess only to the blindly egotistical Keu, Tristan's disguise as *jongleur/ clown*, a low entertainer relying on slapstick routines and tricks of legerdemain to amuse his audience, only imperfectly conceals his courtly persona. If the closed eye, the ridiculous garb, and the confusion that he sows in the streets of Lancien point to the *jongleur* at his most burlesque, his skill as musician and his performance of the 'Lai du Chèvrefeuille', extensions of his overt identity as harper and composer of lays, designate the persona of the courtly poet/lover.[43]

---

[43] The episode of *Tmen* contains, albeit in a gentler tone, the same mockery of the king found in *B*, *Fb*, and *Fo*; for the unwitting Mark is persuaded to employ as watchmen those who have come to Lancien with the express intention of despoiling him of his property and his honor.

The traditional representation of the fool contains another element that renders plausible in literary terms the otherwise wildly improbable situation constituted by Tristan's detailed evocation, in Mark's presence, of his life with Iseut.[44] Madness was considered, especially in the Celtic tradition that so profoundly marks the Tristan poems, to be related both to the gift of divine poetic inspiration[45] and to that of clairvoyance, either in the form of the ability to prophesy the future and to reveal hidden truths or, more prosaically, in the ability to voice unpopular truths before a monarch.[46] The oracular powers of the soothsayer and the orphic powers of the poet coincide in the verities concealed beneath the apparently frivolous discourse of the fool.

In *Fb*, the fool calls himself Picous (and Picolet, 158, 189), a name accorded in popular tradition to a dwarf and seer (Hoepffner, *Folie de Berne* 80; Telfer, '*Picous*').[47] Cloaked in the trappings of folly, Tristan's speeches before the court contain an insistent and aggressive note of truth and, in the mouth of the poor, deranged villein, resemble sibylline utterances. The attribution of the mantle of clairvoyance to Tristan, oblique as it may be in the *Folies*, is predicated on the identification of the sometime musician and hunter with the hidden world of natural things. Nature in this sense is set in opposition to society as is love to the marriage of Mark and Iseut and as is the truth of the *fol naturel*'s speeches to the mendacious forms of social convention maintained by Mark and his queen. The inspiration that shapes the fool's utterances is the gift of the divinity (surely not the same being as that served by Ogrin) that preserved the hero in his 'saut mortel', that acquiesced in Iseut's ambiguous oath, and that has conjoined, watched over, and protected the lovers. The holiness of nature and of natural things invests Tristan as he stands before Mark and, possessed by a god, gives utterance to truths that the king and the courtiers are incapable of apprehending.

---

[44] See Bédier (*Deux poèmes* 92) and Hoepffner (*Folie de Berne* 87) and the solutions proposed by Adler (350–51), Fedrick ('Note'), and Haidu (715, n. 4).

[45] On divine poetic frenzy, see Curtius 146, 474–75.

[46] 'Le fou est également pourvu d'un étrange pouvoir prophétique. ... Apparemment étranger au monde des hommes, le fou est peut-être en contact avec le monde invisible, avec les êtres d'En-Haut. Il entrevoit les choses cachées. Il donne par moments l'impression de participer aux grands mystères du monde' (Ménard, *Rire* 179). See also Welsford 76–112; Swain 2; Ménard, 'Fous' 457–58. On the role of fool as satirist, see Swain 63–64. Examples of fools with the gift of prophecy abound in medieval literature. In *R*, the fool of King Pharamont of Gaule predicts that Tristan will kill Le Morholt (Curtis 1: §§268–70). Lailoken and Merlin, both prophets, become mad (Bernheimer 13). See also Ménard 179, n. 168. In *O*, Tristan the fool declares to Mark: '"Ja kan ich nit geliegen"' (8819). ('"I am incapable of telling a lie."')

[47] Hoepffner understands Iseut's speech at line 378 as an allusion to the 'métier qu'il exerce en ce moment, le métier de devin, celui qui révèle des choses cachées' (*Folie de Berne* 110).

Tristan the Nightingale

Of all of the episodic Tristan poems, *Tros* is most closely linked to the larger context of the work in which it figures, the *Donnei des amanz*. There, it serves as an *exemplum* recounted to a reluctant maiden by an ardent lover to demonstrate the proposition:

> 'K'amie n'est fine ne pure
> Ke ne se met en aventure
> E en perilus hardement
> S'ele aime del tut lealment.' (659–62)

It is also couched in the larger context of the mythic and metaphoric associations linking nature, love, and music in the figure of the nightingale. Finally, it is one of a group of moral tales castigating the uncourtly *vilain* (and the *gelus* who is associated with him). *Tros* constitutes a disguise episode insofar as Tristan conceals his presence and dissembles his form in order to enter into contact with Iseut, although the latter rather than the former is the protagonist of the episode.

Tristan, who has not seen Iseut for a year, returns alone from Brittany to Cornwall where he comes by night to the garden of Mark's palace. Beside a fountain beneath a pine, presumably the same as that beneath which the lovers previously deceived Mark in *B* and *T*, he sits and lays his plans.[48] Having learned in his youth the art of imitating birdsong, he alters his voice to reproduce the song of the nightingale, the popinjay, the oriole, and the other woodland birds.[49] Lying in the arms of the sleeping Mark, Iseut hears his song and knows that her lover is nearby. She is, however, guarded throughout the night by ten knights and a malevolent dwarf. As she hesitates, unsure of what to do,

> Tristrans feseit tel melodie
> Od grant dousur ben loinz oïe
> N'est quer enteins de murdrisur
> Ke de cel chant n'eüst tendrur. (479–82)

Compelled by the sweetness and the urgency of his song, she resolves to go to him in spite of the danger. Slipping stealthily from the arms of her husband, she leaves the bed and crosses the chamber where, miracu-

---

[48] While in *B*, where the discovery of Mark in the tree precedes the opening of the fragment, no mention is made of a fountain, there is a brook in *S* (Ch. 55) and a spring in *Fo* (*funteine* 785).

[49] Tristan also disguises his voice in two other disguise episodes: *Fo* (210) and *B* (3747–48).

lously, the guards are fast asleep.[50] In opening the door of the chamber, however, Iseut awakens the dwarf, who raises the alarm. She strikes him in the face, dislodging four of his teeth. Awakened by the dwarf's cries, Mark comes to the pair, silences the dwarf's accusations, and orders that Iseut be allowed to go where she will, saying that she has been too closely guarded of late. Iseut joins Tristan in the garden, and there the lovers 'meinent lur joie e lur deduit / mut grant pece de cele nuit' (653–54).

Tros, which alludes liberally if subtly to motifs in the aforegoing canon, represents an amplification and a recombination of certain of Tristan's attributes and a joining of these with popular and literary notions concerning the nightingale (see Telfer, 'Evolution'). His song possesses the power to put to sleep the watchful guards and to change Mark's heart; only the dwarf 'de males ars' (598) is proof against its magic. Tristan's use of birdsong as the means to be reunited with Iseut recalls his use of the carved message in *Ch*, another image charged with connotations of nature and the woodland, and presages his use of the 'Lai du Chèvrefeuille' for the same purpose in *Tmen*. Finally, as the nightingale serves frequently as a double of the poet/lover in twelfth-century literature (Pfeffer 73–74), Tristan's song in *Tros* recalls the poetic accounts that he gives of himself in the *Folies*, in *Tmen*, and, by means of the carved message, in *Ch*, evoking for Iseut their shared past and their love just as surely as in those other episodes.

Tristan's ability to imitate birdsong, which partakes equally of his skills as musician, hunter/woodsman, and minstrel,[51] is an elaborate expansion of the topos of the nightingale calling to his mate, a motif absent from the traditional depiction of the nightingale in classical literature but found in the lyrics of the twelfth-century troubadours Marcabru, Bernart de Ventadorn, and Gaucelm Faidit.[52] Like the song of the nightingale, which arouses love, Tristan's poignant melody impels Iseut to quit her prison at great peril.[53] Yet, the physical danger to which Iseut is subjected is paral-

---

[50] At this point, the poet embarks on a digression on the *gelus* (534–88).

[51] Schoepperle notes: 'To imitate birds seems to have been an accomplishment not uncommon among French minstrels of the twelfth and thirteenth century' (*Sources* 289).

[52] Marcabru, 'Bel m'es quan la rana chanta' 5–6 (PC 293, 11); Bernart de Ventadorn, 'Can lo boschatges es floritz' 3–4 (PC 70, 40); Gaucelm Faidit, 'Pel joi del temps qu'es floritz' 1–4 (PC 167, 45), 'Lo rossinolet salvatge' 8–9 (PC 167, 34). It is not impossible that another passage from Marcabru's poem, in which the nightingale is said to be insouciant of winter, may have provided the germ of inspiration for this episode:

> Ples d'orgueilh car el no sen
> Freg ni gel ni glaz ni bisa.   (7–8)

Compare the opening lines of the *Donnei*, where the poet hears the nightingale and the other woodland birds 'Orgoil mener, qu'iver decline' (7).

[53] Cf. 'Philomena cantibus suscitat amores' (*Carmina Burana* 1.2: No. 139, ii, 7–8) and Bernart de Ventadorn, 'Can la verz folha s'espan' 5–8 (PC 70, 38). It may be that the *Tros* poet is alluding to the episode of Cariado and Iseut in *T* (Sn[1] 781–888), the only other episode in the Tristan poems in which avian imagery plays a prominent role, drawing a contrast between the erotic power of Tristan the nightingale and the loathing inspired by the repellant Cariado, bearer of bad tidings and owl of ill omen.

lelled by the mortal danger weighing on the lovesick Tristan, whose pain pierces through his song, moving Iseut to desperation; for since Pliny the nightingale's song has announced its death:[54]

> Tristran dehors e chante e gient
> Cum russinol que prent congé
> En fin d'esté od grant pité.
> Ysoud en ad dolur e ire,
> Plure des oilz, del quer suspire.   (494–98)

Hence, *Tros* also echoes the themes of Tristan's infirmity – a trope for his lovesickness – and his healing through the power of Iseut's love, which are leitmotifs of the return episodes (see below, 'The Ailing Hero').

Concealed in the darkness of the garden, Tristan seems wrapped in the protective cloak of the powers of the woodland; and his song draws on the erotic powers of spring, of nature, and of the *celeste armonie*. The list of birds that Tristan imitates (465–67) echoes the list of those that populate the spring landscape evoked at the opening of the poem (3–5; Pfeffer 155), emphasizing his association with the natural world. The nightingale, a powerful erotic symbol in twelfth-century literature, is an apt metaphor for Tristan embracing his lady in a nocturnal garden of love. His song effects – and celebrates – the triumph of the resourceful lover and his courageous lady over the uncourtly *vilein* and *gelus*, whose coarse emotions cloud their wits:

> Li oiselet, men essiënt,
> Quant il chantent plus doucement,
> S'esforcent plus e seir e mein
> Pur tariër le fel vilein,
> E les gelus ensurquetut,
> Ke joie e chant heent de but;
> Kar a geluz, tut sanz mensunge,
> La nostre joie est fable e sunge.   (41–48)

Through a spurious etymology, the poet associates Mark, *li gelus*, with the '*gelee*, / Ke l'ewe *moille* tent fermee' (551–52), punning on *moille*, 'running, liquid' and *moillier*, 'wife'. Mark's castle is a mythical prison of death from which Tristan frees Iseut as the spring, whose harbinger the nightingale is, frees rivers and streams from the wintry grip of the *gelee*.[55] Ultimately,

---

[54] Telfer, 'Evolution' 31; cf. *Le Bestiaire d'amour rimé* 207–12.
[55] This second image is to be compared with, and is perhaps a deliberate echo of the 'funteine ki ben surt' of *Fo* (701), Tristan's metaphor for love that is freely given.

Tristan's song, like that of the woodland birds, assures the victory of love over jealousy and constraint, of union over separation, of spring over winter, of life over death.[56]

Tristan the Wild Man in the Folie d'Oxford

When, in *Fo*, Tristan, who is wearing an 'esclavine ben velue' (190) and carrying a staff over his shoulder, arrives at the gates of Tintagel, the porter (surely a literary ancestor of the antic gatekeeper of *Macbeth*, II, iii) addresses him jocularly in the following terms:

> 'Entrez, fis Urgan le velu,
> Granz e velu estes assez:
> Urgan en so ben resemblez.'   (242–44)

Since in *T* Tristan slew a giant named Urgan (*S* Ch. 62), the porter's words, the first allusion in the poem to the events of Tristan's past, might seem to characterize the hero as a giant. In fact, because of the emphasis that the porter lays on the fool's hirsuteness, he humourously if obliquely characterizes Tristan as a wild man. Indeed, the disguised hero possesses many of the traditional attributes of that mythical being. Because of the *esclavine ben velue* that he is wearing, he appears to be covered with hair. His features are blackened (211–14), and he carries a staff (219–20) that he will later use as a club. Since Tristan is not greatly above normal height, the porter's 'granz' refers not to his stature but to his musculature.[57] Most

---

[56] Another episode of the Tristan corpus, the Welsh *Ystori Trystan*, is structured around the same controlling image of summer and winter as is *Tros*. When Trystan ap Tallwch and Esyllt, wife of March, flee to the Forest of Clyddon, March complains to Arthur. After a parley in the wood between Gwalchmai, Arthur's representative, and Trystan, Arthur makes peace between uncle and nephew. However, neither will consent to be without Esyllt.

> Then Arthur adjudged her to one while the leaves should be on the wood, and to the other during the time that the leaves should not be on the wood, the husband to have the choice. And the latter chose the time when the leaves should not be on the wood, because the night is longest during that season.   (109–10)

Upon being informed of the judgment, Esyllt craftily evokes the yew, the holly, and the evergreen that keep their leaves throughout the year and thus is enabled to remain always with Trystan. The seasonal metaphor of *Tros* and the *Ystori Trystan*, which recalls the stories in classical mythology of Persephone and Hades and of Orpheus and Eurydice, opposes winter, night, jealousy, separation, and death to spring/summer, day, love, union, and life. Like the Mark of *Tros*, the jealous March is a winter figure, and like the Mark of *B*, who delivers Iseut to Yvain's band of lepers, March, who would claim Iseut during the long winter nights, is a being dominated by a perverse, obsessive lust.

[57] See also 45–46.

important, however, is the fact that in this episode Tristan acts the part of a madman, and madness was the chief means by which a human being might be reduced to the state of wildness.

It seems clear that in reviewing the entire antecedent Tristan corpus, the *Fo* poet, struck by certain elements of Tristan's persona – his suffering for love, his 'madness', his association with the forest, his sexual passion, his conflict with the social Order, and his 'abduction' of Iseut to the Morois – found appropriate the metaphorical characterization of the hero as a wild man. The *Fo* poet did not, however, as did the author(s) of *R*, actually cast the hero in the role of a wild man. Instead, in the porter's off-handed gibe and in the fool's fantastical utterances, he merely sketched the contours of that mythical figure.

In the following scene, Tristan falls in with the porter's jest. Laying about him with his stick, he scatters those who have harassed him, crying after him as after a wolf (247), another creature of the wild. His reply to Mark's question concerning his identity and origins likewise suggests his association with the wild:

> 'Ma mere fu une baleine.
> En mer hantat cume sereine.
> Mès je ne sai u je nasqui.
> Mult sai jo ben ki me nurri.
> Une grant tigre m'aleitat
> En une roche u me truvat.
> El me truvat suz un perun,
> Quidat que fusse sun foün,
> Si me nurri de sa mamele.'   (271–79)

While madness was the chief means by which wild men were made, the theme of the child raised in the wild by beasts was also a commonplace of wild man lore. Children so nurtured grew to adulthood innocent of civilization's conventions, although upon attaining maturity they frequently entered civilized society. For example, *Tristan de Nanteuil*, a fourteenth-century *chanson de geste*, tells of a lost child, the eponymous hero of the epic, who, suckled by a mermaid and later by the wife of a fisherman and nurtured by a savage giant hind, passes the first sixteen years of his life in the wild before taking a wife and becoming a knight.[58] In *Fo*, Tristan's evocation of his fantastical birth and nurture alludes both to his metaphorical depiction as a wild man and, more generally, to his association with the forest and the forces of nature.

---

[58] Given the homonymy of the protagonists' names, it seems likely that the *Tristan de Nanteuil* poet was inspired by the above passage from *Fo*.

In wildman lore, however, one came more often to the state of wildness through intense physical or emotional travail that unseated the reason and caused the victim to revert to the 'natural state'. Tristan, who is 'dolent, mornes, tristes, pensifs' (2), has experienced a plenty of both sorts of suffering in the uneven course of his passion for Iseut. As the *Fo* poet, who clearly found the metaphor of insanity appropriate because of the suffering that Tristan had endured, insists:

> Peine, dolur, penser, ahan
> Tut ensement confunt Tristran.   (13–14)

Metaphorically, then, Tristan's wildness proceeds directly from his insanity, for 'to the Middle Ages wildness and insanity were almost interchangeable terms' (Bernheimer 12). Tristan's figurative degeneration to the wild state in *Fo* is the result of his love malady and serves, like his madness and leprosy, as yet another trope for the effects of his passion.

Like his mythological forebear the satyr, the medieval wild man was wont to carry off damsels to his forest dwelling, there to live with them in a state of sylvan bliss. Tristan, whose actions in *Fo* constitute a figurative abduction of his lady, brashly announces that he has come to Tintagel to seek Iseut (280–91), whom he demands to exchange for a mythical sister (285–87). All this, he ambiguously remarks, in order to serve the king 'pur amur' (291). In the same breath, he evokes an idyllic sojourn in a crystalline dwelling that is an idealized version of the grotto of the Morois (299–308), the scene of his earlier 'abduction' of Iseut.[59]

In the apparently oracular allusions that he makes to the life of the lovers, the disguised Tristan exhibits yet another characteristic of the wild man; for the clairvoyance of the fool was often shared by the wild man who was a civilized hero gone mad.[60] The best-known example of a wild man with the gift of prophecy is that of Merlinus Silvaticus in the twelfth-century *Vita Merlini* of Geoffrey of Monmouth.[61] Tristan, who has declared that Iseut is the cause of his melancholic madness (615–18), evokes in the latter portion of *Fo* the image of Iseut's love as a freely flowing fountain (701–02), a detail that offers a striking parallel to the scene in the *Vita Merlini* in which Merlin's insanity is finally cured by a draught from a magic fountain, as Tristan's madness (wildness) will be by the renewal of Iseut's love.

---

[59] Cf. *Fo* 861–70 and *S* Ch. 64.

[60] Bernheimer notes: 'The lunatic was now also a prophet, whom his mental waywardness had endowed with oracular faculties, while it compelled him also to forsake human company and to seek shelter in the woods' (13). The other, more dehumanized sort of wild man, the bestial forest giant, was aphasic and without the gift of prophecy.

[61] The Lailoken fragments, the immediate source for Geoffrey's depiction of Merlin's madness, give the account of a mad Welsh prophet Lailoken who dwelt in the Caledonian forest (Bruce 1: 141).

In *T*, Tristan the leper (a being who, like the wild man, possesses an extraordinary sexual urge) lies beneath the steps of the palace near death, wrapped, like the fool of *Fo* (190), in an *eschavine velue* (D 631). While fetching wood for the fire, the wife of the porter of Tintagel comes upon him and, misled by his hairy covering and darkened features, 'Cuide que ço deable seit' (D 633). Since the medieval wild man was sometimes identified with the devil and his agents, the incubi (Le Goff and Vidal-Naquet 555),[62] this curious, isolated detail in *T* may well have been the germ of inspiration for the wild man motif in *Fo*, which retains the *eschavine*, the darkened features, and the porter of *T*.

Another episode from *T*, that of the intertwining trees, may have reinforced the association of Tristan with the wild man, who was said to make his home sometimes in caves (cf. the grotto of the Morois and the *salle aux images* in *T*) and sometimes in the trunks of trees. The oak trees that grow from the tombs of the lovers signify that they, and especially Tristan, have been reinvested with their real and original form, that of woodland divinities whose place of habitation is the forest glade and whose special domain is sexual union.

The *Fo* poet was not alone in perceiving a link between the 'mad' Tristan and the figure of the wild man. *R*, whose redaction is probably closer in time to *Fo* than to any of the other Tristan poems except for *Tmen*, contains a madness scene that has no counterpart in the poems (Löseth §§76–80, 101–04). Believing that Iseut has forsaken him for Kaherdin, Tristan takes flight from the world of men. Driven mad by jealousy and love sickness, he flees to the Morois where he lives as a wild man. As he is about to enter the forest, he does battle with a young knight whom, in his frenzy, he slays. In the forest he gives free rein to his sorrow. He refuses to speak and spends eight days beside a fountain where he and Iseut had formerly been happy. His body is black and blue as though he had been beaten. A maiden who comes upon him believes him to be near death and plays upon a harp three lays that he had composed in happier days. The following day he composes a fourth, which he calls the 'lai mortel', 'car il l'a fait pendant la nuit de sa douleur et de sa mort' (Fotitch 19). The lay concluded, he seeks to kill himself but finds no weapon with which to accomplish the act. He then dashes into the heart of the forest, shouting like a 'beste forcenee', for he has utterly lost his reason. There he lives, feeding on the raw flesh of wild animals. He dwells with some shepherds who torment him, shaving his head and dyeing his face. He is called the 'fou de la fontaine' and is cared for by a good hermit.

---

[62] This tendency, first manifested in the writings of the church fathers (notably Jerome), whose mistrust of the vestiges of pagan culture made such an association inevitable, was only enhanced by the wild man's reputation as a ravisher of women (Bernheimer 97, 121).

In Tristan's absence a giant, Taulas de la Montagne, invades and ravages Cornwall. One day Taulas comes to the fountain where Tristan dwells. There the giant defeats a young knight and then does battle with Tristan, who, having utterly forgotten the arts of war, must be instructed by the shepherds. He slays Taulas and almost does as much to the grateful young knight who wishes to take him away to cure him. One day while in pursuit of a stag, Mark chances upon the fountain and observes the madman. Without guessing the latter's identity, he has him brought to Tintagel where the madman's identity is revealed when he is recognized by his faithful Husdent (cf. *Fb* 509–18, *Fo* 901–16). Iseut cares for, bleeds, and cures Tristan, whom Mark then exiles.[63] The representation of Tristan as a wild man in *R*, which develops the suggestion implicit in *Fo* that Tristan, driven mad by love sickness, falls to the degenerate state of wild man, is explicit and unambiguous. Like Yvain in the *Chevalier au Lion* and Merlin in the *Vita Merlini*, he loses his wits through love madness inspired by jealousy and lives the same degrading life in the forest, although his behavior is more violent than theirs.

The presence of the figure of the wild man in medieval art attests to the recognition by the medieval world that there are in man 'basic and primitive impulses clamoring for satisfaction … impulses of reckless physical self-assertion' (Bernheimer 2–3). The 'lawless love' of Tristan and Iseut is such an impulse, which expresses itself first in sexual terms and then, when thwarted, in physical violence. This passion that flies in the face of society and civilized usage is a manifestation of that wildness that Bernheimer calls '[the temptation to] natural and moral anarchy [opposed to] the beneficent rule of Christianity [and] that very principle of hieratic order upon which medieval society was founded' (20). The figure of the wild man, at once savage giant and ravisher of women, incarnates two capital features of Tristan's personality, his great strength and prowess as a warrior and his involuntary and ungovernable passion for Iseut.

The sexual appetite of the wild man was held to be prodigious, a fact that served to indicate his affinity with the *élan vital* of nature and the woodland. The phallic club that he invariably carried and that was sometimes depicted as an entire tree torn by its roots from the ground is also associated with the Tree of Life that embodies the Life Spirit of natural things. The wild man rejoiced at storms and rain. Tristan's *esclavine*, perhaps reminiscence of the coat of Orguillos that homeopathically endowed the wearer with the strength of those fallen warriors whose beards and mustaches composed it (*T Sn*[1] 667–86), resembles the wild man's hairy

---

[63] The topos of the combat between wild man and knight becomes a metaphor for the conflict of Mark (the dominating father-figure and superego) and Tristan (the rebellious id) for possession of Iseut.

coat. This covering, 'the outward sign of his bestial strength and, at the same time, its magical cause' (Bernheimer 10), identified the wild man with the beasts of the woodland whose master he traditionally was.

The medieval wild man incorporated in a single mythological being the attributes of two classes of pagan divinities: divinities of the fertile earth, whose attributes were sexuality and vigor, and demons of the Underworld, whose attributes were ugliness and violence. These qualities unite in the prodigious strength that is the chief characteristic of the wild man, whose identity as woodland divinity subsumes and transcends those of his pagan forbears. As Ménard has remarked, 'dans la pensée mythique du Moyen Age l'homme sauvage n'incarne pas seulement la force brute et les instincts élémentaires. Il n'est pas seulement le satyre prompte à ravir les femmes. Il est aussi un être inspiré qui a un pouvoir surhumain et qui connaît les profonds mystères de la nature' (*Rire* 355).[64] The violent and sexually aggressive madman of *Fo* incarnates the first two characteristics of the wild man, while the third is embroidered in Tristan's association with the woodland, an association explicitly evoked by the *Fo* poet (487–512), and in the suggestion that the mad Tristan possesses oracular powers.

[64] Ménard suggests that Bernheimer neglects this second aspect of the wild man's personality (*Rire* 355, n. 136).

III

TRISTAN VICTIM AND SAVIOR

The Ailing Hero

> Amur est plaie dedenz cors.
> (Marie de France, 'Guigemar' 483)
>
> [Brunor] lui demande s'il aime.
> 'Oui,' répond Tristan; 'je ne
> cuit qe en nostre tens souffrist
> a tant chevalier por amors comme
> j'ai souffert.' (Löseth §480)

The idea that the passion of Tristan and Iseut is a source of suffering is organic to the medieval understanding of the Tristan legend. In the French poems, the lovers are alternately portrayed as beneficiaries of a great joy and victims of intense distress. Since in all but two of the poems Tristan is the focus of the narrative,[1] it is his suffering that is depicted most vividly in the corpus and alluded to most frequently in other medieval texts. The motif of Tristan's suffering is closely linked to that of his sorrow, of the *tristesse* that is alluded to in his name and that, from the moment of his birth, marks him for a life of travail. He suffers as a result of his heroism in the service of the social Order; of Mark's vengefulness; of the hardships that he must undergo in order to effect his clandestine reunions with Iseut; of Iseut's anger, neglect, or (perceived) infidelity;[2] and of his heroism in the service of a personal ideal. His character is a strange and inconsistent mixture of voluntary self-sacrifice and passive acceptance of his role as victim.

The understanding of Tristan's passion as a source of suffering is nowhere more evident than in the contemporary allusions to the Tristan matter, those shorthand summaries of the significance that readers had extracted from the original. Bernart de Ventador's persona affirms:

---

[1] *B* and *Tros* are the exceptions.
[2] An important sub-tradition, which was perhaps part of the pre-*estoire* legend, represents Tristan as the victim of a cruel and unfeeling Iseut (Curtis, 'Philtre').

Plus trac pena d'amor
De Tristan l'amador,
Que·n sofri manhta dolor
Per Izeut la blonda.

('Tant ai mo cor ple de joya', PC 70, 44: 45–48)

The author of *Amadas et Ydoine* declares:

Mais ainc Tristrans si grant doleur
Ne souffri pour Yseu la bloie,
Ne tant mal sans confort de joie,
Com Amadas en a sousfert.   (340–43)

Variations on the formula 'our hero suffered more for love than did even Tristan for the love of Iseut' recur time and again in medieval texts, indicating that Tristan's suffering for love was proverbial and constituted one of the most closely held attributes of his persona.[3]

On one hand, Tristan's suffering was perceived by the medieval reader as an index of the loyalty, constancy, and courtliness of his love. His extravagant misfortunes testified to an equally extravagant fidelity. The more he abased himself or was abased in the service of his lady, the finer was shown to be his *fin' amor*. He is held up time and again as the paragon of the lover constant in adversity:

E Tristantz fon de totz los amadors
Lo plus leals e fes mais d'ardimens.
(Peire Cardenal, 'Alexandris fon le plus conquerens', PC 461,
14: 3–4)

C'onques Tristanz, qui but le berevage,
Pluz loiaument n'ama sanz repentir.
(Châtelain de Couci, 'La douce voiz du louseignol sauvage',
19–20)

In this perspective, Tristan's suffering ennobles him, transforming him into a figure of high tragedy at the same time that it foreshadows the death that will ultimately claim the lovers.

On the other hand, Tristan was also perceived as a hapless victim – of his enemies (Mark and the *losengiers*); of a repressive, inhumane social Order; of the jealousy of his wife; and, above all, of his love for Iseut. While this

---

[3] In addition to the allusions to Tristan's sorrow given here and above ('Tristan's Parentage, Birth, and Naming in *T*'), see *Amadas et Ydoine* 2883–87; Philippe de Remi, *Jehan et Blonde* 423–24; *Le Bel Inconnu* 4334–36; Jean Renart, *Le Lai de l'ombre* 124–126; *The First Continuation of the Old French Perceval* 2: 1039–42; *De Venus la déesse d'Amor* 297–98; *Gliglois* 339–41; *Gautier d'Aupais* 273–75; Arnaut de Maruelh, 'Tant m'abellis e·m plaz' (PC 36, IV) 158–65.

understanding contradicts the notion that Tristan voluntarily engaged in those enterprises that occasioned his suffering – his defense of the social Order and his lady's service, it too colors the narrative and finds expression in the contemporary allusions to the legend. Tristan, who for his misfortune drank of the potion, is depicted as the victim of the vengefulness of his uncle or of the jealous machinations of his wife, Iseut aux Blanches Mains, whose lie concerning the coming of Iseut la Blonde is immediately responsible for the hero's death. 'Sa moylers fets Tristayn morir, / Car no·y jasia', categorically declares Cerveri de Girona (§997). From the thirteenth century onwards, Tristan's name habitually figures in enumerations of celebrated heros brought low by a woman; in certain of those texts it is by no means clear that the woman referred to is Tristan's wife rather than his lover. For the author of *Amadas et Ydoine*, it is Iseut herself who is the ultimate cause of Tristan's misfortunes:

> 'Li cortois Tristans fu traïs
> Et deceüs et mal baillis
> De l'amisté Yseut la bloie.' (5833–35)

In *La Mort le Roi Artu*, Boort declares:

> 'Certes ge ne vi onques preudome qui longuement amast par amors qui au derreain n'en fust tenuz por honniz; et se vos voulez garder as anciens fez des Juïs et des Sarrazins, assez vos en porrait l'en moustrer de ceus que la veraie estoire tesmoigne *qui furent honni par fame*. ... Et a nostre tens meïsmes, n'a pas encore cinc anz que Tristans en morut, li niés au roi Marc, qui si loiaument ama Yseut la blonde que onques en son vivant [il] n'avoit mespris vers lui.'
> (§59: 30–37, 54–58)[4]

All those texts that portray Tristan as a victim of love, whether implicitly or explicitly, attest to the belief in love as a source of suffering. These thirteenth-century allusions merely elaborate – in accordance with the rhetoric of medieval anti-feminism and the poetic topos of the suffering lover – a suggestion that is implicit in the twelfth-century Tristan poems.

At the heart of the legend lies the mythic equation of passion as joy and passion as suffering. In *T* Iseut at the side of the dead Tristan juxtaposes these two elements of the lovers' passion when she recalls

---

4 I have added *il* to clarify the ambiguous syntax of the last clause, an emendation authorized by the linguistic habits of the text's author (or scribe). The third-person singular tonic pronouns are regularly confused in the text (e.g. §59: 6, 28, 39), and *lui*, a variant of *li*, refers here not to Tristan but to Iseut. For other allusions to Tristan's victimization, see *Amadas et Ydoine* 1183–88; Jean Froissart, *Méliador* 9122–33; and Guilhem Augier Novella, 'Per vos, bella douss'amia', PC 205, 4a: 26–27.

'Nostre joie, nostre emveisure,
La paine et la grant dolur
Qu'ad esté en nostre amur.'   (Sn²795–97)

In linking *joie* and *paine, emveisure* and *dolor*, Iseut offers a definition of
their love as an emotion compounded in equal parts of suffering and
beatitude, an idea reinforced by the recurring puns on *amor, amer*, and
mort that place within the single term *amur* the antithetical notions of joy
and pain, of infirmity and healing, of life and death. In the Tristan poems,
the lovers' passion is not simply a force that encompasses life and death; it
represents life within death and death within life, not simply the co-
existence of joy and pain but joy as a form of suffering and suffering as a
component of joy, not simply infirmity and healing but love as an act of
wounding and wounding as a means of healing.

The Sexual Wound and its Healing in T

'Ha! Dex', fait il, 'quel destinee!
C'ai je sofert en tel amor!
Onques de li ne fis clamor
Ne ne me plains de ma destrece;
Por quoi m'asaut? Por quoi me blece?'
(Fb 54–58)

The motif of Tristan's wounds, 'diminished images of the death which
seems to hover always in the background' (Trindade, 'Time' 391), serves as
a generalized metaphor for the hero's suffering for love. The metaphor of
Tristan wounded and healed by love represents a special case of the metaphor of love-sickness and its healing through the ministrations (*mecine*) of
the lady (*mire*). In *T*, the metaphor of a wound to the hero's sexual parts and
its subsequent healing through the act of physical love renders most explicitly the intimate association between Tristan's suffering for love and
the healing qualities of that very love.

   The first of Tristan's wounds, one that is common to all of the 'full'
versions of the legend[5] and that serves as a model for his other wounds, is
that suffered at the hands of Le Morholt:

---

[5] By 'full' (Mod.Fr. *totalisante*), I refer both to the once complete versions of the narrative (*T,
O, R*, and perhaps *B*) and to the would-be complete versions (*G* and perhaps *B*).

'... ma plaie
Que je reçui en Cornuaille
Qant a Morholt fis la bataille
En l'ile ou fui menez a nage
Por desfandre lo treüssaje
Que cil devoient de la terre.'   (*Fb* 97–102)[6]

The other wound that figures in all the texts that preserve the conclusion of the legend is that which is responsible for hero's death.[7] The metaphor of love's pain as a wound is drawn between these two episodes, which frame the 'roman de Tristan et Iseut'. Thomas stresses the symmetries and oppositions that link the two wounds. Each is inflicted with a poisoned weapon. The wound inflicted by Le Morholt, which Tristan suffers for the sake of the social Order, brings him in contact with Iseut who heals him. The wound inflicted by Estult l'Orguillos, which is suffered for the sake of the Counter-Order, separates him from Iseut who is unable to heal him. In the first episode, Tristan's small boat is providentially directed by the wind and the waves to Ireland where healing awaits him. In the last, the ship bearing Iseut is prevented by a storm and then by becalming from arriving in time for Iseut to effect the healing of the wounded hero.[8]

The motif of the healing of the hero by Iseut is present throughout the Tristan poems, particularly in the suggestion that the figurative infirmities of the disguise episodes are healed by her love. However, the motif finds its fullest expression in *T*, which adds two elements not found in the other poems. Thomas makes more concrete the symbolism implicit in the motif by suggesting that Tristan's wounds are healed through the act of physical love with Iseut and, conversely, that they are not healed when he and Iseut are prevented from being reunited. Thomas embellishes this metaphor in two key episodes by suggesting that Tristan's wounds are wounds to the sexual parts.

In *T* and its derivatives, two episodes present the motif of the hero's healing through the ministrations of Iseut's mother and double, Iseut the

[6] The episode is also found or alluded to in *B* 27–28, 50–53, 135–42, 848–57, 2038; *Fb* 77; and *Fo* 327–40.
[7] That is, *O*, the reconstructed *T*, *R*, and MS. B.N.fr. 103. It is inflicted by Mark in *R*, and by a cuckolded husband in *O* and in MS. B.N.fr. 103.
[8] In *T*, the wounding episodes include Tristan's combat with the Irish dragon (*S* Ch. 36), the threat of wounding in this bath after Iseut has discovered Tristan's identity through the breach in the sword (*S* Ch. 43), the leap between the beds (*S* Ch. 55), the battle with the Spanish giant Sn[1] 729–52), the last battle (D 1017–53), and the metatextual episode of Rivalen's wounding (*S* Ch. 11). The extant portion of *B* contains only one wound episode, that found in the leap between the beds (716–35), doublets of which occur in MS. B.N.fr. 103 (Bédier, *Thomas* 2: 354–55) and in *O* (3797–942). Finally, in *R* Mark inflicts on Tristan his fatal wound (Löseth §546), and in MS. B.N.fr. 103 he commands the bramble that grows from Tristan's tomb to Iseut's to be cut away (Bédier, *Thomas* 2: 394).

Queen. On his first voyage to Ireland, Tristan's seemingly incurable wound is healed, according to the accounts of S (Ch. 30), Fo (357–58), G (7741–961), and Sir Tristrem (1200–10), by Iseut's mother.[9] On the second, the 'wound' that he suffers in his combat against the Irish dragon is healed by Iseut's mother, assisted by her daughter (S Ch. 38) or jointly by Iseut and her mother (Fo 423–26).[10] However, as I have noted above ('Music and Love'), Tristan affirms later in T that Iseut alone cured his first wound and that the couple's love dates from the period of his first sojourn in Ireland (D 1214–20). In the account of Tristan's two voyages to Ireland, Thomas would appear to have distanced himself from the account of the *version commune* on this point in order to assert that it is only after the consumption of the potion that the couple falls in love and only at that moment that Iseut fully possesses the power to heal the ailing hero, implying that her healing skills are directly linked to the couple's love. In the Douce fragment of T, however, the dying Tristan seizes on this implication and, in the extremity of his need, revises the account of the first voyage in order to argue to Iseut that as his first wound was healed by her love, so must his last wound be. In doing so, Tristan is once again elaborating a motif that already existed in T although not in the episodes of the first and second voyages to Ireland.

Thomas' first presentation of the motif of the healing by love occurs in the metatextual episode of Rivalen and Blancheflor, which contains in germ the story of Tristan and Iseut and whose function is explicative and premonitory. Blancheflor comes secretly to the chamber where Rivalen is dying from his wounds and lies with him. As a result of their union, Rivalen is healed and Tristan is conceived (S Ch. 12). The motif also figures prominently in the account of Tristan's marriage. Following his marriage to Iseut aux Blanches Mains, Tristan enters the nuptial bed full of desire for

[9] In the *version commune* Tristan is healed by Iseut herself. In B Iseut says to Tristan:
'Molt vos estut mal endurer
De la plaie que vos preïstes
En la batalle que feïstes
O mon oncle. *Je vos gari.*' (50–53)
In Fb Tristan addresses himself to Iseut in the following terms:
'Car de la plaie que jë oi,
Quë il me fist par mi l'espaule, [subject: Le Morholt]
Si issi je de cestë aule:
Me randistes et sauf et sain:
Autres de vos n'i mist la main.' (401–05)
See also Fb 77, 97–98. Tristan is also cured by Iseut in R (Curtis 1: §314). Bédier's ingenious suggestion that Tristan's assumed name on his voyage to Ireland in O, Pro of Jemsetir, is an anagram of 'Iset por mire' (*Thomas* 2: 211) does not take into account the fact that *Jemsetir* is a corrupt reading of an original *yenßhalb*, 'across the sea' (Buschinger, *Tristrant* 95).
[10] In the account of Fb, however, it is again Iseut alone who heals Tristan:
'Del venin del cruiel sarpent
(Panduz soie, se jë en mant!)
Me garesistes sanz mehain.' (Fb 406–408)

the bride who resembles so closely his absent lady. Yet, he finds himself unable to have physical relations with his wife, although he would have been able to do so with Iseut:

> Le desir qu'il ad vers la reïne
> Tolt le voleir vers la meschine;
> Le desir lui tolt le voleir,
> Que nature n'i ad poeir.   (Sn¹597–600)

Arousal is followed by impotence, triggered by the ring that falls from his finger, reminding of him of Iseut. It is as though the curative power afforded him by the love of Iseut, who, he will claim, healed him of the wound inflicted by Le Morholt, has, with the loss of the ring, been lifted, allowing the effects of an old wound to rob him of his potency. Indeed, he pleads the after-effects of just such an infirmity as a pretext for abstaining from conjugal relations with his bride:

> 'De ça vers le destre costé
> Ai el cors une enfermeté,
> Tenu m'ad molt lungement;
> Anoit m'ad anguissé forment.
> Par le grant travail qu'ai eü
> M'est il par le cors esmeü,
> Si anguissusement me tient
> E si pres de la feie me vient
> Que jo ne m'os plus emveisier
> Ne mei pur le mal travaillier.'   (Sn¹629–38)

Tristan's infirmity is by implication centered in the genitals; for he specifies that it is 'pres de la feie', near, that is, to the organ that according to medieval medical theory was the seat of the sexual urge, 'þe place of volupte ... [that] ... exciteþ loue of Venus, and fongiþ diuers passiouns' (Bartholomaeus Anglicus Lib. 5, Cap. 39).

Thomas piously suggests that Tristan's incapacity is a matter of voluntary abstinence, prompted by *amur* and *raisun* (Sn¹ 595–602), a means of retrieving his initial transgression against *fin' amor*:

> Car si ço fin' amur fust,
> La meschine amé ne oüst
> Cuntre volenté s'amie.   (Sn¹319–21)

Yet immediately after this episode the poet embarks on a digression that has only the flimsiest connection with the main narrative: the double story of Arthur's combat with Orguillos and Tristan's with the giant's nephew. This unexpected flashback is justified only by Thomas' statement that, following his departure from England and shortly before his arrival in Brittany (Sn¹ 736), Tristan came to Spain where he defeated a giant, receiving in the process a wound of which Iseut la Blonde had no knowledge. Although Thomas neglects to say so, there can be little doubt that he intends his readers to understand that this wound is the infirmity of which Tristan complains on his wedding night:

> Tristrans i fu forment naufré
> E el cors blecé e grevé.
> Dolent em furent si amis,
> Mais li jaianz i fu ocis;
> E pois icele naufreüre
> N'oï Ysolt nul aventure.   (Sn¹749–54)

Thomas' otherwise unmotivated juxtaposition of the episode of Tristan's wedding night with those of Arthur's combat against Orguillos and Tristan's against the Spanish giant suggests that Tristan's abstinence arises not from choice but from a physical incapacity, implicitly a wound to the sexual parts, a suggestion at odds with his earlier insistence on his protagonist's courtliness.[11]

Apparently a digression within a digression, the episode of Arthur and Orguillos, like that of Rivalen and Blancheflor, serves an important explicative function. A doublet of Tristan's combat with the Spanish giant, which it introduces, it signifies that the castration motif implicit in the severed beards of the giant's victims is likewise present in the linked episodes of Tristan's combat with the Spanish giant and Tristan's wedding night. Specifically, it reinforces the connection between Tristan's wound, inflicted by the nephew and double of the castrating Orguillos, and Tristan's infirmity that he holds responsible for his sexual incapacity on his wedding night.[12] Tristan's sexual wound, symbolized by his sexual incapacity, cannot be healed by the counterfeit Iseut, who lacks the power to overcome that incapacity or to heal that wound as Iseut would, through the act of physical love, have been able to do. Only when he is next reunited with Iseut in the following episode does Tristan, whose feigned leprosy, like his impotence, is a trope for his infidelity, find healing and renewed vigor (D 721–23).

---

[11] A failure to understand the relationship between these three episodes has led critics to widely divergent interpretations of the function and meaning of the paired episodes of Arthur and Orguillos and Tristan and the Spanish giant. Barteau has called the double episode a 'songerie d'Iseut' (119), while Trindade has alluded to Thomas' 'embarrassment' at having to include the story of the beard-stealing giant ('Time' 395), which Fourrier terms 'une intentionnelle plaisanterie' (96) and Grigsby 'un symbole pour relier la légende du roi Arthur à son roman' (125, n.39).

[12] As Estult, who stole the lady of another Tristan, is a double of Orguillos, so both castrating giants are doubles of Mark, who 'stole' Tristan's lady.

The episode of Arthur and Orguillos also draws a connection between Tristan's wound suffered at the hands of the Spanish giant, who is a taker of beards (Sn[1] 732–42), and that inflicted by Estult; for the second is connected to Arthur's combat by the homonymy of the names of the antagonists, Orguillos (Sn[1] 664) and Estult l'Orgillus (D 1019), the first by the juxtaposition of the two episodes in the narrative. Both are by implication sexual wounds. The wound that Tristan receives at the hands of Estult is inflicted 'par mi la luingne' (D 1047), a phrase that may be translated with some precision as 'in the loins', for the English expression conveys the same polysemantic ambiguity as the Anglo-Norman from which it derives and as the Latin *lumbus* in which both have their ultimate origin. 'Loins' and *'la luingne'* refer literally to the lower back, but through a semantic shift each term is employed as a euphemism for the sexual parts. The motif of the healing of the hero's wound through the act of physical love is again present in the episode of the final wound; for, as in the episode of Tristan and Le Morholt, the hero is wounded beyond hope of salvation, save, he asserts, that afforded by Iseut:

> Nuls ne set en cest mal mecine
> Nequident s'Ysolt la reïne
> Icest fort mal en li saveit
> E od li fust, ben le guareit.   (D 1077–80)

Thus, Tristan sends Kaherdin to Iseut, charging his friend to remind her specifically of the physical love that the couple enjoyed in times past and of the occasion on which she healed the wound that he sustained in his combat with Le Morholt, conveniently forgetting that it was the mother and not the daughter who was responsible for his cure:

> 'Dites li qu'ore li suvenge
> Des emveisures, des deduiz
> Qu'eümes jadis jors e nuiz,
> Des granz peines, des tristurs
> E des joies e des dusurs
> De nostre amor fine e veraie
> Quand ele jadis guari ma plaie.'   (D 1214–20)

When Iseut does not come in time, Tristan succumbs to the effects of his wound. When she finally arrives only to learn that she has come too late, Iseut too evokes her healing powers, lamenting:

> 'Si jo fuisse a tens venue,
> Vie vos oüse, amis, rendue,
> E parlé dulcement a vos
> De l'amur qu'ad esté entre nos.'   (Sn[2] 790–93)

She then embraces her dead lover, simulating the act of physical love in an effort to revive him:

> Embrace le, si s'estent,
> Baise la buche e la face
> E molt estreit a li l'enbrace,
> Cors a cors, buche a buche estent.   (Sn²809–12)

Her efforts are in vain, however, and she dies in his arms:

> Son espirit a itant rent,
> E murt dejuste lui issi
> Pur la dolur de sun ami.   (Sn²813–15)

This simulacrum of the healing sexual act is not, however, without effect, for it results in the symbolic healing of the lovers, who are reincarnated in the form of intertwining trees. In this final image, *joie* and *paine*, *emveisure* and *dolor*, *amor* and *mort* become one. Wounding has become a means to healing, pain a means to joy, death a means to life.

The Corrupt and Corrupting Humor

> Dieu! quel boire! Or sont entrez en la rote
> qui jamais ne leur fauldra jour de leurs vies,
> car ilz ont beü leur destruction et leur mort.
> Cil boire leur a semblé bon et moult doulz,
> mais oncques doulceur ne fu si chier achetee
> comment ceste sera.
> (MS. B.N.fr. 103, Bédier, *Thomas* 2: 341)

The metaphoric equation of love and suffering also finds expression in a number of episodes that depict Tristan as the victim of an infirmity charactized by a corruption of the blood, either a humoral change or a poisoning. In *Fb*, the 'mad' Tristan laments:

> 'Mais li boivre de trosseroil
> M'a si emblé et cuer e sans
> Que je nan ai autre porpans,
> Fors tant quë en amor servir.'   (309–12)

This statement makes explicit the understanding central to this group of metaphors that the consumption of the potion resulted in a corruption of the hero's blood.

The first of these metaphors is that which depicts the potion, whose tragic potential is stressed throughout the poems, as a poison or an intoxicant. In *T*, Tristan makes the potion responsible for the lovers' tragedy:

> '... [li] beivre qu'ensemble beümes
> En la mer quant suppris en fumes.
> El beivre fud la nostre mort,
> Nus n'en avrum ja mais confort;
> A tel ure duné nus fu
> A nostre mort l'avum beü.' (D 1221–26)

At the moment of her death, Iseut links the fatal *beivre* to the biblical metaphor of the bitter chalice (Matthew 26: 39; John 18: 11):

> 'Quant a tens venir n'i poi
> E jo l'aventure n'oi,
> E venue sui a la mort,
> De meisme le beivre avrai confort.' (*TSn²* 802–05)

In *Fo*, the metaphor is more specific. Angry and frightened at the accuracy of the fool's account of her life with Tristan and at his insistence that he is indeed her lover, Iseut expostulates furiously:

> 'N'est mie vair, einz est mensunge;
> Mais vus recuntez vostre sunge:
> Anuit fustes ivre al cucher
> E l'ivrece vus fist sunger.' (455–58)

To this the fool replies:

> 'Vers est: d'itel baivre sui ivre
> Dunt je ne quid estre delivre.' (459–60)

He goes on to recount the episode of the consumption of the potion, concluding:

> 'Vus en beüstes e j'en bui.
> Ivrë ai esté tut tens puis,
> Mais male ivrece mult i truis.' (472–74)

The metaphor of Tristan's drunkeness parallels that of his madness, for in both cases his senses are disordered and his actions beyond the control of his will. If, like Beroul, the *Fo* poet draws a parallel between passion and sleep, he emphasizes the negative aspects of this metaphor. The summer sunshine has been replaced by darkness. The period since the consumption of the potion is likened by Tristan to a night of drunken slumbers, a dark delusion from which one awakens not to healing but to madness. Following Iseut's lead, he asserts that their love is a drunkard's yarn and a madman's hallucination (*mensunge, sunge*) so long as she refuses to validate the truth of his narrative and, hence, of their love. Only when he partakes again of Iseut's love as of a draught from a healing fountain (see below) will he be delivered from his *male ivrece* and his insanity.

A metaphor closely allied to that of the potion as intoxicant is that of the potion as poison, an ambiguity preserved in the English *intoxication*. Chrétien de Troyes speaks of the 'bevraje ... don Tristans fu anpoisonez' ('D'Amors, qui m'a tolu a moi' 28–29). *Fb* contains the suggestion, made explicit nowhere else in the French poems, that the potion was incorrectly compounded, resulting in disastrous consequences for those who partook of it.[13] Tristan declares plaintively:

> 'Cil boivre fu fait *a envers*
> De plusors herbés mout divers.'   (318–19)

In *Fb*, Tristan's madness is depicted as the result of a specific physiological process, the alteration of the sanguine humor through the action of the *vin herbé*, aggravated by the effects of the hardships and suffering that it produced and whose symbol it was. His statement that '"Mon san ai an folor changiee"' (*Fb* 315) contains, in addition to the pun on *san* ('sang'/ 'sens'), a reference to a specific humoral change, the production of melancholic adust through the agency of the potion. Melancholic adust was a degenerate humor produced by a corruption of the blood that resulted in a melancholy disposition and even in madness; and Brengvein, who in *Fb* says to the fool, '"Plains estes de melancholie"' (275), is referring as much to Tristan's physiology as to his psychology.

Tristan's physical infirmity, symbolized by his disguise as leper, parallels his mental infirmity, symbolized by his disguise as madman; for, like madness, leprosy was held in medieval medical theory to arise at times from an alteration of the blood. In the case of leprosy, the humoral change, which also resulted in the production of melancholy adust, was generated by a malfunction of the liver (Guy de Chauliac 401), the organ that controlled the amorous propensities of the body. As the malfunctioning of the organ governing the erotic predilections of the body generated a corrupt humor that produced leprosy, a disease characterized in part by an unnatural sexual lust, so did an excess of mental turmoil, induced by the consumption of the potion, generate a corrupt humor that inflamed the blood, producing madness and a supernormal sexual urge in its victims.

There existed, however, an antidote to the potion's poison. Lamenting

---

[13] See also *Fb* 345–47 and Curtis, 'Philtre'.

Iseut's refusal to recognize him under his disguise in *Fo*, Tristan taxes her with having forgotten their love (691–96). If the pain that Tristan suffers for his passion is implicitly a terrible thirst, Iseut's love, which he compares to a fountain of clear water, has the power to quench that thirst:

> 'Mult valt funteine ki ben surt,
> Dunt li reuz est bon e ben curt,
> E de l'ure k'ele secchist,
> K'ewe n'i surt n'ewe n'en ist,
> Si ne fet gueres a priser:
> Ne fait amur, quant volt boiser.'   (701–06)

The motif of the draught from a healing fountain as an antidote to a poison, a commonplace of medieval literature, serves frequently as a metaphor for the remedy for unhappy love.[14] The metaphor of the fountain in *Fo* alludes to the 'spring of wholesome water' that flows beside the lovers' grotto in the Morois in *T* (*S* Ch. 64), an image that serves as the objective correlative for the happiest, most satisfying period of the couple's troubled relationship, during which time, their needs entirely fulfilled by the presence of the other, 'they gave little thought to who would give them food and drink' (*S* Ch. 64).[15] In addition, it may constitute an oblique reference to the leper episode in *T* in which Tristan, disguised as a leper and hence presumably

---

14 E.g. the following passage from the *Bestiaire d'amour rimé*:
> Le sers quant il l'a trangloutie
> La serpent que il a flairie,
> Qui tout l'eschaufe et envenime,
> Dont il vait querre medecine
> Au brueil, de la clere fontainne.
> Dont la bele m'ot o s'alainne
> Empli de douce souastume,
> Qui le cuer en amours m'alumme.   (1241–48)

The stag, particularly when it combats and kills the snake, is a traditional symbol for Christ, with whom, as we see below, Tristan is associated in the metaphor of the *vin herbé*. For the metaphorical association of Tristan with a hunted stag, see above, 'Tristan the Hunter'.

15 Likewise, in *Tros* satisfaction in love is compared to a spring freshet newly released from winter's grip (543–88). See above, 'Tristan the Nightingale'. Paradoxically, the ill-compounded *vin herbé* of *Fb*, like the healing fountain of *Fo*, is limpid:
> 'Do buverage empli la cope;
> Mout par fu clers, n'i parut sope.'   (*Fb* 436–37)

Like a medicine with dangerous side-effects, the potion is the source of beatitude when the lovers are united but one of terrible suffering when circumstances separate them. The beneficent and maleficent draughts, which are in reality one, are objective correlatives for the two faces of Tristan's love. In a lay from *R* Tristan sings:
> 'Tant est chis boires dous et sades
> Que il sane bien les malades.
> Mors fui et deviegn fors et rades,
> Chis boires est dous, non pas fades.'   (Fotitch 16, ii, 1–4)

The explicit phallic reference in verse 3 recalls two episodes from *T*: Tristan's impotence and his resuscitation and reincarnation in the form of an oak tree.

consumed by the same *grant ardor* evoked in *B*, returns to England to plead for Iseut's forgiveness and favors. The cup that he uses as a begging bowl is figuratively filled when his wish to be reunited in love and sexual congress with his lady is fulfilled. In *Fo*, the final act of reconciliation between the fool and the incredulous Iseut occurs when she takes water and, imitating the effects of the 'funteine ki ben surt', washes from the fool's face the dye with which he had disguised himself, symbolically washing away the effects of his madness.

In *Fb*, a similar metaphor is employed within the context of an allusion to the Biblical account of the miracle at Cana:

> 'Mais cil Dex qui reigne sanz fin,
> Qui as noces Archetreclin
> Lor fu tant cortois botoillier
> Que l'eve fist en vin changier,
> Icel Dex me mete en corage
> Quë il me giet d'icest folage!'   (352–357)

This passage must be read in the perspective of Tristan's previous declarations that, as a result of consuming the potion, '"Mon san ai an folor changiee"' (315) and '"Li boivre ... m'a ... emblé et cuer e sans"' (309–310) and of the pun on *san/sans* ('sang'/'sens') contained therein. In theological terms the miracle at Cana was a precursor of the miracle of the transubstantiation in which, as water was turned to wine at Cana, so at the Last Supper (and in its ritual commemoration in the Eucharist) was (is) wine turned to blood. Implicit, moreover, in Tristan's reference to the miracle at Cana is the equation of his passion with Christ's (see below, 'Tristan the Trickster'). Tristan's allusion to the miracle at Cana expresses in metaphorical terms his wish that the madness (*folor*, *folage*) produced by the intoxicating *vin herbé* be transformed into sanity (*san[s]*) and satisfaction in love, that his corrupted blood (*san[s]*) be made whole.

The motif of the poisoned wound is so prominent in the Tristan corpus that its occurrence must be accounted for on two levels. While on the mimetic level, the poisoned wound reflects the reality of infection that must inevitably have been the consequence of most battlefield wounds in medieval warfare, the motif is also linked metonymically to the other episodes of the poisoning that signify the hero's subjection to a dolorous passion precipitated by the consumption of the potion. In *T* Tristan's first and last wound are inflicted with a poisoned blade.[16] Chertsey Tile 20

---

[16] The hero is also poisoned by the venom from the tongue that he cuts from the head of the Irish dragon and places in his breeches (*S* Ch. 36). *R* adds several examples of poisoned wounds not found in the French poems. In one episode, Tristan is wounded with a poisoned arrow as he sleeps by a lad whose father the hero had earlier slain (Bédier, *Thomas* 2: 363). In an

depicts the grotesque effects of the wound inflicted by Le Morholt, while the effects of that inflicted by Estult are described in the following terms:

> Li venims espant par tut le cors,
> Emfler le fait dedenz e dehors;
> Nercist e teint, sa force pert,
> Li os sunt ja mult descovert.   (D 1069–72)

The metaphor of the poisoned wound, like that of the ill-compounded potion, equates the passion with a corruption of the blood. The element common to each is the understanding that the poison produces a terrible, unrelieved pain that symbolizes Tristan's anguish at his separation from Iseut (*T* D 1087–91; *Fo* 333–42).

Finally, the metaphor of the potion as poison is extended from the definition of passion as suffering for love to that of passion as dying for love. In the following centuries this metaphor, which may owe its popularity in *trouvère* poetry to the influence of the Tristan legend, was reduced to the status of the most banal cliché. Yet, in the Tristan poems, where it lies at the heart of the legend, it exists in its primitive, literal form. Thomas concludes his romance with the assertion:

> Tristrans *mur*ut pur sue a*mur*,   [i.e. d'Iseut]
> E la bele Ysolt par tendrur.   (Sn² 818–19)

Following their consumption of the potion in *G*, the lovers confess their love to one another in a dialogue built upon 'un concetto latin très répandu dans les écoles' (Delbouille, 'Premier roman' 283). The conceit, which Gottfried is assumed to have borrowed from a lost passage of *T*, puns on *lameir*, which conjoins the senses of *amare* ('aimer'), *amarum* ('amer'), and *mare* ('la mer'):

> Der Minnen vederspil Isot,
> '*Lameir*' sprach si 'daz ist min not,
> *Lameir* daz swæret mir den muot,
> *Lameir* ist, daz mir leide tuot.'
> Do si *lameir* so dicke sprach,
> Er bedahte unde besach

---

alternate version of the last wound, a version common to B.N.fr. 103 and to *O*, Tristan is wounded with a poisoned sword by the cuckholded husband Bedalis whose wife Tristan's friend Ruvalen had debauched (Bédier, *Thomas* 2: 382; *O* 9201–21). Finally, in *R* the mortal wound that Tristan receives from Mark is inflicted with a poisoned lance given the king by the fairy Morgain (Löseth §546).

Anclichen unde cleine
Des selben wortes meine.
Sus begunder sich versinnen,
Lameir daz wære 'minnen',
Lameir 'bitter', *la meir* 'mer':
Der meine der duht in ein her.   (11985–96)[17]

In the extant passages of *T*, Thomas consistently links the terms *mer*, *amur*, *amer*, *mort*, and *murrir* in such a way as to suggest that he is punning on them as well, echoing a pun originally found in the lost portion of his romance and preserved in its entirety only in *G*:

'A tel ure duné nus fu
A nostre *mort* l'avum beü.
De mes dolurs li deit menbrer
Que suffert ai pur li *amer*.'   (D 1225–28)

'Pur vostre *amur* m'estuet *murrir*.'   (D 1762)

'*Mort* estes pur la meie *amur*,
E jo *meur*....'   (D 1813–14)

The puns on *amur* and *mort* are an extended metaphor for the ambiguous nature of the lovers' passion. Yet, the conceit adds a second element to the equation in punning on *mer*, *amer* ('aimer'), and *mort*. The potion (poison) was drunk at sea, 'toujours la même, pourtant si changeante et muable comme la nature de ses héros en proie à leur passion' (Bertolucci-Pizzorusso, 'Cour' 72). On one hand, the ambiguous image of the ocean symbolizes the beneficient effects of the philtre and the love that it induces as well as the profound unconsciousness of that passion. In the first voyage to Ireland, Tristan set forth to seek relief and death and instead found Iseut and healing. On the other, it conveys the virulence of that potion and the passion's potential for misfortune and suffering:

'Del beivre qu'ensemble beümes
En *la mer* quant suppris en fumes.
El beivre fud *la* nostre *mort*.'   (D 1221–23)

It specifically evokes the tempest at sea that will, in the penultimate episode of the romance, blow Iseut's ship off course, preventing her from reaching Tristan in time to save him, transforming the voyage for healing into a voyage of death.

---

[17] See Bédier, *Thomas* 1: 146, n. 1; 2: 53–55; Fourrier 69–70. Echos of the same pun are found in the anonymous song 'La Froidors ne la jalee' (R 517), in MS. B.N. fr. 103 (Bédier, *Thomas* 2: 376), and in *R* (Fotitch 14, i).

Yet the final image of the intertwining trees subsumes the antithetical qualities of the lovers' passion in a single lexeme *(a)mor*, allowing the reader to make transformations of the following type in Thomas' text:

> La bele raïne, sa amie,
> En cui est *sa mort* [*s'amur*] e sa vie.   (T¹ 121–22)[18]

The death and transfiguration of the lovers is the culmination of a series of parallel metaphors – of love as physical hardship, disease, a wound, a mental disorder, a poisoning. Summarized in the pun on *amor* and *mort*, these meet and are transcended in the linked images of the love-death and the lovers' metamorphosis and regeneration as intertwining trees.

Tristan the Trickster

> Tristrans ... molt savoit de gille,
> Car Amors li ensaigne bien.
> *(Tros 3878–79)*

In his seminal essay, 'On the Psychology of the Trickster Figure', Carl Jung explains the trickster figure as an archetype in evolution whose development and change correspond to the development of the human psyche from the nearly total unconsciousness of the primitive to the increasingly higher stages of consciousness of civilized man (*Four Archetypes* 135–152). Since the forces that reside in the unconscious are both incomprehensible and destructive in nature, Jung equates this psychological evolution with an evolution that is at once intellectual and moral: '[The trickster's] nature is more exactly defined ... if one conceives him as a *process* that begins with evil and ends with good' (*Alchemical Studies* 228),[19] and that transforms the meaningless into the meaningful (136). Yet Jung also notes the tenacity of the less civilized elements of the archetype in the psyche of civilized man. 'The darkness and the evil,' he observes, 'have not gone up in smoke, they have merely withdrawn into the unconscious owing to loss of energy, where they remain unconscious so long as all is well with the conscious' (146).

While Jung does not explicitly establish such categories, it is possible to identify four types that correspond to the various stages of the trickster's

---

[18] Cf. *R*, Fotitch 1, viii, x; 5, xxi.
[19] In this passage Jung is discussing the trickster Mercurius.

evolution outlined in his essay. The first of these, corresponding to the entity that Jung has named the 'Shadow', is the stumblebum or numbskull – a figure whose chief characteristic is his deep unconsciousness, untempered by the controlling functions of the conscious mind and who, for that reason, personifies the counter-tendencies of the unconscious: ineptitude, clumsiness, puerility, and fatuity. He is, in short, a summation of all the inferior traits that reside in the unconscious and that the conscious attempts to dominate or to correct (150). In contrast, the second type of trickster, the perverse imp, is consciously and willfully evil and tricks for the sheer pleasure of inflicting malicious and gratuitous harm on others. This figure, which personifies the hostile, aggressive, and destructive impulses of the subconscious, represents an advance in consciousness from the simple, unconscious stupidity of the stumblebum. The most important component of the personality of the trickster is desire, most frequently sexual desire, although hunger, the desire for gain, and other specific desires also reflect the urges of his libido. Thus, the third type is the purposeful, self-centered trickster who tricks in order to satisfy specific personal wants.[20] Fourth, the trickster may take the form of a culture hero. Prometheus, who stole fire from heaven to give to Man and who was made to suffer for the sake of his people, exhibits the two essential characteristics of the culture hero. Through his suffering, he approximates a savior figure; through his 'craft' (craftsmanship and craftiness), he permits the satisfaction of the collective desires of his people.[21] In two respects, the trickster as culture hero manifests an evolutionary advance over the purposeful deceiver who tricks to satisfy personal desires. He represents a progression from the individual to the collective and from the asocial to the social, the final steps in the subjugation of the unconscious to the civilizing and socializing instincts of the conscious.

The numerous inconsistencies and radical oppositions within the trickster's character have presented a major obstacle to an understanding of the archetype, and one is tempted to ask whether the term 'trickster' ought properly designate figures as apparently diverse as the stumblebum, the perverse imp, the purposeful deceiver, and the culture hero. Makarius has advanced an anthropological interpretation of the trickster figure that, in offering a coherent explanation for the inconsistencies in his behavior, resolves the problems inherent in the formulation of a satisfactory defini-

[20] Of this figure Radin writes:
  n a world that has no beginning and no end, an ageless and Priapus-like protagonist is
  tured strutting across the scene, wandering restlessly from place to place, attempt-
   successfully and unsuccessfully, to gratify his voracious hunger and his un-
     ted sexuality.   (167–68)
    ble character of trickery as constructive ingenuity and deceitful fraud is also
     the Old French *engin*. See Hanning, '"Engin' in Twelfth-Century Courtly Texts',
     107.

tion of his nature. She observes that many primitive societies erect elaborate taboos against contact with blood, especially that associated with the sexuality of the female – with defloration, the menstrual cycle, and birth. Prohibitions against incest and the murder of a blood relation constitute extensions of the blood taboo. However, in the same societies there exist magical rituals of great potency that utilize the proscribed blood and, hence, depend on the violation of the blood taboo for their efficacy. The benefits accruing to the individual who performs this dangerous magic are in proportion to the sacrosanctity of the violated taboo. Yet this violation, which is necessarily anti-social and subversive, even if the advantages so obtained profit the entire society, must inevitably call down upon the violator the punishment reserved to those who transgress society's most powerful prohibitions. Since the society stands to gain from the violation of its own taboos, a figure emerges whose task it is to violate his society's interdictions in order to obtain for it the magical powers thus liberated and then to take upon himself the punishment due such a transgression (25). This is the role that the trickster assumes, shouldering the guilt of the collectivity, which he expiates through the sacrifice of his own person. In his self-elected victimization, he exemplifies the stumblebum; in his malicious flouting of societal prohibitions, the perverse imp; in his desire, the purposeful deceiver; and in his self-sacrifice for the sake of the collectivity, the culture hero. The succession of roles that he plays explains the affection, gratitude, and veneration that he evokes and the ridiculous mishaps and tragic misfortunes to which he inevitably falls victim (41).

Since it is traditional to think of the heroes of courtly romance as uniformly possessed of the characteristics appropriate to the chivalric ideal, Tristan the knight and *fin amant* might seem an unlikely candidate for study as a trickster figure. Traditionally, it has been assumed that Tristan's uncourtliness was of a kind with that of Yvain or Lancelot, each an essentially courtly figure who is immediately chastized and instantly repentent for any show of uncourtly behavior towards his lady. Their adoption of uncourtly garb or behavior – Yvain's madness in *Le Chevalier au Lion* or Lancelot's penance in *Le Chevalier de la Charette* – is the price exacted of those who uphold the courtly ethic, their outward abasement the sign of an essential, underlying courtliness. Tristan's uncourtliness, however, differs in kind from that of his chivalric counterparts – and nowhere more radically than in the so-called *version courtoise* of the Tristan poems.[22]

---

[22] A handful of studies have considered the problem of Tristan's uncourtliness, particularly in Thomas' romance (Rozgonyi; Barteau 174–78; Jonin, *Personnages* 177–335; Hunt, 'Significance').

Thomas links his trickery to his uncourtly infidelity. Torn between his obligations to Iseut and to his wife, Tristan laments:

> 'Ne sai a la quele *mentir*,
> Car l'une me covient *traïr*
> E *decevre* e *enginnier*,
> U anduis, ço crei, *trichier*;
> Car tant m'est ceste aprocée   [i.e. Iseut aux Blanches Mains]
> Que Ysolt est ja *enginnée*.
> Tant ai amée la réïne
> Qu'*enginnée* est la meschine,
> Et jo forment *enginné* sui.'   (Sn¹ 461–69)

His adoption of a series of grotesque, degrading disguises; his renunciation of the chivalric ideal of armed combat in favor of guile, deceit, and trickery; his role as victim; and, most of all, his failure to keep faith with Iseut and his marriage to the other Iseut are radically inconsistent with the chivalric and courtly ideal.

The Tristan poems stress the native craftiness of the hero and invoke the topos of wits sharpened by love (e.g. *Tmen* 3878–79, quoted above).[23] As Tristan reminds Iseut in *Fo*:

---

[23] Although unquestionably Iseut and Brengvein also act as tricksters in the Tristan poems, most prominently in *B*, it is Tristan who is portrayed most frequently in that role. (Indeed, in the poems, the term *trickster* is applied only to Brengvein [*la tricherresse*, *B* 519].) Jonin examines the episodes of the tryst at the tree and Iseut's *escondit* and concludes that in *B* Iseut is the prime mover of conspiracies and that beside her Tristan appears 'pauvre et simple' ('Esprit celtique' 412). He writes: 'La passion des amants leur fait courir de mortels dangers. Ils en échappent et ils le doivent parfois à la vaillance de Tristan, mais plus souvent encore à l'esprit d'Iseut' (416). Jonin argues that the motif of the woman trickster is a feature of Celtic literature that was absent from Classical comedy, and he stresses the use of the ambiguous oath as characteristic of the heroines of Irish literature, whose 'digne héritière' he finds Iseut to be (419). However, Jonin overstates his case in apportioning to Tristan the feats of arms and to Iseut and Brengvein those of wits. It is true that in *B* Tristan's role as trickster is more restricted than in any other of the French poems, while Iseut's obtains its greatest development there. Yet Tristan can hardly be characterized as 'pauvre et simple' or as subservient to the superior intelligence of his lady. If, in the two episodes in question, Iseut takes the lead in mounting the trick, Tristan possesses the ready wit to follow that lead in a manner that insures the success of the deception. In the episode of the tryst at the tree, it is Iseut who first perceives the presence of the king in the pine tree and who opens the deceptive dialogue. Yet Tristan immediately grasps the situation and plays his role to perfection, remaining behind to deliver a piteous monologue designed to convince the king beyond all doubt of the lovers' innocence. If Iseut excels in verbal trickery, as in the tryst at the tree and the episode of the *escondit*, Tristan also possesses a high degree of this skill, which he exhibits in the scene of *vérité cachée* that he plays before Mark in 3741–77 (as he does again in *Fb*, *Fo*, and *Tmen*). In *T*, those tricks perpetrated by Iseut and Brengvein are, with one exception (Iseut's clandestine voyage to Brittany, D 1367–1780), confined to that portion of the narrative during which Tristan and Iseut live at Mark's court. In contrast, Tristan's tricks are to be found in every part of the narrative.

'Cum amanz ki trop sunt destraiz
Purpensent de mainte veidise,
Dë engin, dë art, de cuintise,
Cum il purunt entre assembler,
Parler, envaiser e juër,
Si feïmes nus: senez fumes.'   (732–37)

Tristan's feigned madness, which he assumes out of love for Iseut (*Fo* 153–56), is an example of the oxymoron of the wise fool, his folly in reality a deeper cleverness:

'Feindre mei fol, faire folie:
Dunc n'est ço sen e grant veisdie?
Cuintise est, quant n'ai lieu e tens:
Ne puis faire nul greniur sens.
Tels me tendra pur asoté
Ke plus de lu serai sené,
E tels me tendra pur bricun
K'avra plus fol en sa maisun.'   (*Fo* 179–186)

Two fundamental aspects of Tristan's character point to his identification with the trickster figure: his duplicity and his victimization. The first is exemplified by his trickery in the service of his love for Iseut and by the inconstancy of that love, the second by the degrading personae he adopts, by his involuntary suffering for love, and by his self-sacrifice on behalf of the Counter-Order.

In the broadest perspective, the depiction of Tristan as a trickster in the Tristan poems conveys not only the difficulties that the hero must surmount in satisfying, through his trickery, the urges of his passion, but, more important, the profound unconsciousness of those urges. Tristan is a creature of the subconscious, of the libido; and, to the extent that the demands of his libido conflict with the rules of society, he is an asocial trickster and outlaw. However, the urges that he experiences are those of all mankind, and in satisfying them, Tristan acts as the culture hero on behalf of his society, an erotic Counter-Order defined not in the narrow, legalistic terms epitomized by Mark's marriage of convenience to Iseut but in broader, more humane terms that abolish the tension between societal proscription and individual desire.

While Tristan's tricking clearly identifies him with the higher, more evolved types of the trickster figure, his desire, born of the potion consumed in ignorance, has its roots in the depths of his subconscious. Because of the suffering that it occasions him, that desire may be thought of as a counter-tendency, albeit one that possesses the capacity to ennoble its victim.[24] As the unwilling victim of his passion, Tristan resembles the stumblebum.

In the disguise episodes the manner of Tristan's tricking explicitly suggests that of the perverse imp. In B, Tristan, disguised as a leper, mocks Mark and humiliates the felonious barons (3563–864). He plays a capering, simian, demonic trickster who derives immense pleasure from the ridiculous discomfiture that he inflicts on his enemies. Upon seeing the barons mired in the Mal Pas, he gives vent to a maniacal demonstration of joy:

> Qui donc veïst henap casser
> Qant li ladres le henap loche,
> O la coroie fiert la boche
> Et o l'autre des mains flavele.   (3820–23)

This episode represents the farthest swing of the pendulum away from the figure of the courtly knight and towards that of the malicious imp, a figure that we will again glimpse, albeit more distantly, beneath the mask of the clown in the *Folies* and in *Tmen*.

Because his passion, although rooted in the unconscious, still allows him the exercise of his conscious mind in comprehending and in satisfying it, Tristan is more closely associated with the higher types of the trickster, the purposeful deceiver and the culture hero. The majority of his tricks, directed toward the gratification of his desires or toward the protection of himself and his lady, are those of the purposeful deceiver. Beroul draws an explicit parallel between Tristan and Renart, the most fully developed example of the purposeful deceiver in medieval French literature, when he writes: 'Tristran set molt de Malpertis' (4285).[25] Finally, Tristan the trickster serves the Counter-Order as culture hero as Tristan the knight has served the social Order in that capacity.

Tristan's tricks, which are designed to shield the lovers from Mark's wrath, to further his liaison with Iseut by beguiling the vigilance of the king and his cohorts, or to punish the enemies of the couple, stand in opposition to his acts of physical strength and courage as knight.[26] Indeed, it is a given of the tricking episodes that open confrontation with his enemies will avail Tristan nothing. Thus, like Odysseus, he must lay aside his arms and rely on his wits and his protean changes of form to advance the lovers' cause. The feature common to all of Tristan's tricks is the out-

---

[24] In *Fb*, Tristan's loss of the king's favor is said to have been the result of Tristan's 'non savoir' (38).

[25] For a full discussion of the relation of the French Tristan poems to the *Roman de Renart*, see Tregenza; Regalado. On Renart as a trickster figure, see Lomazzi.

[26] While acts of extraordinary physical ability may occasionally be used to effect a trick (e.g. 'the leap between the beds' in *B* 693–754 and *Fo* 725–54 or the 'saut mortel' in *B* 909–964), these may be considered rather as permutations of the deception motif discussed below.

witting of a victim through a deliberate distortion of perceived reality: a misleading statement or act, a lie, a change of form, or an extraordinary physical feat. Tristan's tricks may be divided into two categories: (a) those that rely on deception and (b) those that involve a change of form, a special type of deception.

Tristan's very life begins with a trick. In *T*, Roald perpetrates the infant's concealment and false birth and concocts his spurious identity in order to protect Tristan from the vengefulness of his father's enemy, Duke Morgan.[27] Later, Tristan, who was conceived out of wedlock and who does not discover his true identity until Roald finds him at Mark's court is accused by Duke Morgan of being a bastard ignorant of his origins. In fact, because of the irregular circumstances of his birth, the orphan Tristan, like the bastard whom he resembles, enjoys a freedom of action similar to that of the hero of a *picaresque* novel, a freedom denied to the conventional aristocratic hero of medieval romance whose origins inalterably determine his identity and destiny. This liberty, which for the *picaro* translates into freedom of movement, is in Tristan's case the freedom to change identities and allegiances at will and to live beyond the pale of society. Moreover, his education in the arts of the courtier and noble, normally a means to insure allegiance to one's class and to its codes of legality and morality, serves him well in the life of outlaw and clandestine traveler that he leads after his exile from Mark's court. During this period he will utilize to good advantage all of those arts – military, musical, linguistic, and cynegetic – that he learned in the household of Roald.

The first motive for Tristan's trickery (for which the trick of the hero's false birth may serve as paradigm) is self-preservation. Tristan's frequent lies concerning his identity fall into this category.[28] Likewise, during the lovers' sojourn at Mark's court preceding Tristan's exile, the king's suspicions concerning the lovers are repeatedly aroused and must, with a lie or a trick, be laid once more to rest. In this manner, the precarious equilibrium of the lovers' union, whose potential for discovery and punishment exposes the couple to constant danger, is perpetuated.[29] In *T*, Mark also

[27] In *R*, Merlin, a great trickster and shape-shifter, appears to Tristan's mother just before the hero's birth (Curtis 1: §§226–27).

[28] Upon his arrival in Mark's kingdom in *T*, he identifies himself first as a hunter separated from his companions (*S* Ch. 20) and then as the son of a merchant of Ermenie (*S* Ch. 21). On his first voyage to Ireland the hero claims to be one Tantris, a merchant or petty noble (*S* Ch. 30; *Fo* 315–316, 325–364; *Fb* 183). On his second voyage, he asserts that he is a rich merchant (*S* Ch. 34–35). The leap between the beds (*B* 729–30 and *Fo* 744) and the 'saut mortel' (*B* 909–964) also constitute tricks for self-preservation.

[29] Tricks perpetrated by Tristan, Iseut, and Brengvein whose purpose is to allay Mark's suspicion include the substitution of Brengvein for Iseut in the nuptial bed (*T S* Ch. 46); the contest of wits between Mark and Iseut (*T S* Ch. 53); the tryst at the tree (*B* 2–254, *T S* Ch. 55, *Fo* 793–814); Iseut's ambiguous oath (*B* 4196–216, *T S* Ch. 59, *Fo* 815–32); and Ogrin's mendacious letter to Mark (*B* 2556–618). Two tricks, while not successful in deceiving the king, prevent the

drinks the *vin herbé* (S Ch. 46) and so, like Tristan, has no choice but to love Iseut, a fact that explains the ease with which the lovers are able repeatedly to dupe the king who, explains Iseut, '"Quel talent qu'ait, amer m'estuet"' (D 216).[30] The second motive for the deceptions practiced by Tristan and Iseut is to permit the reunion of the lovers.[31] The clandestine journeys of Tristan to Cornwall or England and, in the last instance, of Iseut to Brittany permit the lovers to be reunited following Tristan's permanent exile. The episode of the intertwining trees in *T* represents the last of the lovers' tricks to effect a clandestine reunion. A third motive for the hero's tricks is vengeance against his and Iseut's enemies.[32] The most singular trick for revenge occurs in the scene at the Gué du Mal Pas in *B* where Tristan first ridicules Mark in veiled but wounding terms, then lures the evil barons onto the marshy ground that gives the Mal Pas its name. Beroul's decision to depict Tristan as a leper in this scene was undoubtedly conditioned in part by the widely held conviction that lepers were exceedingly devious and crafty. Guy de Chauliac writes, '[Les lépreux] sont fins et trompeurs, furieux, et se veulent trop ingerer sur le peuple' (404). In the *Folies* and in *Tmen*, Tristan again mocks his uncle with barbed assertions whose wounding irony and occasional obscenity are comprehensible to whomever has penetrated the secret of Tristan's disguise.

From the very earliest stages of the legend, Tristan is a shape-shifter.[33] The most obvious example of his shape-shifting in the French poems is his adoption of a disguise, a motif that has been discussed above. However, two variations on the form-changing motif may be mentioned. On two occasions in the Tristan poems (*B* 3985–4074, *Tmen*, and on numerous occasions in *R*), Tristan adopts the incognito of an anonymous knight, bearing arms that carry no device. On these occasions he simply divests himself of an inconvenient identity without bothering to replace it with another. The disguise of Kaherdin (Tristan's agent and metaphorical

---

lovers from being taken *in flagrante delicto*: Tristan's leap between the beds (*B* 679–754, *T S* Ch. 55, *Fo* 725–54) and Tristan's flight following the discovery of the lovers in the garden (*T C* 17–52, *Fo* 941–54).

[30] See also D 207–15, 257–62, 282–90.

[31] In the episode of 'Harpe contre Rote', Tristan tricks an Irish baron and rescues Iseut from her abductor (*T S* Ch. 50). The device of the chips in the stream (*T S* Ch. 54; *Fo* 775–92) allows the lovers to fix a rendezvous during Tristan's temporary exile from Mark's court.

[32] The combat episode in *B* (3985–4074), while not, strictly speaking, a trick, relies on the use of an incognito.

[33] The Welsh triad 'Three Enchanter Knights' ascribes magical shape-shifting powers to Tristan:

> Three enchanter knights were in Arthur's court; Menw ap Teirgwaed, and Trystan ap Tallwch, and Cai Hir ap Cynyr Varvoc. The (magical) attributes of these, to change themselves into whatever shape they wished when hardship came upon them, and for this reason they were called enchanter knights, since no one was able to overcome them by might and valour. (Bromwich, 'Remarks' 54, n. 94)

double) as a merchant when he journeys to England to carry Iseut back to Brittany (*TD* 1092–524), constitutes a form-change at one remove, effected through the use of a surrogate.

When in *T* Tristan is exiled from Mark's court and definitively separated from Iseut, his emotional state abruptly alters for the worse, and he consents to the ill-fated marriage with Iseut aux Blanches Mains. Subsequently, he adopts a series of disguises in order to return to England to be reunited with Iseut la Blonde. As Hunt has recently demonstrated, the change in Tristan's sentiments and his resulting marriage constitute, in Thomas' eyes, the central problem of the romance ('Significance'). Indeed, Tristan himself, wrestling with the implications of the ill-fated marriage, repeatedly employs the words *trichier, enginnier, decevre, engin,* and *tricherie* to designate his own actions.[34] At first he protests against the unspoken accusation that in marrying the other Iseut he is guilty of deceiving his beloved: '[M'amur] vers li ne pois trichier' (Sn[1] 78). Yet he protests overmuch, and his declarations of innocence serve only to inculpate him. His assertion that he is incapable of deceiving Iseut is called into question by his complaint that he has been the dupe of their love:

> La nostre amur tant se desevre
> Qu'ele n'est fors pur mei decevre.   (Sn[1] 7–8)

or of Iseut's natural feminine guile:

> '... [jo] me plain
> Del change e de la trischerie
> Que envers moi fait Ysode m'amie.'   (T[1] 30–32)

   In that portion of *T* that recounts the period of the hero's exile, marriage, and clandestine reunions with Iseut, each effected by a chameleon-like change of form, the theme of Tristan as protean shape-shifter serves as a generalized metaphor for the mutability of the hero's passion, a topic on which Thomas discourses at length in the first Sneyd fragment. The poet reminds his audience of the changeability of the human psyche:

> Oez merveilluse aventure,
> Cum genz sunt d'estrange nature,
> Que en nul lieu ne sunt estable:
> De nature sunt si changable,
> Lor mal us ne poent laissier,
> Mais le buen puent changer.   (Sn[1] 233–38)

---

[34] E.g. Sn[1] 8, 78–82, 422–23, 451, 461–70, 482, 489–92, 555–59, 563–65.

According to Thomas, such fickleness arises from the fact that man's desires, infinite and insatiable, far outstrip the possibilities of satisfaction. Pre-eminently a creature of desire, the tricky Tristan is a permanent dupe of this 'novelerie [qui] le deceit' (Sn[1] 271), a vice that Thomas denounces with religious fervor:

> Mais trop par aiment novelerie
> Homes e femmes ensement,
> Car trop par changent lor talent
> E lor desir e lor voleir
> Cuntre raisun, cuntre poeir.   (Sn[1] 292–96)

While *novelerie* signifies any change in the object of one's desires, for Thomas it refers more specifically to the permanent impulse of the libido to seek satisfaction in new objects of sexual desire. It is *novelerie* that draws Tristan to Iseut aux Blanches Mains, and the poet introduces the account of Tristan's marriage with the observation that 'Sis [i.e. Tristan's] corages mue sovent, / E pense molt diversement' (Sn[1] 1–2). Tristan's monologue that follows (Sn[1] 5–182) takes the form of an interior debate concerning his impending marriage. Caught in a turmoil of conflicting emotions, each of which pulls at a different facet of his psyche, Tristan fears that *novelerie* has caused Iseut, who is living as Mark's wife, to forget her lover, his memory effaced by the pleasure that she takes in her spouse's embraces:

> 'Ne la blam pas s'ele mei oblie,
> Car pur mei ne deit languir mie:
> Sa grant belté pas nel requirt,
> Ne sa nature n'i afirt,
> Quant de lui ad sun desir,   [i.e. de Marc]
> Que pur altre deive languir.
> Tant se deit deliter al rei
> Oblier deit l'amur de mei,
> En sun seignur tant deliter
> Que sun ami deit oblier.'   (Sn[1] 97–106)

This passage expresses the shadowy belief, implicit throughout Thomas' poem, that the lovers' passion brings about a forgetfulness of duty, person, and rank.[35]

Behind this belief lies another, even more terrible: the conviction that sexual pleasure effaces the exterior world and with it the memory of persons with whom one might formerly have shared that pleasure; for Eros, a

---

[35] See also Sn[1] 189–92 and B 2147–262, especially Tristan's lament: '"Oublïé ai chevalerie"' (2165).

jealous god, strives ceaselessly to guard his prerogatives against the claims of Amor. The effacement of the beloved through the satisfaction of the sexual urge with another raises the specter of a still more menacing form of mutability, the dissolution of the self through the indifference of the other. The fear of this eventuality is linked in Tristan's mind with his tormented conviction of woman's inability to resist the imperatives of the sexual urge, which he terms the 'naturel fait' (Sn¹ 518) and which Thomas calls 'Ço que la nature volt' (Sn¹ 604). In speaking of Iseut's conjugal relations with Mark, Tristan says: 'Naturelment li estuit faire' (Sn¹ 109), an expression of his dispairing conviction that as long as Iseut lives as Mark's wife, her sexual appetites satisfied, she will have little heed of her absent lover.[36] These beliefs cause Tristan paroxysms of jealousy, pain, anger, and uncertainty and introduce a second motive of instability into the hero's psyche, already prey to the urgings of *novelerie*.

As Thomas depicts it, the passion of Tristan and Iseut has little of the cerebral or the courtly. On two occasions, the poet asserts that Tristan's marriage to the second Iseut violates the canons of *fin'amor*:

Car si ço fin' amur fust,	
La meschine amé ne oüst	[subject: Tristan]
Cuntre volenté s'amie.	(Sn¹ 319–21)
Se de fin' amur l'amast	[subject: Tristan, object: Iseut]
L'altre Ysolt nen espusast.	(Sn¹ 329–30)

Rather, the passion is subliminal, blood-deep, and unreasoning, possessed of the ungovernable blindness of Natura and the libido. Madness, disease, and injury serve as its metaphors. It thrives on proximity and physical satisfaction. When circumstances separate the lovers, the passion is apt to fix upon another object. Indeed, the latter portion of Thomas' poem turns on the tension between the antinomian concepts of the instability produced by the sexual urge and the ideal of a love powerful enough to overcome this instability.

This then is Thomas' vision of a world without permanence, of a love without memory, ultimately no more than an abstract urging of the flesh. The sudden shifts in Tristan's mind and intentions in this passage make clear the effect that his jealousy exercises upon him, transforming him into a chimerical being moved and metamorphosed by the ebb and flow of his passion. The Tristan of the first Sneyd fragment who, believing that Iseut has forgotten him, consents to a marriage with Kaherdin's sister is the

---

36 Tristan's misogyny is similar to that of Baudelaire who, in his *Journaux intimes*, expostulated: 'La femme est *naturelle*, c'est-à-dire abominable' ('Mon coeur mis à nu', *Oeuvres complètes* 1272).

same Tristan who, in the final episode of the romance, cannot believe that Iseut will come to Brittany to save him, a lack of faith that results in his death and that of Iseut. This mercurial being shifts his outward appearance as quickly as his emotions change. Indeed, the metamorphoses that he undergoes are changes not of form only but of substance. In the poems, Tristan not merely impersonates but becomes a penitent (*T*), a leper (*T*, *B*), and a madman (*Fb*, *Fo*), each degrading disguise translating a different aspect of his mind's disorder. The trickster figure is an expression of the unconscious with its hidden content of assorted impulses and desires that find expression in a multiplicity of outward forms; in Tristan the trickster the man of many minds is rendered by the man of many faces.

Jung has noted the trickster's approximation to a savior figure 'in confirmation of the mythological truth that the wounded wounder is the agent of healing, and that the sufferer takes away suffering' (136). Prometheus, chained to a mountain top, his liver torn by a griffon-vulture in punishment for his theft of the celestial fire, is the paradigm of the trickster as culture hero and suffering savior figure. In *T*, Tristan, who imparts to his society esoteric and previously unknown wisdom – the art of the hunt – plays the role of culture hero. In certain respects, Tristan, whose suffering casts him in the role of victim, also approximates a savior figure; for in the savior figure the trickster archetype comes a full circle and, in the final stage, that of wounded culture hero, rejoins the first, that of suffering stumblebum.

The Tristan poems serve a cathartic and healing function in mediating the 'impulses of reckless physical self-assertion' (Bernheimer 3) and the temptation to natural and moral anarchy that exist in the psyche of each human being, constantly threatening the individual's well-being and the fabric of society. These impulses are incarnate in Tristan's passion with its potential for individual suffering and the dislocation of the social mechanism and with its potential for beatitude. Lévi-Strauss has written concerning the trickster figure that 'mythical thought always works from the awareness of oppositions towards their progressive mediation' (188). He notes that, because of his ambiguous and equivocal nature, the trickster serves as a mediating figure in mythic literature, resolving dualities, antitheses, and contradictions (190–91). Hanning offers a slightly different construction, observing: 'Through *engin*, characters and authors of chivalric romances are repeatedly shown to be at work gilding over intractable realities with a facade of chivalry and idealistic love' (135).

Viewed in their socio-psychological dimension, the Tristan romances serve to conjure or to purge the dangerous elements in the human psyche by bringing them within the ken and hence the control of the conscious.[37]

---

[37] What Jung has written of the Winnebago trickster cycle was, for a period and for a certain

These dangerous elements are of two sorts. On one hand, there is the individual's fear of the consequences of defective love – of loving (or being loved) too little, too much, or in the wrong manner. On the other, there is the collective fear of the consequences to the social Order of an adulterous (and implicitly incestuous) 'lawless love' like that of Tristan and Iseut, of a violation of the blood taboo. In focusing in the person of its hero the tensions that arise from the threat of such a passion to the individual and to the collective organism, the Tristan poems give expression to and therefore relieve those fears.

Thomas addresses his work not to the happy few but to all lovers, particularly those whose love has been fraught with adversity:

> Tumas fine ci sun escrit:
> A tuz amanz saluz i dit,
> As pensis e as amerus,
> As emvius, as desirus,
> As enveisiez e as purvers,
> [A tuz cels] ki orunt ces vers.... (Sn²820–25)

To them – and to his reader – he offers his work, and the example of his hero and heroine, as a specific against the ills of unhappy love:

> Que as amanz deive plaisir,   [subject: l'estoire]
> E que par lieus poissent troveir
> Choses u se puissent recorder:
> Aveir em poissent grant confort,
> Encuntre change, encontre tort,
> Encuntre paine, encuntre dolur,
> Encuntre tuiz engins d'amur! (Sn²833–39)

Chief among the *engins d'amur*, which bring about *change, tort, paine*, and *dolur*, are not only absence and enforced separation but also *novelerie*, unsteadfastness, infidelity, and love unable to sustain itself in the face of those ills. The pain experienced by Tristan le Nain at the abduction of his lady, by Tristan at Iseut's apparent renunciation, and by Iseut at Tristan's death symbolizes and embodies the suffering occasioned by those *engins*.

---

social class – the courtly society to which the poets destined their works – also true of the French Tristan poems:

> ... the story of the trickster is not in the least disagreeable to the Winnebago consciousness or incompatible with it but, on the contrary, pleasurable and therefore not conducive to repression. It looks, therefore, as if the myth were actively sustained and fostered by consciousness. This may well be so, since that is the best and most successful method of keeping the shadow figure conscious and subjecting it to conscious criticism (145).

Hardly the paragon of faithful lovers, Tristan '*l'Amerus*' in *T* incarnates the failings of all lovers, which he expiates through his death.

When Tristan champions the cause of Tristan le Nain, the former's passion and the actions that it inspires take on a social dimension, assimilating the protagonist to the figure of the trickster as culture hero. In order for Tristan to fulfill his obligation to *tuz amanz*, the people of the Counter-Order, he must take upon himself their sins against ideal love and their consequent suffering, must be put to death for their sake. Having violated the taboos established by the moral and social Order, he becomes a sacrificial victim, healing their suffering through his and rendering them whole through his death. Thus, Tristan (and Iseut with him) will die at the hands of the enemies of the Counter-Order: the rival and abductor, Estult; the wife, Iseut aux Blanches Mains; and implicitly the husband, Mark, who has threatened the lovers on so many occasions and who continues to separate them at a moment when Iseut's presence alone is capable of saving Tristan's (and her own) life.[38] His and Iseut's suffering and death are figuratively a ritual sacrifice that serves to take away suffering and to preserve their people, the Counter-Order of *tuz amanz*, from the evils that imperfect love may bring.

On the social level, the problem is posed in different terms.[39] Central to the structure of the Tristan poems is the tension between the Christian conception of a societal morality that demands and enforces the repression of an adulterous, anti-social passion like that of Tristan and Iseut and the contrary belief in the goodness, even the sanctity of such a passion. This tension, reflected in the conflict between Tristan, outlaw and lover, and Mark, king and husband, is further mirrored in a series of oppositions within the trickster/hero: his flight from and longing for reintegration into society, his degradation and nobility, his infidelity and constancy, his weakness and strength. In their mythopoeic function of mediating in an exemplary manner those oppositions, the Tristan poems cast their hero in the role of savior-victim, destroyed by those oppositions whose antithetical imperatives he is punished for transgressing. Thomas offers Tristan's death and subsequent reincarnation, through which the hero transcends those oppositions, as an example through which the medieval reader of his poem might find the strength and understanding to transcend the same dualities in his own life.

---

[38] Makarius 42. In *R*, which once again makes explicit what is implicit in the poems, Mark actually puts Tristan to death by wounding him with a spear as he harps for Iseut (Löseth §546).

[39] Payen has analyzed the political pressures on Beroul's Mark to reassert the priority of the moral Order by persecuting the lovers and by banishing Tristan. For Payen, the essential conflict in *B* is the challenge to the central authority by the rebel barons who attack Tristan in order to undermine Mark's power ('Ordre moral').

IV

INTERTEXTUALITY AND THE ELABORATION
OF MEANING
IN THE OLD FRENCH TRISTAN POEMS

> A travers les règles et les techniques de la
> rhétorique d'une part et à partir d'une tradi-
> tion de récits légendaires, que les roman-
> ciers nomment 'estoire', le texte poétique, et
> plus particulièrement le texte narratif, ap-
> paraît moins comme le résultat d'une con-
> ception originale que comme le produit d'une
> ré-écriture spécifique, à la fois travail et jeu
> d'ajustement des formes entre elles: jeux
> d'invention et de disposition, recherche de
> correspondances symboliques et formelles
> par le recours aux gloses et amplifications.
> (Walter, 'Solstice' 7)

Philippe Walter's concise description of the mechanism by which the
Tristan poems evolved is especially pertinent and perspicacious in the
distinction that it draws between 'le texte poétique' and 'le texte narratif',
between what I would term the metaphorical and narrative dimensions of
those poems. Central to Walter's analysis, and to my own, is a recognition
of the fact that the 'estoire', the received Tristan narrative of the twelfth
century was an imperfectly homogeneous body of texts within which only
certain material was perceived by the poets as canonical and only certain
versions authoritative. It was not, as Bédier contended, 'un poème
régulier, composé à une haute époque, dès le début du XIIe siècle, par un
homme de génie ... [non] pas une vulgate informe, mais déja un de ces
organismes supérieurs dont toutes les parties sont liées par une synergie
telle que toutes souffrent de la moindre atteinte à l'une d'entre elles'
(*Thomas* 2: 186–87). Nevertheless, as I have argued above, it is also virtually
certain that these more or less traditional tales orbited around a fixed
narrative core and that the most innovative transformations of the Tristan
matter were effected in those portions of the narrative, most notably the
return episodes, that were independent of this fixed core that they glossed
and amplified.

That the French poets of the Tristan matter continued throughout the twelfth century to borrow narrative motifs from a variety of exogenous (i.e. non-Tristanian) sources is beyond question, and a large body of scholarship has been devoted to the cataloguing of these borrowings. Yet, the Tristan poets manifestly thought of themselves as working within a self-contained, if not necessarily a unified, tradition; and their most significant and most striking transformations of the canon were the product of an increasing tendency to play upon and off of the givens of that tradition. While this self-referentiality is most apparent in the episodic poems, which are extended allusions that depend for their comprehensibility on a knowledge of the canonical narrative, it is no less pervasive in the romances of Thomas and Beroul, detailed – and sometimes highly critical – commentaries on that narrative.

Because each identity that Tristan adopts carried a pre-existing set of literary and extra-literary associations, the depiction of the protagonist was a function of the interplay between an existing (or pretextual) body of knowledge, belief, and meaning (e.g., the literary commonplaces and popular beliefs concerning music, love and love-sickness, the hunt, and madness that informed the depiction of Tristan's social and disguise identities) and the interpretation of that knowledge imposed by a given poet. In the process of retelling and embellishing the canonical Tristan matter, the French poets regularly singled out and transformed narrative elements present in the preceding corpus, investing them with a metaphorical resonance that was merely potential in their source(s). By the second half of the twelfth century, this process of metaphorical development resulted in the elaboration of a complex network of significant connections among the narrative elements of the French Tristan poems; and subsequent texts were composed with reference to this nexus of meanings, allusions to which constitute a major source of meaning in the poems. Even the most original of these metaphorical developments, the *Fo* poet's ironical depiction of Tristan as a wild man, had its genesis in a network of significant links between the new motif and narrative elements of the antecedent tradition: Tristan's suffering for love, his 'madness', his association with the forest, his sexual passion, his conflict with the social Order, and his 'abduction' of Iseut to the Morois. Meaning in each new text was generated by the deployment of a complex and sophisticated battery of rhetorical devices, most prominently by the cultivation of parallelisms and antitheses in metaphorical and narrative structure within the new text and between it and the texts of the antecedent canon.

Elements furnished by four different contexts are at play in the complex interaction of external influence, internal referentiality, and personal invention that characterizes the development and evolution of the Old French Tristan narrative. The broadest extra-literary context for the poems is the body of largely unconscious archetypal or mythic knowledge upon which the medieval poet drew in depicting his protagonist. A second extra-literary context for the poems is comprised of the sum of the poet's conscious knowledge and beliefs about the workings of the material and spiritual world, similar in many respects to the one that he himself inhabited, in which he placed his characters. In the case of Tristan's identities, this context is the information and received beliefs pertaining to each of the social states depicted by the poets. The literary context, like the extra-literary, is double, comprising both an external and an internal dimension. The external literary context, reflecting contemporary literary usage (especially rhetorical conventions), established canons of literary meaning (especially received equations of metaphorical meaning), and a rich repertoire of narrative motifs, is constitutued by the non-Tristanian literary canon of the twelfth century (i.e., by the totality of non-Tristanian texts known to the twelfth century, whether composed in that century or earlier). The internal context is constitutued by the corpus of Tristan narratives known to the poets. While the distinction between the literary and the extra-literary is frequently blurred, since most originally non-literary constructs of belief and meaning eventually receive literary expression, the distinction is useful in discriminating between those intellectual constructs that are grounded in non-literary belief and that only sporadically find literary expression and those artificial and self-sufficient literary constructs that are largely, if never entirely, divorced from a non-literary scheme of knowledge and belief. The belief that leprosy was transmitted by sexual congress is an example of the former; the metaphor of love as a wasting illness an example of the latter.

The motif of the intertwining trees, the trickster archetype, the belief in the relation of madness to poetic inspiration and clairvoyance, and the figure of the marvelous musician whose powers derive from his affinity with the forces of nature are examples of mythic material utilized by the Tristan poets. While a number of these motifs were known to the Tristan poets through texts that were in circulation in twelfth-century France, others, and sometimes the same ones, appear to have been nurtured by more immediate contact with the living mythology of the Celtic world. The figure of the marvelous musician is one such case; for, fixed in Western literary tradition by the figures of David and Orpheus, it was enriched and revitalized in the twelfth century through the influence of a similar tradition in Celtic mythology. The rhetorical figure of the *locus amoenus* crystallizes in literary form aspects of the mythology of the Other World, particularly as it found expression in classical literature. Yet the *loci amoeni* depicted in the Tristan poems are shaped by myths about the natural world incorporating pre-literary beliefs that transcend the figure of the *locus amoenus*. In like manner, although the hunt as a metaphor for the amorous pursuit was a literary commonplace in twelfth-century France, the depiction of Tristan as a hunter draws on mythic constructs of great antiquity, echoes of which are found throughout classical literature. The descent into the belly of the whale, another literary motif of considerable antiquity, has its origins in an archetypal quest narrative that is pre-literary. Conversely, while the clairvoyance of the wild man was part of the mythology of that fantastical being, it is most probable that the *Fo* poet's knowledge of this motif derived not from a living mythological tradition but from a literary source, Geoffrey of Monmouth's *Vita Merlini*. Hence, while the Tristan poets drew on a vast reservoir of mythic material that was known to them only through literary sources, they utilized other material that was derived directly or at little distance from mythological traditions that remained vital and viable in the twelfth century.

Similarly, the depiction of the several social and disguise identities that Tristan adopts was variously shaped by the poets' knowledge of and be-liefs about those estates as they actually existed in twelfth-century society and by the conventions governing their literary representation. A belief in the innate trickiness of the leper, the sexual incontinence of the madman, or the efficacy of a pilgrimage in curing affliction apparently reflect a primarily non-literary understanding of the material and spiritual world; and their utilization in a literary text constitutes a secondary phenom-enon.[1] In contrast, Thomas' ideological convictions about the obligations imposed by *fin'amor* represent an intellectual construct that was primarily literary. Convictions about the real determinative force of genealogy and etymology, the received beliefs of chivalric and clerical culture respect-ively, were ultimately responsible for the composition of the episode of Tristan's parents and for the puns on *triste/Tristan* and *amare/amarum/mare*, although here again literary tradition was a contributing factor; for the genealogical preface was a common feature of twelfth-century literature and the *amare/amarum/mare concetto* a commonplace of the schools.

The Tristan poems are highly 'literary' in two senses: they are highly self-conscious artefacts crafted with all the rhetorical resources available to twelfth-century literary culture and they are composed within the con-text of an antecedent canon of Tristan texts. Beliefs like those in the curative powers of music and love or in the erotic appeal of chivalric prowess were items of common cultural information that had been highly embellished, even stylised, in a long literary tradition stretching back to

---

[1] A special category must be reserved for religious beliefs, which, while 'extra-literary' in origin, frequently figure in secular literary texts. For the purposes of this discussion, re-ligious convictions, like that in madness as a punishment visited by God upon a sinner guilty of transgressing divine law, are considered 'extra-literary', not because their origins are extra-textual (for of course they are not) but because religious convictions belong, nominally at least, to a different order of belief from literary knowledge.

biblical and classical literature.[2] The *Tros* poet, who alludes liberally if subtly to musical motifs in the aforegoing canon, amplifies and recombines certain of Tristan's attributes (notably, his skill in music and the hunt) in light of popular notions and literary conceits concerning the nightingale.

Intertextuality itself becomes an important literary motif in the Tristan poems. The *Folies* are the most innovative in exploiting the notion of an ongoing tradition to create a narrative situation that demands a retelling of the antecedent narrative, while *Ch* and *Tmen* develop the fiction that the literary use of antecedent episodes of the Tristan narrative plays a determinative role in subsequent episodes. *Ch* is, in essence, an account of the literary composition of an episode by Tristan himself, the ongoing events of whose life become intermingled with the composition of a series of works celebrating them. In *Tmen* Tristan is a performer reciting for the pleasure and edification of the queen (and the reader) a text of his own making that treats of an incident from their shared past. He is simultaneously a poet engaged in composing a living episode to which he will subsequently give literary form. The *Fo* poet exploits with the greatest originality and complexity of any of the Tristan poets the intertextuality motif, making extensive narrative and metaphorical allusions to the antecedent corpus. Finally, like the disguise motif, which inverts and plays on the reality of Tristan's overt identities, the intertextual motif frequently inverts and plays on the events of the narrative in the lovers' misleading, fantastical, or mendacious discourse about the past.

In their extensive reliance on and exploitation of the possibilities afforded by intertextuality, both as a literary technique and as a narrative motif, the Tristan poems differ in degree only and not in kind from the mainstream of twelfth and thirteenth-century secular literature. If adaptation, *amplificatio*, and cyclical composition were the norm in medieval literature, seldom were they practiced with the degree of conscious application exercised by the Tristan poets. This difference arises, I believe, from the peculiar character of the Tristan matter, which, as I have argued above, was composed of a fixed core *within* which space was reserved for invention and innovation. The Tristan matter differs even from the Renart tales that in so many respects it resembles in that the latter were essentially self-contained stories constituting an open-ended cycle and having little in common beyond the fundamental traits of their protagonist's character, while the former was grounded in a narrative whose beginning and end-

---

[2] It was undoubtedly the existence of the motifs of the curative powers of music and love as literary commonplaces that authorized the ironies of the *Fo* poet, who played one off against another; for in *Fo* Tristan's own music is incapable of healing his love madness, which is susceptible only to the healing qualities of Iseut's love.

ing were not only fixed but of such a character as to exercise a determinative influence over the form of any new tales composed about the lovers. Unlike Chrétien's unfinished *Perceval*, the Tristan matter did not admit of open-ended expansion or unchecked serial development, for it was constrained by the 'facts' of the core narrative, especially its culminating event, the death of the lovers, with respect to which all other episodes of the legend had to be situated. Unlike the *romans antiques*, adaptations of fully constituted literary texts, its narrative, which was not fully drawn, provided the possibility for internal expansion. It was, however, the very narrowness of the limits within which the story of the lovers could be rewritten that gave to the extant French poems, which occur relatively late in the evolution of the matter, their great narrative compression and dramatic intensity. Subsequent rewritings of the matter, beginning with the French prose romance, burst the mold of the core narrative, submerging the surviving elements in a flood of extraneous narrative detail. It may be, as I have hypothesized elsewhere ('*Mouvance*'), that the nature and intensity of this tale of adulterous love and tragic death made its destruction inevitable. It may simply be that the imperatives to which the twelfth and early thirteenth-century poems were constrained were no longer determinative for later generations and new literary tastes. Whatever the case, the poems were entirely eclipsed by the literary fashions of the thirteenth century and, if the manuscript tradition is a reliable guide, passed entirely from the consciousness of Western European culture (save in Scandinavia) until their rediscovery in the nineteenth century.

WORKS CONSULTED

Abbreviations

BBIAS *Bulletin Bibliographique de la Société Internationale Arthurienne /*
       Bibliographical Bulletin of the International Arthurian Society
CCM   *Cahiers de Civilisation Médiévale*
CFMA   Classiques Français du Moyen Age
SATF   Société des Anciens Textes Français
TCFMA Traductions des Classiques Français du Moyen Age
TLF   Textes Littéraires Français
TLL   *Travaux de Linguistique et de Littérature Publiés par le Centre de*
       Philologie et de Littératures Romanes de l'Université de Strasbourg
ZFSL   *Zeitschrift für Französische Sprache und Literatur*
ZRP   *Zeitschrift für Romanische Philologie*

I

PRIMARY SOURCES

Unless otherwise specified, all textual quotations are taken from the first edition listed under each rubric. Under 'Other Edition(s)' are cited editions that contain important commentary or textual notes.

A. The Old French Tristan Poems

Beroul's *Tristran* [B]

Ewert, Alfred. *The Romance of Tristran by Beroul. A Poem of the Twelfth Century*. I. *Introduction, Text, Glossary, Index*. II. *Introduction, Commentary*. 2 vols. Oxford: Blackwell, 1939, 1970.

Other Editions:

Roques, Mario and Lucien Foulet. *Béroul. Le Roman de Tristan, poème du XIIe siècle, édité par Ernest Muret. Quatrième édition revue par L. M. Defourques*. CFMA 12. Paris: Champion, 1947.

Muret, Ernest. *Le Roman de Tristan par Béroul et un anonyme, poème du XIIe siècle*. SATF. Paris: Firmin Didot, 1903. New York: Johnson Reprint Corp., 1965.

Thomas' *Tristan* [T]

Wind, Bartina H. *Thomas. Les Fragments du roman de Tristan, poème du XIIe siècle. Edités avec un commentaire*. TLF 92. Geneva: Droz; Paris: Minard, 1960.

Other Editions:

Wind, Bartina H. *Les Fragments du roman de Tristan, poème du XIIe siècle par Thomas. Edités avec commentaire*. Leiden: Brill, 1950.

Bédier, Joseph. *Le Roman de Tristan par Thomas, poème du XIIe siècle*. SATF. 2 vols. I. *Texte*. Paris: Firmin-Didot, 1902. II. *Introduction*. Paris: Firmin-Didot, 1905.

The *Folies Tristan* of Bern [Fb] and Oxford [Fo]

Payen, Jean-Charles. *Tristan et Yseut. Les Tristan en vers. 'Tristan' de Béroul, 'Tristan' de Thomas, 'Folie Tristan' de Berne, 'Folie Tristan' d'Oxford, 'Chèvrefeuille' de Marie de France. Edition nouvelle comprenant texte, traduction, notes critiques, bibliographie et notes*. Paris: Garnier, 1974. 247–97.

Other Editions:

Dean, Ruth J. and Elspeth M. Kennedy. 'Un Fragment anglo-normand de la *Folie Tristan* de Berne'. *Moyen Age* 79 (1973): 57–72.

Hoepffner, Ernest. *La Folie Tristan d'Oxford, publiée avec commentaire*. Publications de la Faculté des Lettres de l'Université de Strasbourg, Textes d'Etude 8. 1938. 2nd. ed. revised and corrected, Paris: Belles Lettres, 1943.

———. *La Folie Tristan de Berne, publiée avec commentaire*. Publications de la Faculté des Lettres de l'Université de Strasbourg, Textes d'Etude 3. 1934. 2nd ed. revised and corrected, Paris: Belles Lettres, 1949.

Bédier, Joseph. *Les Deux Poèmes de la Folie Tristan*. SATF. Paris: Firmin-Didot, 1907. New York and London: Johnson Reprint Co., 1965.

Marie's *Lai du Chèvrefeuille* [Ch]

Payen, Jean-Charles. *Les Tristan en vers.* 299–302.

Other Editions:

Rychner, Jean. *Les Lais de Marie de France.* CFMA. Paris: Champion, 1966.

Ewert, Alfred. *Marie de France: Lais.* Blackwells' French Texts. 1944. Oxford: Blackwell, 1969.

Tristan Rossignol [Tros]

Paris, Gaston. 'Le Donnei des amants'. *Romania* 25 (1896): 497–541. The episode of *Tristan rossignol* comprises lines 453–662 of the 'Donnei des amanz'.

Tristan Ménestrel [Tmen]

Williams, Mary. *Gerbert de Montreuil. La Continuation de Perceval.* CFMA 28. Paris: Champion, 1922. 1: 3309–4832.

Other Edition:

Bédier, Joseph and Jessie L. Weston. 'Tristan Ménestrel. Extrait de la Continuation de *Perceval* par Gerbert'. *Romania* 35 (1906): 497–530.

B. *Eilhart von Oberge's* Tristrant [O]

Buschinger, Danielle. *Eilhart von Oberg. Tristrant. Edition diplomatique des manuscrits et traduction en français moderne avec introduction, notes et index.* Göppinger Arbeiten zur Germanstik 202. Göppingen: Alfred Kümmerle, 1976.

C. *The French Prose Romance*

Since there exists no single edition either of the dominant version of the French prose *Tristan* or of MS. B.N.fr. 103, I cite all those editions publishing portions of the text. In quoting from or citing the text, I identify parenthetically the version used.

The Dominant Version of the French Prose *Tristan* [R]

Löseth, Eilert. *Le Roman en prose de Tristan, le roman de Palamède et la compilation de Rusticien de Pise. Analyse critique d'après les manuscrits de Paris.* Paris: Bouillon, 1891. New York: Burt Franklin, 1970.

Curtis, Renée L. *Le Roman de Tristan en prose.* 3 vols. I. Munich: Hueber, 1963 (corresponds to Löseth §§1–38); II. Leiden: Brill, 1976 (corresponds to Löseth §§39–86); III. Cambridge: D. S. Brewer, 1985 (corresponds to Löseth §§87–91).

Fotitch, Tatiana and Ruth Steiner. *Les Lais du roman de Tristan en prose d'après le manuscrit de Vienne 2542.* Münchener Romanistische Arbeiten 38. Munich: Fink, 1974.

Murrell, E. S. 'The death of Tristan from Douce ms. 189'. *PMLA* 43 (1928): 343–83.

The Variant Version of the French Prose *Tristan* Preserved by Paris, MS. B.N.fr. 103 (composed between 1340 and 1450) and Eight Printed Editions (published between 1489 and 1533) [MS B.N.fr. 103]

Bédier, Joseph. *Le Roman de Tristan par Thomas, poème du XIIe siècle.* SATF. Paris: Firmin-Didot, 1905. 2: 321–95.

Bédier, Joseph. 'La Mort de Tristan et d'Iseut, d'après le manuscrit fr. 103 de la Bibliothèque Nationale, comparé au poème allemand d'Eilhart d'Oberg'. *Romania* 15 (1886): 481–510.

Tristan, 1489. Introductory note by C. E. Pickford. London: Scolar Press, 1976.

D. *The Derivatives of Thomas'* Tristan

Brother Robert's Old Norse *Tristrams saga ok Ísöndar* [S]

Schach, Paul, trans. *The Saga of Tristram and Ísönd.* Lincoln: University of Nebraska Press, 1973.

Other Edition:

Kölbing, Eugen. *Die nordische und die englische Version der Tristan-Sage.* I. *Tristrams Saga ok Ísondar mit einer literar-historischen Einleitung, deutscher Uebersetzung und Anmerkungen zum ersten Mal herausgegeben.* Heilbronn: Henninger, 1878.

Gottfried von Strassburg's *Tristan* [G]

Ranke, Friedrich. *Gottfried von Straßburg. Tristan und Isold. Text.* 7th ed. Berlin: Weidmann, 1963.

The Middle English *Sir Tristrem* [E]

McNeill, George P. *Sir Tristrem.* Scottish Text Society 8. Edinburgh: Blackwood, 1886. New York: Johnson Reprint Corp., 1966.

The Italian *Tavola Ritonda*

Polidori, Filippo-Luigi. *La Tavola Ritonda, o l'Istoria di Tristano; testo di lingua citato dagli accademici della Crusca ed ora per la prima volta pubblicato secondo il codice della Mediceo-Laurenziana.* Collezione di Opere Inedite o Rare di Scrittori Italiani dal XIII al XVI Secolo. 2 vols. Bologna: G. Romagnoli, 1864–65.

E. Allusions to the Tristan Matter

Williams, Harry F. 'Allusions à la légende de Tristan'. *BBIAS* 12 (1960): 91–96.

Bédier, Joseph. 'Allusions à la légende de Tristan dans la littérature du moyen âge'. *Le Roman de Tristan par Thomas, poème du XIIe siècle.* SATF. Paris: Firmin-Didot, 1905. 2: 397–400.

Sudre, Léopold. 'Les Allusions à la légende de Tristan dans la littérature du moyen âge'. *Romania* 15 (1886): 534–57.

Michel, Francisque. *Tristan. Recueil de ce qui reste des poëmes relatifs à ses aventures, composés en françois, en anglo-normand et en grec dans les XII et XIII siècles.* 3 vols. London: Pickering; Paris: Techener, 1835–38.

F. The Iconography of the Tristan Matter

General

Loomis, Roger Sherman and Laura Hibbard Loomis. *Arthurian Legends in Medieval Art.* 1938. New York: Kraus Reprint Corp., 1966.

The Chertsey Tiles

Loomis, Roger Sherman. *Illustrations of Medieval Romance on Tiles from Chertsey Abbey*. University of Illinois Studies in Language and Literature 2.2. Urbana: University of Illinois, 1916.

Paris, MS. B.N.fr. 112, fo. 239. Miniature.

Payen, Jean-Charles. *Les Tristan en vers*. Plate 7.

G. *Associated Classical and Medieval Texts*

Abelard. *Abélard. Historia Calamitatium, texte critique avec une introduction*. Ed. Jacques Monfrin. Bibliothèque des Textes Philosophiques, Textes et Commentaires. 2nd ed. Paris: J. Vrin, 1962.

Adam of Fulda. *De Musica*. In *Scriptores ecclesiastici de musica sacra potissimum. Ex variis Italiæ, Galliæ & Germaniæ codicibus manuscriptis collecti*. Ed. Martin Gerbert. 3 vols. 1784. Berlin: C. Reinecke, 1905. 3: 329–81.

Ambroise. *L'Estoire de la guerre sainte; histoire en vers de la troisième croisade (1190–92), publiée et traduite d'après le manuscrit unique du Vatican*. Ed. and trans. Gaston Paris. Collection de documents inédits sur l'histoire de la France. Paris: Imprimerie Nationale, 1897.

Amadas et Ydoine, roman du XIIIe siècle. Ed. John R. Reinhard. CFMA 51. Paris: Champion, 1926.

Arnaut de Maruelh. *Les* Saluts d'amour *du troubadour Arnaud de Mareuil, textes publiés avec une introduction, une traduction, et des notes*. Ed. Pierre Bec. Bibliothèque Méridionale 31. Toulouse: Edouard Privat, 1961.

Arrigo da Settimello (Henricus Samariensis). *De Diversitate Fortunae et Philosophiae Consolatione*. In *Historia Poetarum et Poematum Medii Aevi Decem, Post Annum a Nato Christo CCCC, seculorum*. Halae Magdeb.· Novi Bibliopolii, 1721.

Aucassin et Nicolette, chantefable du XIIIe siècle. Ed. Mario Roques. CFMA 41. Paris: Champion, 1969.

Bartholomaeus Anglicus. *On the Properties of Things. John Trevisa's Translation of 'Bartholomaeus Anglicus. De Proprietatibus Rerum'. A Critical Text*. Eds. M. C. Seymour, et al. 2 vols. Oxford: Clarendon, 1975.

La Bataille Loquifer. Ed. Monica Barnett. Medium Aevum Monographs, ns 6. Oxford: Blackwell, 1975.

Bernart de Ventadorn. *Bernard de Ventadour, troubadour du XIIe siècle. Chansons d'Amour. Edition critique avec traduction, introduction, notes et glossaire*. Ed. Moshé Lazar. Bibliothèque Française et Romane, Série B, 4. Klincksieck: Paris, 1966.

Le Bestiaire d'amour rimé, poème inédit du XIIIe siècle. Ed. Arvid Thordstein. Etudes Romanes de Lund 2. Lund: Gleerup; Copenhagen: Munksgaard, 1941.

Boethius. *Anicii Manlii Severini Boethii Opera. Pars I. Philosophiae Consolatio.* Ed. Ludovicus Bieler. Corpus Christianorum, Series Latina 94. Turnhout: Brepols, 1957.

Carmina Burana, mit Benutzung der Vorarbeiten Wilhelm Meyers, kritisch herausgegeben von Alfons Hilka und Otto Schumanm. 2 vols. Heidelberg: Carl Winter, 1930–1961.

Cerveri de Girona (Guilhem de Cervera). *Les 'Proverbes' de Guylem de Cervera, poème catalan du XIIIe siècle.* Ed. Antoine Thomas. *Romania* 15 (1886): 25–108.

Le Châtelain de Couci. *Chansons attribuées au Chastelain de Couci (fin du XIIe-début du XIIIe siècle).* Ed. Alain Lerond. Publications de la Faculté des Lettres et Sciences Humaines de Rennes 7. Paris: Presses Universitaires de France, 1964.

Chaucer, Geoffrey. *Chaucer's Major Poetry.* Ed. Albert C. Baugh. New York: Appleton-Century-Crofts, 1963.

Chrétien de Troyes. *Les Romans de Chrétien de Troyes, édités d'après la copie de Guiot (Bibl. nat. fr. 794). I. Erec et Enide.* Ed. Mario Roques. CFMA 80. Paris: Champion, 1952.

——. *Les Romans de Chrétien de Troyes, édités d'après la copie de Guiot (Bibl. nat. fr. 794). II. Cligés.* Ed. Alexandre Micha. CFMA 84. Paris: Champion, 1970.

——. *Les Romans de Chrétien de Troyes, édités d'après la copie de Guiot (Bibl. nat. fr. 794). III. Le Chevalier de la charrete.* Ed. Mario Roques. CFMA 86. Paris: Champion, 1958.

——. *Yvain (Le Chevalier au lion). The Critical Text of Wendelin Foerster with Introduction, Notes and Glossary by T. B. W. Reid.* Manchester: Manchester University Press, 1942.

——. *Le Roman de Perceval ou le conte du Graal, publié d'après le MS fr. 12576 de la Bibliothèque Nationale.* Ed. William Roach. TLF 71. Geneva: Droz; Paris: Minard, 1959.

——. 'D'Amors, qui m'a tolu a moi' (R 1664). *Christian von Troyes. Sämtliche Erhaltene Werke, nach allen bekannten Handschriften. 5. Der Percevalroman (Li Contes del graal).* Ed. Alfons Hilka. Halle: Niemeyer, 1932. 801–03.

Christine de Pisan. *Lavision-Christine. Introduction and Text.* Ed. Sister Mary L. Towner. Washington, D.C.: Catholic University of America, 1932. New York: AMS Press, 1969.

The Continuations of the Old French Perceval of Chrétien de Troyes. II. The First Continuation. Redaction of MSS EMQU. Eds. William Roach and Robert H. Ivy. Philadelphia: University of Pennsylvania, 1950.

Durmart le Galois: roman arthurien du treizième siècle. I. *Texte.* II. *Etude.* Ed. Joseph Gildea. Villanova, Pa.: Villanova Press, 1965–66.

'La froidor ne la jalee' (anonymous song, R 517). Ed. Wilhelm Wackernagel. *Altfranzösische Lieder und Leiche, aus Handschriften zu Bern und Neuenburg, mit grammatischen und litterarhistorischen Abhandlungen.* Bern: Schweighauserische Buchhandlung, 1846. No. 33.

Froissart, Jean. *Méliador, par Jean Froissart, roman comprenant les poésies lyriques de Wenceslas de Bohème, Duc de Luxembourg et de Brabant.* Ed. Auguste Longnon. SATF. 3 Vols. Paris: Firmin Didot, 1895–1899. New York: Johnson Reprint Corp., 1965.

Gaucelm Faidit. *Les Poèmes de Gaucelm Faidit, troubadour du XIIe siècle. Edition critique.* Ed. Jean Mouzat. Les Classiques d'Oc 2. Paris: Nizet, 1965.

Gautier d'Aupais, poème courtois du XIIIe siècle. Ed. Edmond Faral. CFMA 20. Paris: Champion, 1919.

Gautier de Coinci. *Les Miracles de Nostre Dame par Gautier de Coinci.* Ed. V. Frédéric Koenig. TLF. 4 vols. Geneva: Droz, 1955–70.

Geoffrey of Monmouth. *Life of Merlin. Geoffrey of Monmouth. Vita Merlini. Edited with Introduction, facing translation, textual commentary, name notes, index and translations of the* Lailoken *tales.* Ed. and trans. Basil Clarke. Cardiff: University of Wales Press, 1973.

Gerbert de Montreuil. *La Continuation de Perceval.* Ed. Mary Williams. 2 Vols. CFMA 28, 50. Paris: Champion, 1922–25.

Giron le Courtois, Etude de la tradition manuscrite et analyse critique. Ed. Roger Lathuillère. Publications romanes et françaises 86. Geneva: Droz, 1966.

Gliglois, A French Arthurian Romance of the Thirteenth Century. Ed. Charles H. Livingston. Harvard Studies in Romance Languages 8. Cambridge: Harvard UP, 1932. New York: Kraus Reprint Corp., 1966.

Guilhem Augier Novella. 'Die Gedichte des Guillem Augier Novella'. Ed. Johannes Müller. *ZRP* 23 (1899): 47–78.

Guy de Chauliac. *La Grande Chirurgie de Guy de Chauliac, Chirurgien, Maistre en Médecine de l'Université de Montpellier, composée en l'an 1363.* Ed. E. Nicaise. Paris: F. Alcan, 1890.

Isidore of Seville. *Etymologiarum sive originum libri XX.* Ed. W. M. Lindsay. Oxford: Clarendon Press, 1911.

Henri de Ferrières. *Les Livres du roi Modus et de la royne Ratio.* Ed. Gunnar Tilander. 2 Vols. Paris: SATF, 1932.

Hildegard von Bingen. *Causae et curae.* Ed. Paul Kaiser. Leipzig: Teubner, 1903.

Huon le Roi. *Le Vair Palefroi, conte courtois du 13e siècle.* Trans. Jean Dufournet. TCFMA 22. Paris: Champion, 1977.

Jean Renart. *L'Escoufle, roman d'aventure. Nouvelle édition d'après le manuscrit 6565 de la Bibliothèque de l'arsenal.* Ed. Franklin Sweetser. TLF. Geneva: Droz, 1974.

———. *Le Lai de l'ombre.* Ed. Félix Lecoy. CFMA 104. Paris: Champion, 1979.

———. *Le Roman de la Rose ou de Guillaume de Dole.* Ed. Félix Lecoy. CFMA. Paris: Champion, 1962.

Marcabru. J.-M.-L. Dejeanne. *Poésies complètes du troubadour Marcabru, publiées avec traduction, notes et glossaire.* Bibliothèque Méridionale 1st ser. 12. Toulouse: Privat; Paris: Picard, 1909.

Marie de France. *The Fables of Marie de France: An English Translation.* Trans. Mary Lou Martin. Foreword by Norris J. Lacy. Birmingham, Ala.: Summa, 1984.

La Mort le roi Artu, roman du XIIIe siècle. Ed. Jean Frappier. TLF 58. Geneva: Droz; Paris: Minard, 1964.

Ovidius Naso, Publius. *Ovid. Metamorphoses, with an English Translation.* Ed. and trans. Frank Justus Miller. Loeb Classical Library. I. *Books I–VIII.* Cambridge: Harvard UP; London; Heinemann, 1916. II. *Books IX–XV.* New York: Putnam; London: Heinemann, 1916.

Peire Cardenal. *Poésies complètes du troubadour Peire Cardenal (1180–1278): Texte, traduction, commentaire, analyse des travaux antérieurs, lexique.* Ed. René Lavaud. Bibliothèque Méridionale, 2e série 34. Toulouse: Privat, 1957.

Philippe de Remi. *Oeuvres poétiques de Philippe de Remi, Sire de Beaumanoir.* Ed., Hermann Suchier. SATF. 2 vols. Paris: Firmin Didot, 1884–85.

Philippe Mousket. *Chronique rimée de Philippe Mouskés.* Ed. F.-A.-F.-T. de Reiffenberg. 2 vols. Brussels: Hayez, 1836–1838.

Raoul de Houdenc. *Sämmtliche Werke.* II. *La Vengeance de Raguidel, altfranzösischer Abenteuerroman.* Ed. M. Friedwagner. Halle, 1909. Geneva: Slatkine, 1975.

Recueil d'arts de seconde rhétorique. Ed. Ernest Langlois. Paris: Imprimerie Nationale, 1902.

Renaut de Beaujeu. *Le Bel Inconnu ou Giglain fils de Messire Gauvain et de la Fée aux Blanches Mains, poème de la Table Ronde par Renauld de Beaujeu, publié d'après le manuscrit unique de Londrès.* Ed. C. Hippeau. Collection des Poètes Français du Moyen Age 3. Paris, 1860. Geneva: Slatkine, 1969.

Robert de Boron. *The Didot-Perceval. According to the Manuscripts of Modena and Paris.* Ed. William Roach. Philadelphia: University of Pennsylvania Press, 1941.

Le Roman de la Poire. Ed. Christiane Marchello-Nizia. SATF. Paris: Picard, 1984.

Le Roman de Renart, édité d'après le manuscrit de Cagné. Ed. Mario Roques. 5 vols. CFMA 78, 79, 81, 85, 88. Paris: Champion, 1948–1960.

Sir Orfeo. Ed. A. J. Bliss. Oxford English Monographs. Oxford: Oxford University Press, 1954.

Thomas Malory. *The Works of Sir Thomas Malory*. Ed. Eugène Vinaver. 3 vols. Oxford: Clarendon, 1947.

Tristan de Nanteuil, chanson de geste inédite. Ed. K. V. Sinclair. Assen: Van Gorcum, 1971.

The Tristan Legend: Texts from Northern and Eastern Europe in Modern English Translation. Ed. Joyce Hill. Leeds Medieval Studies 2. Leeds: Graduate Center for Medieval Studies, 1977.

De Venus la déesse d'Amor. Ed. Wendelin Foerster. Bonn: Max Cohen, 1880.

Virgil. *The Ecologues. The Latin Text with a Verse Translation and Brief Notes*. Trans. Guy Lee. Harmondsworth, Middlesex: Penguin, 1984.

The *Vulgate Merlin. The Vulgate Version of the Arthurian Romances edited from manuscripts in the British Museum*. II. *Lestoire de Merlin*. Ed. H. Oskar Sommer. Washington: The Carnegie Institute of Washington, 1908.

Wace. *Le Roman de Brut de Wace*. Ed. Ivor Arnold. 2 vols. Paris: SATF, 1938–1940.

Walter Map. *De Nugis Curialium. Courtiers' Trifles*. Ed. and trans. M. R. James. Rev. by C. N. L. Brooke and R. A. B. Mynors. Oxford: Clarendon, 1983.

'The Welsh Triads'. Ed. Rachel Bromwich. *Arthurian Literature in the Middle Ages. A Collaborative History*. Ed. Roger Sherman Loomis. Oxford: Clarendon, 1959. 44–51.

'Ystori Trystan'. 'A Welsh Tristan Episode'. Ed. Tom Peete Cross. *Studies in Philology* 17 (1920): 93–110.

II

TRISTAN STUDIES

A. Bibliographies

Shirt, David J. *The Old French Tristan Poems: A Bibliographical Guide*. Research Bibliographies and Checklists 28. London: Grant & Cutler, 1980.

Adams, Robert Dana Walden. *A Tristan Bibliography*. University of Southern California Language and Literature Series 4. Los Angeles: University of Southern California Press, 1943.

Küpper, Heinz. *Bibliographie zur Tristansage*. Deutsche Arbeiten der Universität Köln 17. Jena: Diederich, 1941.

B. Critical Studies

Adams, Alison. 'The Metaphor of *folie* in Thomas' *Tristan*'. *Forum for Modern Language Studies*. 17 (1981): 88–90.

Adams, Alison and Timothy D. Hemming. ' "Chèvrefeuille' and the Evolution of the Tristan Legend'. *BBIAS* 28 (1976): 204–13.

———. 'La Fin du *Tristan* de Béroul'. *Moyen Age* 79 (1973): 449–68.

Adler, Alfred. 'A Structural Comparison of the Two *Folies Tristan*'. *Symposium* 6 (1952): 349–58.

Adolf, Helen. 'Tristan aux enfers'. *BBIAS* 6 (1954): 100–01.

Aitken, D. F. 'The "Voyage à l'aventure" in the "Tristan" of Thomas'. *Modern Language Review* 23 (1928): 468–72.

Andrieu, Gabriel with Jacques Piolle and May Plouzeau. '*Le Roman de Tristan' de Béroul. Concordancier complet de formes graphiques occurrentes.* Aix-en-Provence: Université de Provence, Centre de Recherches et d'Etudes Linguistique, 1974.

Anson, John S. 'The Hunt of Love: Gottfried von Strassburg's *Tristan* as Tragedy'. *Speculum* 45 (1970): 594–607.

Atanassov, Stojan. 'Les modèles narratifs dans le *Tristan* de Thomas'. *Actes du 14e Congrès International Arthurian. Rennes, 16–21 Août 1984.* 2 vols. Rennes: Presses Universitaires de Rennes 2, 1985. 1: 1–15.

Barteau, Françoise. *Les Romans de Tristan et Iseut: Introduction à une lecture plurielle.* Collection 'L'. Paris: Larousse, 1972.

Batts, Michael S. *Gottfried von Strassburg.* New York: Twayne, 1971.

Baumgartner, Emmanuèle. *Tristan et Iseut: De la légende aux récits en vers.* Etudes Littéraires 15. Paris: Presses Universitaires de France, 1987.

———. *Le 'Tristan en prose'. Essai d'interprétation d'un roman médiéval.* Publications Romanes et Françaises 133. Geneva: Droz, 1975.

———. 'Sur les pièces lyriques du *Tristan* en prose'. *Etudes de langue et de littérature du moyen âge offertes à Félix Lecoy par ses collègues, ses élèves et ses amis.* Paris: Champion, 1973. 19–25.

Baumgartner, Emmanuèle and Robert-Léon Wagner. ' "As enveisiez e as purvers": Commentaire sur les vers 3125–3129 du *Roman de Tristan* de Thomas'. *Romania* 88 (1967): 527–37.

Bertin, Gerald A. 'The Oedipus Complex in *Tristan et Iseut*'. *Kentucky Foreign Language Quarterly* 5 (1958): 60–65.

Bertolucci-Pizzorusso, Valeria. 'La cour et les images de la cour dans le *Tristan* de Béroul'. *Actes du 14e Congrès International Arthurian. Rennes, 16–21 Août 1984.* 2 vols. Rennes: Presses Universitaires de Rennes 2, 1985. 1: 70–88.

———. 'La Retorica nel *Tristano* di Thomas'. *Studi Mediolatini e Volgari* 6–7 (1959): 25–61.

Blakeslee, Merritt R. 'Les Allusions aux romans de Tristan dans l'oeuvre de Jean Renart: Etude des sources'. *Tristan et Iseut, mythe européen et mondial. Actes du Colloque des 10, 11 et 12 janvier 1986.* Göppingen: Kümmerle Verlag, 1987.

———. '*Mouvance* and Revisionism in the Transmission of Thomas of Britain's *Tristan*: The Episode of the Intertwining Trees'. *Arthurian Literature* 6 (1986): 124–56.

———. '*Mal d'Acre, Malpertuis,* and the Date of Beroul's *Tristran*'. *Romania* 106 (1985): 145–72.

———. 'The Authorship of Thomas's *Tristan*'. *Philological Quarterly* 64 (1985): 539–556.

———. 'Tristan the Trickster in the Old French Tristan Poems'. *Cultura Neolatina* 44 (1984): 167–90.

———. 'The Pattern(s) of the Heroic Biography: Structure and Sense in the *Tristan* of Thomas of Britain'. *Michigan Academician* 9 (1978–79): 375–90.

Blanchot, Maurice. 'Orphée, Don Juan, Tristan'. *La Nouvelle Nouvelle Revue Français* No. 15 (March 1954): 492–501.

Bogdanow, Fanni. 'Theme and Character: the two faces of King Mark'. *Actes du 14e Congrès International Arthurian. Rennes, 16–21 Août 1984.* 2 vols. Rennes: Presses Universitaires de Rennes 2, 1985. 1: 89–109.

Bouchard, Constance B. 'The Possible Nonexistence of Thomas, Author of *Tristan and Isolde*'. *Modern Philology* 79 (1981–1982): 66–72.

Branca, Daniela Delcorno. *I romanzi italiani di Tristano e la 'Tavola Ritonda'.* Pubblicazioni della Facoltà di Lettere e Filosofia della Università di Padova 45. Florence: Leo S. Olschki, 1968.

Brault, Gerard J. 'Le Rituel de la chasse dans le *Tristan* de Thomas'. *Actes du 14e Congrès International Arthurian. Rennes, 16–21 Août 1984.* 2 vols. Rennes: Presses Universitaires de Rennes 2, 1985. 1: 112–19.

———. 'Isolt and Guenevere: Two Twelfth-Century Views of Women'. *The Role of Woman in the Middle Ages.* Ed. Rosemarie Thee Morewedge. Albany: State University of New York Press, 1975. 41–64.

Bromwich, Rachel. 'Some Remarks on the Celtic Sources of *Tristan*'. *Transactions of the Honourable Society of Cymmrodorion* (1953). 32–60.

Bruckner, Matilda Tomaryn. 'The Representation of the Lovers' Death: Thomas' *Tristan* as Open Text'. *Tristania* 9 (1983–84): 49–61.

Brusegan, Rosanna. '*La folie de Tristan*: de la loge du Morrois au palais de verre'. *La Légende de Tristan au Moyen Age. Actes du Colloque des 16 et 17 janvier 1982.* Ed. Danielle Buschinger. Göppinger Arbeiten zur Germanistik 355. Göppingen: Kümmerle, 1982. 49–59.

Burgess, Glyn S. and Merritt R. Blakeslee. '*D'Acre, Dagres, Degies*: Une note sur le v. 3849 du *Tristran* de Béroul'. In collaboration with Glyn S. Burgess. Forthcoming in *Romania*.

Buschinger, Danielle. 'La Composition numérique du *Tristrant* d'Eilhart von Oberg'. *CCM* 16 (1973): 287–94.

———. 'La Structure du *Tristrant* d'Eilhart von Oberg'. *Etudes Germaniques* 27 (1972): 1–26.

Cahné, C. *Le Philtre et le venin dans 'Tristan et Iseut'*. Paris: Nizet, 1975.

Caulkins, Janet Hillier. 'Le Jeu du surnaturel et du féodal dans le *Tristan* de Béroul'. *Mélanges d'histoire littéraire, de linguistique et de philologie romane offerts à Charles Rostaing*. Liège: Association des Romanistes de l'Univ. de Liège, 1974. 1: 131–140.

———. 'The Meaning of *pechié* in the *Romance of Tristran* by Béroul'. *Romance Notes* 13 (1971–72): 545–49.

———. 'Béroul's Concept of Love as Revealed in *Tristan et Iseut*'. *BBIAS* 21 (1969): 150.

Cazenave, Michel. *Le Philtre et l'amour, la légende de Tristan et Iseut*. Paris: J. Corti, 1969.

Cluzel, Irénée-M. 'Les plus anciens troubadours et la légende amoureuse de Tristan et Iseut'. *Mélanges de linguistique et de littérature romanes à la mémoire d'Istvàn Frank*. Annales Universitatis Saraviensis 6. Saarbrucken: Universität des Saarlandes, 1957. 155–70.

———. 'La reine Iseut et le harpeur d'Irlande'. *BBIAS* 10 (1958): 87–98.

Combarieu, M. de. 'Le Jour et la nuit dans *Le Roman de Tristan* de Béroul (Poème du XIIe siècle)'. *Tristania* 2.1 (November 1976): 12–31.

Cormier, Raymond J. 'Open Contrast: Tristan and Diarmaid'. *Speculum* 51 (1976): 589–601.

Curtis, Renée L. 'The Humble and the Cruel Tristan: A New Look at the Two Poems of the *Folie Tristan*'. *Tristania* 2.1 (November 1976): 3–11.

———. 'Le Philtre mal préparé: le thème de la réciprocité dans l'amour de Tristan et Iseut'. *Mélanges de langue et de littérature du Moyen Age et de la Renaissance offerts à Jean Frappier*. 2 Vols. Geneva: Droz, 1970. 1: 195–206.

———. 'Bédier's Version of the *Prose Tristan*'. *Tristan Studies*. Munich: Fink, 1969. 58–65.

———. 'The Manuscript Tradition of the *Prose Tristan* (Part I)'. *Tristan Studies*. Munich: Fink, 1969. 66–91.

Dannenbaum, Susan. 'Doubling and *Fine Amor* in Thomas' *Tristan*'. *Tristania* 5.1 (autumn 1979): 3–14.

De Caluwé, Jacques. 'Dieu et l'amour dans les *Folies Tristan*'. *Marche Romane* 30.3–4 (1980): 55–61.

Delbouille, Maurice. 'Le Fragment of Cambridge et la genèse des *Folies Tristan*'. *TLL* 16.1 (1978): 117–29.

———. 'Le Premier *Roman de Tristan*'. *CCM* 5 (1962): 273–86, 419–35.

Delpino, Marcella. 'Elementi celtici ed elementi classici nel 'Tristan' di Thomas'. *Archivum Romanicum* 23 (1939): 312–36.

Denomy, Alexander J. 'Tristan and the Morholt: David and Goliath'. *Medieval Studies* 18 (1956): 224–32.

Ditmas, E. M. R. 'Béroul the Minstrel'. *Reading Medieval Studies* 8 (1982): 34–74.

Dufournet, Jean. 'Présence et fonction de la lèpre dans le *Tristan* de Béroul'. *Mélanges de Linguistique, de littérature et de philologie médiévales, offerts à J. R. Smeets*. Leiden, 1982. 87–103.

Eckard, Gilles. 'A propos d'un passage de la *Folie Tristan* de Berne'. *TLL* 16.1 (1978): 161–68.

Eisner, Sigmund. *The Tristan Legend: A Study in Sources*. Evanston: Northwestern University Press, 1969.

Ewert, Alfred. 'On the Text of Béroul's *Tristran*'. *Studies in French Language and Mediaeval Literature Presented to Professor Mildred K. Pope*. Manchester: University Press, 1939. 89–98.

Fedrick, Alan. 'The Account of Tristan's Birth and Childhood in the French Prose *Tristan*'. *Romania* 89 (1968): 340–54.

——. 'A Note on the *Folie Tristan de Berne*'. *Medium Aevum* 32 (1963): 125–29.

Ferrante, Joan M. 'Artist Figures in the Tristan Stories'. *Tristania* 4.2 (May 1979): 25–35.

——. *The Conflict of Love and Honor. The Medieval Tristan Legend in France, Germany and Italy*. The Hague-Paris: Mouton, 1973.

Foulet, Alfred. 'Jehan Tristan, Son of Saint Louis, in History and Legend'. *Romance Philology* 12 (1958–59): 235–40.

Foulet, Lucien. 'Marie de France et la légende de Tristan'. *ZRP* 32 (1908): 161–183, 257–89.

——. 'Thomas and Marie in their relation to the *conteurs*'. *Modern Language Notes* 22 (1908): 205–08.

François, Carlo. '*Tristan et Iseut*: Poème d'amour et manuel de la ruse'. *Mercure de France* 338 (Jan.–April, 1960): 611–25.

Frappier, Jean. 'La Reine Iseut dans le *Tristan* de Béroul'. *Romance Philology* 26 (1972–73): 215–28.

——. 'Sur le mot *Raison* dans le *Tristan* de Thomas d'Angleterre'. *Linguistic and Literary Studies in Honor of Helmut A. Hatzfeld*. Washington: Catholic University of America Press, 1964. 163–76.

——. 'Structure et sens du *Tristan*: version commune, version courtoise'. *CCM* 6 (1963): 255–80, 441–54.

Friedman, Arlene H. 'A Case for Béroul's *Tristan* as an *Embourgeoisement* of the Tristan Legend'. *Cultura Neolatina* 36 (1976): 9–32.

Gallais, Pierre. 'Les Arbres entrelacés dans les romans de Tristan et le mythe de l'arbre androgyne primordial'. *Mélanges de langue et de littérature médiévales offerts à Pierre Le Gentil, Professeur à la Sorbonne, par ses collègues, ses élèves et ses amis*. Paris: SEDES, 1973. 295–310.

Gay, Lucy M. 'Heraldry and the *Tristan* of Thomas'. *Modern Language Review* 23 (1928): 472–75.

Grenier-Braunschweig, Laurette. 'L'énigme de la *Folie Tristan* d'Oxford'. *Actes du 14e Congrès International Arthurian. Rennes, 16–21 Août 1984*. 2 vols. Rennes: Presses Universitaires de Rennes 2, 1985. 1: 241–56.

Grigsby, John L. 'L'Empire des signes chez Béroul et Thomas: "Le sigle est tut neir"'. *Marche Romane* 30.3–4 (1980): 115–25.

Grisward, Joël H. 'A propos du thème descriptif de la tempête chez Wace et chez Thomas d'Angleterre'. *Mélanges de langue et de littérature du Moyen Age et de la Renaissance offerts à Jean Frappier*. 2 vols. Geneva: Droz, 1970, 375–89.

Gunnlaugsdóttir, Alfrún. *Tristán en el Norte*. Reykjavík: Arna Magnússonar, 1978.

Haidu, Peter. 'Text, Pretextuality and Myth in the *Folie Tristan d'Oxford*'. *MLN* 88 (1973): 712–17.

Halverson, John. 'Tristan and Iseult: The Two Traditions'. *ZFSL* 93 (1983): 217–96.

Heimerle, Magda. *Gottfried und Thomas. Ein Vergleich*. Frankfurt: Diesterweg, 1942.

Heller, Bernard. 'L'Epée symbole et gardienne de chasteté'. *Romania* 36 (1907): 36–49.

——. 'L'Epée symbole et gardienne de chasteté (supplément)'. *Romania* 37 (1908): 162–63.

Henry, Albert. 'Sur les vers 320–338 du *Tristan* de Béroul'. *TLL* 16.1 (1978): 209–15.

Hilka, Alfons. 'Der Tristanroman des Thomas und die *Disciplina clericalis*'. *ZFSL* 45 (1919): 38–46.

Hoepffner, Ernest. 'Die *Folie Tristan* und die *Odyssee*'. *ZRP* 40 (1920): 232–35.

——. 'Thomas d'Angleterre et Marie de France'. *Studi Medievali* ns 7 (1934): 8–23.

Holden, Anthony. 'Note sur la langue de Béroul'. *Romania* 89 (1968): 387–99.

Horrent, Jules. 'La Composition de la *Folie Tristan* de Berne'. *Revue Belge de Philologie et d'Histoire* 25 (1946–47): 21–38.

Hunt, Tony. 'The Significance of Thomas's *Tristan*'. *Reading Medieval Studies* 7 (1981): 41–61.

——. 'Aristotle, Dialectic, and Courtly Literature'. *Viator. Medieval and Renaissance Studies* 10 (1979): 95–129.

——. 'Abelardian Ethics and Béroul's *Tristran*'. *Romania* 98 (1977): 501–40.

Jackson, W. T. H. 'Artist and Performance in Gottfried's *Tristan*'. *Tristania* 1.1 (November 1975): 3–13.

Jonin, Pierre. 'L'Esprit celtique dans le roman de Béroul'. *Mélanges de langue et de littérature médiévales offerts à Pierre Le Gentil, Professeur à la Sorbonne, par ses collègues, ses élèves et ses amis*. Paris: SEDES, 1973. 409–20.

———. *Les Personnages féminins dans les romans français de Tristan au XIIe siècle. Etude des influences contemporaines*. Publ. des Annales de la Fac. des Lettres d'Aix-en Provence, ns 22. Gap: Ophrys, 1958.

Kelly, Douglas. *'En uni dire (Tristan*, Douce 839) and the Composition of Thomas's *Tristan'*. *Modern Philology* 67 (1969–70): 9–17.

Kunstmann, Pierre. 'Texte, intertexte et autotexte dans le *Tristan* de Thomas d'Angleterre'. *The Nature of Medieval Narrative*. Eds. Minnette Grunmann-Gaudet and Robin F. Jones. French Forum Monographs 22. Lexington: French Forum, 1980.

Larmat, Jean. 'La Souffrance dans le *Tristan* de Thomas'. *Mélanges de langue et de littérature françaises du moyen-âge offerts à Pierre Jonin*. Senefiance 7. Aix-en-Provence: CUER MA; Paris: Champion, 1979. 369–85.

Leach, Henry Goddard. 'Tristan in the North'. *Angevin Britain and Scandinavia*. Harvard Studies in Comparative Literature 6. Cambridge, Mass.: Harvard UP, 1921. Millwood, NY: Kraus, 1975. 169–98.

Lecoy, Félix. 'L'Episode du harpeur d'Irlande et la date des *Tristan* de Béroul et de Thomas'. *Romania* 86 (1965): 538–45.

Le Gentil, Pierre. 'Sur l'épilogue du *Tristan* de Thomas'. *Mélanges de littérature du Moyen Age et du XXe siècle offerts à Mademoiselle Jeanne Lods*. Collection de l'Ecole Normale Supérieure de Jeunes Filles 10. Paris, 1978. 1: 365–70.

———. 'A propos du mariage de Tristan et de la colère de Brangain dans le roman de Thomas'. *Mélanges de philologie romane offerts à Charles Camproux*. Montpellier: Centre d'Estudis Occitans, 1978. 1: 401–05.

———. 'L'Episode du Morois et la signification du *Tristan* de Béroul'. *Studia Philologica et Litteraria in Honorem L. Spitzer*. Bern: Francke, 1958. 267–74.

———. 'La Légende de Tristan vue par Béroul et Thomas: Essai d'interprétation'. *Romance Philology* 7 (1953–54): 111–29.

Legge, M. Dominica. 'Le Problème des *Folies* aujourd'hui'. *Mélanges de littérature du Moyen Age et du XXe siècle offerts à Mademoiselle Jeanne Lods*. Collection de l'Ecole Normale Supérieure de Jeunes Filles 10. Paris, 1978. 1: 371–77.

———. 'Place-Names and the Date of Beroul'. *Medium Aevum* 38 (1969): 171–74.

———. 'The Unerring Bow'. *Medium Aevum* 25 (1956): 79–83.

Lejeune-Dehousse, Rita. 'La Coupe de la légende de Tristan dans *L' Escoufle* de Jean Renart'. *The Medieval Alexander Legend and Romance Epic. Essays in Honour of David J. A. Ross*. Eds. Peter Noble, Lucie Polak et Claire Isoz.

Millwood, New York-London: Kraus International Publications, 1982. 119–24.

———. 'Les Noms de Tristan et Iseut dans l'anthroponymie médiévale'. *Mélanges de langue et de littérature du Moyen Age et de le Renaissance offerts à Jean Frappier.* 2 Vols. Geneva: Droz, 1970. 2: 625–30.

———. 'Les 'influences contemporaines' dans les romans français de Tristan au XIIe siècle. A Propos d'un livre récent'. *Moyen Age* 66 (1960): 143–62.

———. 'Rôle littéraire d'Aliénor d'Aquitaine et de sa famille'. *Cultura Neolatina* 14 (1954): 1–57.

Loomis, Roger Sherman. 'Problems of the Tristan Legend. Bleheris; the Diarmaid Parallel; Thomas's Date'. *Romania* 53 (1927): 82–102.

Lot-Borodine, Myrrha. 'Tristan et Lancelot'. *Medieval Studies in Memory of Gertrude Schoepperle Loomis.* Paris: Champion; New York: Columbia University Press, 1927. 21–47.

Loth, Joseph. 'Contributions à l'étude des romans de la Table Ronde. VI. Le Cornwall et le roman de Tristan'. *Revue Celtique* 33 (1912): 258–310.

Lyle, E. B. 'Orpheus and Tristan'. *Medium Aevum* 50 (1981): 305–08.

Lyons, Faith. '"Vin herbé" et "Gingembras" dans le roman breton'. *Mélanges de langue et de littérature du Moyen Age et de la Renaissance offerts à Jean Frappier.* 2 Vols. Geneva: Droz, 1970. 2: 689–96.

Lutoslawski, W. 'Les Folies de Tristan'. *Romania* 15 (1886): 511–33.

Marx, Jean. 'La Naissance de l'amour de Tristan et Iseut dans les formes les plus anciennes de la legende'. *Romance Philology* 9 (1955–1956): 167–73.

———. 'Observations sur un épisode de la légende de Tristan'. *Recueil de travaux offert à M. Clovis Brunel, Membre de l'Institut, Directeur Honoraire de l'Ecole des Chartes, par ses amis, collègues et élèves.* 2 vols. Mémoires et Documents Publiés par la Société de l'Ecole des Chartes 12. Paris: Société de l'Ecole des Chartes, 1955. 2: 265–73.

Micha, Alexandre. 'Tristan et Cligès'. *Neophilologus* 36 (1952): 1–10.

Muret, Ernest. 'Eilhart d'Oberg et sa source française'. *Romania* 16 (1887): 288–363.

Newstead, Helaine. 'The Harp and the Rote: An Episode in the Tristan Legend and its Literary History'. *Romance Philology* 22 (1968–69): 463–70.

———. 'The Enfances of Tristan and English Tradition'. *Studies in Medieval Literature in Honor of Professor Albert Croll Baugh.* Philadelphia: University of Pennsylvania Press, 1961. 169–85.

———. 'The Origin and Growth of the Tristan Legend'. *Arthurian Literature in the Middle Ages. A Collaborative History.* Ed. Roger S. Loomis. Oxford: Clarendon, 1959. 122–33.

——. 'The Tryst Beneath the Tree: An Episode in the Tristan Legend'. *Romance Philology* 9 (1955–1956): 269–84.

——. 'Kaherdin and the Enchanted Pillow: An Episode in The Tristan Legend'. *PMLA* 65 (1950): 290–312.

Noble, Peter S. *Beroul's 'Tristan' and the 'Folie de Berne'*. Critical Guides to French Texts 15. London: Grant & Cutler, Ltd., 1982.

——. 'Beroul's 'Somewhat Softened Feminine View'?' *Modern Language Review* 75 (1980): 746–52.

Novati, Francesco. 'Un nuovo ed un vecchio frammento del *Tristran* di Tommaso'. *Studj di Filologia Romanza*. 2 (1887): 369–515.

Olsen, Thorkil Damsgaard and Hanne Ruus. 'Emotional Patterns in the *Tristram's Saga*'. *Actes du 14e Congrès International Arthurian. Rennes, 16–21 Août 1984*. 2 vols. Rennes: Presses Universitaires de Rennes 2, 1985. 2: 456–64.

Padel, Oliver J. 'Béroul's Geography and Patronage'. *Reading Medieval Studies* 9 (1983): 84–94.

——. 'The Cornish Background of the Tristan Stories'. *Cambridge Medieval Celtic Studies* 1 (1981): 53–81.

Payen, Jean-Charles. 'Tristan, l'*amans-amens* et le masque dans les *Folies*'. *La Légende de Tristan au Moyen Age. Actes du Colloque des 16 et 17 janvier 1982*. Ed. Danielle Buschinger. Göppinger Arbeiten zur Germanistik 355. Göppingen: Kümmerle, 1982. 61–68.

——. 'Le palais de verre dans la "Folie d'Oxford". De la folie métaphorique à la folie vécue ou le rêve de l'île déserte de l'exil: notes sur l'érotique des "Tristan"'. *Tristania* 5.2 (spring 1980): 17–27.

——. 'Le peuple dans les romans français de *Tristan*: La "povre gent" chez Béroul, sa fonction narrative et son statut idéologique'. *CCM* 23 (1980): 187–198.

——. 'Ordre moral et subversion politique dans le *Tristan* de Béroul'. *Mélanges de littérature du Moyen Age et du XXe siècle offerts à Mademoiselle Jeanne Lods*. Collection de l'Ecole Normale Supérieure de Jeunes Filles 10. Paris, 1978. 1: 473–484.

——. 'Lancelot contre Tristan, la conjuration d'un mythe subversif (Réflexions sur l'idéologie romanesque au Moyen Age)'. *Mélanges de langue et de littérature médiévales offerts à Pierre Le Gentil, Professeur à la Sorbonne, par ses collègues, ses élèves et ses amis*. Paris: SEDES, 1973. 617–32.

Pensom, Roger. 'Rhetoric and Psychology in Thomas's *Tristan*'. *Modern Language Review* 78 (1983): 285–97.

Picozzi, Rosemary. *A History of Tristan Scholarship*. Kanadische Studien zur deutschen Sprache und Literatur 5. Bern and Frankfurt: Herbert Lang, 1971.

Poirion, Daniel. 'Le *Tristan* de Béroul: récit, légende et mythe'. *L'Information Littéraire* 26.5 (November-December 1974): 199–207.

Polak, Lucie. '*Tristan* and *Vis and Ramin*'. *Romania* 95 (1974): 216–34.

———. 'The Two Caves of Love in the *Tristan* by Thomas'. *Journal of the Warburg and Courtauld Institutes* 33 (1970): 52–69.

Raynaud de Lage, Guy. 'Les Romans de Tristan au XIIe siècle'. *Grundriss der romanischen Literaturen des Mittelalters. IV. Le Roman jusqu'à la fin du XIIIe siècle (Partie historique)*. Heidelburg: Carl Winter, 1978. 212–30.

———. 'Faut-il attribuer à Béroul tout le "Tristan"? (suite et fin)' *Moyen Age* 70 (1964): 33–38.

———. 'Trois notes sur le *Tristan* de Béroul'. *Romania* 83 (1962): 522–26.

———. 'Faut-il attribuer à Béroul tout le "Tristan"?' *Moyen Age* 64 (1958): 249–70.

Regalado, Nancy F. 'Renart and Tristan: Two Tricksters'. *L'Esprit Créateur* 16 (1976): 30–38.

Reid, Thomas Bertram Wallace. *The 'Tristran' of Beroul: A Textual Commentary*. Oxford: Blackwell; New York: Barnes and Noble, 1972.

———. 'The *Tristran* of Beroul: One Author or Two?' *Modern Language Review* 60 (1965): 352–58.

———. 'On the Text of the *Tristran* of Béroul'. *Medieval Miscellany Presented to Eugène Vinaver by Pupils, Colleagues and Friends*. Eds. F. Whitehead, et al. Manchester: University Press; New York: Barnes & Noble, 1965. 263–88.

Remigereau, François. '*Tristan, maître de vénerie* dans la tradition anglaise et dans le roman de Thomas'. *Romania* 58 (1932): 218–37.

Ribard, Jacques. 'Le *Tristan* de Béroul, un monde de l'illusion?' *BBIAS* 31 (1979): 229–44.

Robertson, James Duncan. 'On the Text of the Berne *Folie Tristan*'. *Romania* 98 (1977): 95–104.

———. 'Literary Tradition and Poetic Realization in the *Folies Tristan*'. Diss. Princeton University, 1972.

Roncaglia, Aurelio. 'Commento a cinque versi del 'Tristano' di Tommaso'. *R. Accademia di Scienze, Lettere, ed Arti in Modena. Atti e Memorie* 5th ser. 11 (1953): 3–16.

Röttiger, Wilhelm. *Der heutige Stand der Tristanforschung*. Programm des Wilhelm-Gymnasiums zu Hamburg: Bericht über das Schuljahr 1896–7. Hamburg: Lütcke and Wulff, 1897.

———. *Der Tristan des Thomas, ein Beitrag zur Kritik und Sprache desselben*. Diss. Göttingen: Kaestner, 1983.

Rougemont, Denis de. *L'Amour et l'Occident*. 1939. 10/18. Paris: Plon, 1972.

Rozgonyi, Eva. 'Pour une approche d'un Tristan non-courtois'. *Mélanges offerts à René Crozet à l'occasion de son soixante-dixième anniversaire*. Eds. Pierre Gallais and Yves-Jean Riou. Poitiers: Société d'Etudes Médiévales, 1966. 2: 821–28.

Saly, A. 'Tristan chasseur'. *La Chasse au moyen âge. Actes du Colloque de Nice (22–24 juin 1979)*. Publications de la Faculté des Lettres et des Sciences Humaines de Nice 20. Paris: Belles Lettres, 1980. 435–42.

Sandqvist, Sven. *Notes textuelles sur le* Roman de Tristan *de Béroul*. Etudes Romanes de Lund 39. Malmö: LiberFörlag, 1984.

Sargent-Baur, Barbara Nelson. 'Between Fabliau and Romance: Love and Rivalry in Béroul's *Tristran*'. *Romania* 105 (1984): 292–311.

Schach, Paul. 'Some Observations on the Influence of *Tristrams saga ok Isöndar* on Old Icelandic Literature'. *Old Norse Literature and Mythology: A Symposium*. Ed. Edgar C. Polomé. Austin: University of Texas Press, 1969. 81–129.

———. 'The Reeves Fragment of *Tristrams Saga ok Ísöndar*'. *Einarsbók. Afmæliskveðja til Einars Ól. Sveinssonar*. Eds. Bjarmi Guðnason, Halldór Halldórsson and Jonas Kristjánsson. Reykjavík: n.p., 1969. 296–308.

———. 'The Style and Structure of *Tristrams Saga*'. *Scandinavian Studies. Essays Presented to Dr. Henry Goddard Leach on the Occasion of his Eighty-Fifth Birthday*. Eds. Carl F. Bayerschmidt and Erik J. Friis. Seattle: University of Washington Press, 1965. 63–86.

———. 'Tristan and Isolde in Scandinavian Ballad and Folktale'. *Scandinavian Studies* 36 (1964): 281–97.

———. 'An Unpublished Leaf of *Tristrams Saga*: AM 567 Quarto, XXII, 2'. *Research Studies (Washington State University)* 32 (1964): 50–62.

———. 'Some Observations on *Tristrams Saga*'. *Saga-Book of the Viking Society* 15 (1957–59): 102–29.

Schaefer, Jacqueline T. 'Tristan's Folly: Feigned or Real?' *Tristania* 3.1 (November 1977): 3–16.

Schoepperle, Gertrude. *Tristan and Isolt. A Study of the Sources of the Romance. Second Edition, expanded by a bibliography and critical essay on Tristan scholarship since 1912 by Roger Sherman Loomis*. New York: Burt Franklin, 1970.

———. 'Sur un vers de la *Folie Tristan* de Berne'. *Romania* 40 (1911): 86–88.

Schwartz, Jacques. 'Le Roman de Tristan et la légende de Pélée'. *Mélanges de langue et de littérature du Moyen Age et de la Renaissance offerts à Jean Frappier*. 2 Vols. Geneva: Droz, 1970. 2: 1001–03.

Shoaf, Judith P. 'Thomas's *Tristan* and the *Tristrams Saga*: Versions and Themes'. Diss. Cornell University, 1978.

Snow, Ann. 'Wilt, *wilde, wildenære*: a study in the interpretation of Gottfried's *Tristan*'. *Euphorion* 62 (1968): 365–77.

Telfer, Jean M. 'The Evolution of a Mediaeval Theme'. *The Durham University Journal* 45 (1952–53): 25–34.

———. '*Picous (Folie Tristan de Berne*, line 156)'. *French Studies* 5 (1951): 56–61.

Thomas, M. F. 'The Briar and the Vine: Tristan Goes North'. *Arthurian Literature* 3 (1983): 53–90.

Tómasson, Sverrir. 'Hvenær var Tristrams Sögu Snúið?' *Gripla* 2 (1977): 47–78 (with English summary).

Tregenza, W. A. 'The Relation of the Oldest Branch of the *Roman de Renart* to the Tristan poems'. *Modern Language Review* 19 (1924): 301–05.

Trindade, W. Ann. 'Hommage à Gaston Paris. A Reappraisal of Gaston Paris' Celebrated Essay on the Tristan Legend'. *Actes du 14e Congrès International Arthurien. Rennes, 16–21 Août 1984.* 2 vols. Rennes: Presses Universitaires de Rennes 2, 1985. 2: 635–45.

——. 'Time, Space, and Narrative Focus in the Fragments of Thomas's *Tristan'. Romance Philology* 32 (1978–1979): 387–96.

——. 'The Enemies of Tristan'. *Medium Aevum* 43 (1974): 6–21.

Van Hamel, Anton G. 'Tristan's Combat with the Dragon'. *Revue Celtique* 41 (1924): 331–49.

Vàrvaro, Alberto. 'L'utilizzazione letteraria di motivi della narrativa popolare nei romanzi di Tristano'. *Mélanges de langue et de littérature du Moyen Age et de la Renaissance offerts à Jean Frappier.* Publications Romanes et Françaises 112. 2 vols. Geneva: Droz, 1970. 2: 1057–75.

——. 'La Teoria dell'archetipo tristaniano'. *Romania* 88 (1967): 13–58.

——. *Beroul's 'Romance of Tristran'.* Trans. John C. Barnes. Manchester: University Press; New York: Barnes & Noble, 1972.

Vinaver, Eugène. 'La Forêt de Morois'. *CCM* 11 (1968): 1–13.

——. 'Pour le commentaire du vers 1650 du *Tristan* de Béroul'. *Studies in Medieval French. Presented to Alfred Ewert in honour of his seventieth birthday.* Oxford: Clarendon, 1961. 90–95.

——. 'The Prose *Tristan'. Arthurian Literature in the Middle Ages. A Collaborative History.* Ed. Roger S. Loomis. Oxford: Clarendon, 1959. 339–47.

——. 'The Love Potion in the Primitive Tristan Romance'. *Medieval Studies in Memory of Gertrude Schoepperle-Loomis.* New York: Columbia UP; Paris: Champion, 1927. 75–86.

——. *Etudes sur le 'Tristan' en prose. Les sources; les manuscrits, bibliographie critique.* Paris: Champion, 1925.

Walter, Philippe. 'Tristan et la mélancholie (contribution à une lecture médicale des textes français en vers sur Tristan)'. *Actes du 14e Congrès International Arthurien. Rennes, 16–21 Août 1984.* 2 vols. Rennes: Presses Universitaires de Rennes 2, 1985. 646–57.

——. 'Orion et Tristan, ou la sémantique des étoiles'. *Le Soleil, la lune et les étoiles au moyen âge. Sénéfiance* 13. Aix-en-Provence: CUER MA, 1983. 437–49.

——. 'Le Solstice de Tristan'. *TLL* 20.2 (1982): 7–20.

Whitehead, Frederick. 'Tristan and Isolt in the Forest of Morrois'. *Studies in*

French Language and Mediaeval Literature Presented to Professor Mildred K. Pope. Manchester: University Press, 1939. 393–400.

Whitteridge, Gweneth. 'The *Tristan* of Béroul', in *Medieval Miscellany Presented to Eugène Vinaver by Pupils, Colleagues and Friends*. Eds. F. Whitehead, et al. Manchester: University Press; New York: Barnes & Noble, 1965. 337–56.

——. 'The Date of the *Tristan* of Beroul'. *Medium Aevum* 28 (1959): 167–71.

Wind, Bartina H. 'Quelques remarques sur la versification du *Tristan* de Thomas'. *Neophilologus* 33 (1949): 85–94.

——. 'Eléments courtois dans Béroul et dans Thomas'. *Romance Philology* 14 (1960–1961): 1–13.

——. 'Les versions françaises du *Tristan* et les influences contemporaines. A propos d'un livre récent'. *Neophilologus* 45 (1961): 278–86.

——. 'Nos incertitudes au sujet du *Tristan* de Thomas'. *Mélanges de langue et de littérature du Moyen Age et de la Renaissance offerts à Jean Frappier*. Geneva: Droz, 1970, 2: 1129–38.

Witte, Arthur. 'Der Aufbau der ältesten Tristandichtungen'. *Zeitschrift für deutsches Altertum und deutsche Literatur* 70 (1933): 161–95.

York, Ernest C. 'Isolt's Ordeal: English Legal Customs in the Medieval Tristan Legend'. *Studies in Philology* 68 (1971): 1–9.

Zingarelli, Nicola. 'Tristano e Isotta'. *Studi Medievali* ns 1 (1928): 48–58.

III

GENERAL STUDIES

Babcock-Abrahams, Barbara. '"A Tolerated Margin of Mess": The Trickster and his Tales Reconsidered'. *Journal of the Folklore Institute* 11 (1975): 147–186.

Barber, Richard W. *The Knight and Chivalry*. New York: Scribners, 1970.

Barker-Benfield, B. C., Assistant Librarian, Department of Western Manuscripts, Bodleian Library, Oxford University. Letters to author. January 28, 1985, August 8, 1985.

Barnes, Geraldine. 'The *Riddarasögur* and Mediaeval European Literature'. *Mediaeval Scandinavia* 8 (1975): 140–158.

Bernheimer, Richard. *Wild Men in the Middle Ages: A Study in Art, Sentiment, and Demonology*. Cambridge: Harvard University Press, 1952.

Blakeslee, Merritt R. '*Lo Dous Jocx Sotils*: La Partie d'échecs amoureuse dans la poésie des troubadours'. *Cahiers de Civilisation Médiévale* 28 (1985): 213–222.

Bloch, R. Howard. *Etymologies and Genealogies. A Literary Anthropology of the French Middle Ages.* Chicago and London: The University of Chicago Press, 1983.

Bloomfield, Morton W. 'Allegory as Interpretation'. *New Literary History* 3 (1971–72): 301–317.

Brody, Saul Nathaniel. *The Disease of the Soul: Leprosy in Medieval Literature.* Ithaca and London: Cornell University Press, 1974.

Brown, Norman O. *Hermes the Thief: The Evolution of a Myth.* 1947. New York: Random-Vintage, 1969.

Bruce, James Douglas. *The Evolution of Arthurian Romance from the Beginnings down to the Year 1300.* 2 vols. Second Edition with a supplement by Alfons Hilka. Göttingen: Vandenhoeck & Ruprecht; Baltimore: Johns Hopkins Press, 1928.

Campbell, Joseph. *The Hero with a Thousand Faces.* Bollingen Series 17. Princeton: Princeton University Press, 1949.

———. *The Masks of the Gods: Creative Mythology.* New York: Viking Press, 1968.

Colman, E. A. M. *The Dramatic Use of Bawdy in Shakespeare.* London: Longman, 1974.

Cosman, Madeleine Pelner. *The Education of the Hero in Arthurian Romance.* Chapel Hill: The University of North Carolina Press, 1965.

Cougoul, Jacques-Guy. *La Lèpre dans l'ancienne France.* Bordeaux: Delmas, 1943.

Crane, Susan. *Insular Romance. Politics, Faith, and Culture in Anglo-Norman and Middle English Literature.* Berkeley: University of California Press, 1986.

Crist, Larry S. 'Deep Structures in the *chansons de geste*: Hypotheses for a Taxonomy'. *Olifant* 3 (1975–1976), 3–35.

Curtius, Ernst Robert. *European Literature and the Latin Middle Ages.* Trans. Willard R. Trask. Bollingen Series 36. Princeton: Princeton University Press, 1973.

Deloffre, Frédéric. 'Stylistique et critique d'attribution'. *Au Bonheur des mots: Mélanges en l'honneur de Gérald Antoine.* Nancy: Presses Universitaires de Nancy, 1984. 509–520.

Demetz, Peter. 'The Elm and the Vine: Notes Toward the History of a Marriage Topos'. *PMLA* 73 (1958): 521–32.

Doob, Penelope B. R. *Nebuchadnezzar's Children: Conventions of Madness in Middle English Literature.* New Haven-London: Yale University Press, 1974.

Dragonetti, Roger. *La Technique poétique des trouvères dans la chanson courtoise. Contribution à l'étude de la rhétorique médiévale.* Bruges: De Tempel, 1960.

Duby, Georges. *The Knight, the Lady, and the Priest: The Making of Modern Marriage in Medieval France*. Trans. Barbara Bray. New York: Pantheon, 1983.

———. 'Dans la France du Nord-Ouest au XIIe siècle: les "jeunes" dans la société aristocratique'. *Annales: Economies, Sociétés, Civilisations* 19 (1964): 835–46.

Duggan, Joseph J. 'Ambiguity in Twelfth-Century French and Provençal Literature: A Problem or a Value?' *Jean Misrahi Memorial Volume. Studies in Medieval Literature*. Ed. Hans R. Runte, Henri Niedzielski, William L. Hendrickson. Columbia, South Carolina: French Literature Publications, 1977. 136–49.

Entwistle, William J. *The Arthurian Legend in the Literatures of the Spanish Peninsula*. New York: Phaeton, 1975.

Faral, Edmond. *Les Jongleurs en France au moyen âge*. 1910. New York: Burt Franklin, 1970.

Ferrante, Joan M. *Woman as Image in Medieval Literature from the Twelfth Century to Dante*. New York and London: Columbia UP, 1975.

Foucault, Michel. *Histoire de la folie a l'âge classique*. 2nd. edition. Bibliothèque des Histoires. Paris: Gallimard, 1972.

Fourrier, Anthime. *Le Courant réaliste dans le roman courtois en France au Moyen Age*. I. *Les Débuts (XIIe siècle)*. Paris: Nizet, 1960.

Frappier, Jean. 'Orphée et Proserpine ou la lyre et la harpe'. *Mélanges de langue et de littérature médiévales offerts à Pierre Le Gentil, Professeur à la Sorbonne, par ses collègues, ses élèves et ses amis*. Paris: SEDES, 1973. 277–94.

———. *Chrétien de Troyes, nouvelle édition revue et augmentée, illustrée*. Connaissance des Lettres 50. Paris: Hatier, 1968.

———. 'Vues sur les conceptions courtoises dans les littératures d'oc et d'oïl au XIIe siècle'. *CCM* 2 (1959): 135–156.

Frazer, James George. *The New Golden Bough*. Ed. Theodor H. Gaster. New York: Mentor, 1964.

Friedman, John Block. *Orpheus in the Middle Ages*. Cambridge: Harvard University Press, 1970.

Frye, Northrop. *Anatomy of Criticism: Four Essays*. Princeton: Princeton University Press, 1957.

Gardner, Edmund Garratt. *The Arthurian Legend in Italian Literature*. 1930. New York: Octogon, 1971.

Godefroy, Frédéric. *Dictionnaire de l'ancienne langue française et de tous les dialectes, du IXe au XVe siècle*. 10 vols. Paris: Vieweg, 1881–1902. Paris: Librairie des Sciences et des Arts, 1937.

Graves, Robert. *The Greek Myths*. 2 vols. Baltimore: Penguin, 1955.

Guiette, Robert. *Questions de littérature*. Romanica Gandensia 8. Gand, 1960.

Haidu, Peter. *Lion-queue-coupée. L'écart symbolique chez Chrétien de Troyes.* Geneva: Droz, 1972.

Hanning, Robert W. *The Individual in Twelfth-Century Romance.* New Haven and London: Yale University Press, 1977.

Halvorsen, Eyvind. 'Problèmes de la traduction scandinave des textes français du Moyen Age'. *Les Relations littéraires franco-scandinaves au Moyen Age. Actes du colloque de Liège, avril 1972.* Ed. Maurice Grave. Paris: Les Belles Lettres, 1975. 247–74.

Helle, Knut. 'Anglo-Norwegian Relations in the Reign of Håkon Håkonsson (1217–63)'. *Mediaeval Scandinavia* 1 (1968): 101–114.

Hotson, Leslie. *The First Night of* Twelfth Night. New York: Macmillan, 1954.

James, Edwin Oliver. *Seasonal Feasts and Festivals.* New York: Barnes and Noble, 1961.

Johnsen, Arne Odd. 'Les relations intellectuelles entre la France et la Norvège (1150–1214)'. *Le Moyen Age* 57 (1951): 247–68.

Jongkees, A. G. '*Translatio Studii*: les avatars d'un thème médiéval'. *Miscellanea Mediaevalia in memoriam Jan Frederik Niermeyer.* Groningen: Wolters, 1967.

Jung, Carl G. *Four Archetypes: Mother, Rebirth, Spirit, Trickster.* Trans. R. F. C. Hull. Bollingen Series 215. Princeton: Princeton University Press, 1959.

———. *Alchemical Studies.* Trans. R. F. C. Hull. Princeton: Princeton University Press, 1967.

Kalinke, Marianne E. *King Arthur North-by-Northwest. The* matière de Bretagne *in Old Norse-Icelandic Romances.* Bibliotheca Arnamagnæana 37. Copenhagen: C. A. Reitzels, 1981.

Koenig, V. Frederic. 'Counter-Notes on Jean Renart'. *Modern Language Notes* 55 (1940): 8–16.

———. 'New Studies on Jean Renart: The Date of the *Escoufle*'. *Modern Philology* 32 (1934–35): 343–52.

Lazar, Moshé. *Amour courtois et 'fin'amors' dans la littérature du XIIe siècle.* Bibliothèque Française et Romane, Série C, 7. Paris: Klincksieck, 1964.

Leach, Henry Goddard. 'The Relations of the Norwegian with the English Church, 1066–1399, and their Importance to Comparative Literature'. *Proceedings of the American Academy of Arts and Sciences* 44.20 (May 1909): 531–60.

Lecoy, Félix. 'Sur la date du *Guillaume de Dole*'. *Romania* 82 (1961): 379–402.

Le Goff, Jacques. *La Civilisation de l'Occident médiéval.* 1964. Paris: Flammarion, [1982].

Le Goff, Jacques and Pierre Vidal-Naquet. 'Lévi-Strauss en Brocéliande'. *Critique* 325 (June 1974): 541–71.

Lejeune-Dehousse, Rita. *L'Oeuvre de Jean Renart. Contribution à l'étude du genre romanesque au moyen âge.* Bibliothèque de la Faculté de Philosophie et Lettres de l'Université de Liége 61. Liége: Faculté de Philosophie et Lettres; Paris: E. Droz, 1935.

——. 'Le *Roman de Guillaume de Dole* et la principauté de Liège'. *CCM* 17 (1974): 1–24.

Lévi-Strauss, Claude. 'The Structural Study of Myth'. *Journal of American Folklore* 78 (1955), 428–44.

Leyerle, John. 'The Game and Play of Hero'. *Concepts of the Hero in the Middle Ages and the Renaissance. Papers of the 4th & 5th Annual Conferences of the Center for Medieval & Early Renaissance Studies, State University of New York at Binghamton, 2–3 May 1970, 1–2 May 1971.* Eds. Norman T. Burns and Christopher J. Reagan. Albany: State University of New York Press, 1975. 49–82.

Lomazzi, Anna. 'L'eroe come *trickster* nel *Roman de Renart*'. *Cultura Neolatina* 40 (1980): 55–65.

Loomis, Roger Sherman. *Arthurian Literature in the Middle Ages: A Collaborative History.* Oxford: Clarendon, 1959.

Makarius, Laura. 'Le Mythe du "trickster"'. *Revue de l'Histoire des Religions* 175 (1966): 17–46.

Ménard, Philippe. 'Les Fous dans la société médiévale. Le témoignage de la littérature au XIIe et au XIIIe siècle. *Romania* 98 (1977): 433–59.

——. *Le Rire et le sourire dans le roman courtois en France au Moyen Age (1150–1250).* Publications Romanes et Françaises 105. Geneva: Droz, 1969.

Micha, Alexandre. 'Le Mari jaloux dans la littérature romanesque des XIIe et XIIIe siècles'. *Studi Medievali* ns 17 (1951): 303–20.

Neaman, Judith S. *Suggestion of the Devil. The Orgins of Madness.* Garden City: Doubleday, 1975.

Patch, Howard Rollin. *The Other World According to Descriptions in Medieval Literature.* Cambridge: Harvard University Press, 1950.

Paton, Lucy Allen. *Studies in the Fairy Mythology of Arthurian Romance. Second Edition; enlarged by a Survey of Scholarship on the Fairy Mythology since 1903 and a Bibliography by Roger Sherman Loomis.* New York: Burt Franklin, 1960.

Pauphilet, Albert. *Le Legs du Moyen Age. Etudes de littérature médiévale.* Melun: Librairie D'Argences, 1950.

Payen, Jean Charles. *Le Motif du repentir dans la littérature française médiévale (des origines à 1230).* Publications Romanes et Françaises 98. Geneva: Droz, 1967. 331–364.

Pfeffer, Wendy. *The Change of Philomel. The Nightingale in Medieval Litera-*

ture. American University Studies, Comparative Literature 14. New York, Bern, Frankfurt: Peter Lang, 1985.

Pelan, Margaret M. *L'Influence du 'Brut' de Wace sur les romanciers français de son temps*. Paris: Droz, 1931. Geneva: Slatkine, 1974.

Poirion, Daniel. 'Fonction de l'imaginaire dans l'Escoufle'. *Mélanges de langue et de littérature françaises du moyen âge et de la renaissance offerts à Monsieur Charles Foulon*. Rennes: Institut de France, Université de Haute-Bretagne, 1980. 287–93.

Propp, Vladimir. *Morphologie du conte, suivi de 'Les Transformations des contes merveilleux', et de E.Mélétinski, 'L'Etude structurale et typologique du conte'*. Trans. Marguerite Derrida, Tzvetan Todorov and Claude Kahn. Collection Poétique. Paris: Le Seuil, 1965.

Psichari, Jean, and H.Gaidoz. 'Les Deux Arbres entrelacés'. *Mélusine* 4 (1888–89): cols. 60–62, 85–91.

Radin, Paul. *The Trickster: A Study in American Indian Mythology*. 1954. New York: Schocken, 1972.

Raglan, Lord. *The Hero: A Study in Tradition, Myth and Drama*. London: Watts, 1949.

Rank, Otto. *The Myth of the Birth of the Hero and Other Writings*. Ed. Philip Freund. 1914. New York: Vintage-Knopf, 1964.

Remy, Paul. 'La lèpre, thème littéraire au Moyen Age. Commentaire d'un passage du roman provençal de *Jaufré'. Moyen Age* 52 (1946), 195–242.

Richards, Peter. *The Medieval Leper and his Northern Heirs*. Towota, New Jersey: Rowman & Littlefield, 1977.

Righter, William. 'Myth and Interpretation'. *New Literary History* 3 (1971–72): 319–44.

Rogers, Katharine M. *The Troublesome Helpmate: A History of Misogyny in Literature*. Seattle and London: University of Washington Press, 1966.

Ryding, William W. *Structure in Medieval Narrative*. The Hague: Mouton, 1971.

Swain, Barbara. *Fools and Folly during the Middle Ages and the Renaissance*. New York: Columbia University Press, 1932.

Thiébaux, Marcelle. *The Stag of Love: The Chase in Medieval Literature*. Ithaca and London: Cornell University Press, 1974.

Tobler, Adolf and Erhard Lommatzsch. *Altfranzösisches Wörterbuch. Adolf Toblers nachgelassene Materialien bearbeitet und mit Unterstützung der Preussischen Akademie der Wissenschaften herausgegeben von Erhard Lommatzsch*. Berlin: Weidmann, 1925– (presently completed through volume 10 [T], Wiesbaden: Steiner, 1976).

Togeby, Knud. 'La Chronologie des versions scandinaves des anciens textes français'. *Les Relations littéraires franco-scandinaves au Moyen Age. Actes du colloque de Liège, avril 1972*. Ed. Maurice Grave. Paris: Les Belles Lettres, 1975. 183–91.

Welsford, Enid. *The Fool; His Social and Literary History*. New York: Ferrar & Rinehart, 1935.

Weston, Jessie L. *From Ritual to Romance*. Cambridge: Cambridge University Press, 1920. Garden City: Anchor, 1957.

Woledge Brian and Ian Short. 'Liste provisoire de manuscrits du XIIe siècle contenant des textes en langue française'. *Romania* 102 (1981): 1–17.

Zink, Georges. 'Les Poèmes arthuriens dans les pays scandinaves'. *Les Relations littéraires franco-scandinaves au Moyen Age. Actes du colloque de Liège, avril 1972*. Ed. Maurice Grave. Paris: Les Belles Lettres, 1975. 77–95

Zumthor, Paul. *Essai de poétique médiévale*. Collection Poétique. Paris: Le Seuil, 1972.

INDEX

Curtis, Renée L., 97, 108
Curtius, Ernst Robert, 50, 65, 86
Cycle de Guillaume, 2, 19

Diarmaid, 18
Dannenbaum, Susan, 17
David, 18, 28, 30, 34–35, 129
de Rougemont, Denis, 3
deduit, (se) deduire, 44–45
Delbouille, Maurice, 10
Delpino, Marcella, 2
Denomy, Alexander J., 28
disguises, 59–95
    the disguise as adynaton, 65–67
    the disguise as metaphor, 61–67
    the *fou*, 72–86, 90–95
    inversion of values, 61–67
    the leper, 66–67, 118, 120
    narrative functions, 59–61
    the nightingale, 87–90
    the pilgrim, 60, 68–69
    Tristan als Mönch, 9, 60
Ditmas, E. M. R., 6
Donnei des amanz, 1, 2, 9, 37–38, 43, 62, 67,
    72, 87–90
Doob, Penelope B. R., 28, 73, 76, 81
Duby, Georges, 14, 43
Duggan, Joseph J., 3
Durrell, Lawrence, 76
Durmart le Galois, 16

Eilhart von Oberge, *Tristrant* [O], 1, 6, 9,
    10, 14, 31, 32, 51, 59, 65, 69, 70, 72, 73,
    80, 81, 82, 86, 100, 101, 102, 110
    Pro of Jemsetir, 102
Eisner, Sigmund, 18
Ewert, Alfred, 6

Faral, Edmond, 80
La Farce de Maître Pathelin, 19
Feast of Saint John, 52, 70, 75
Fedrick, Alan, 86
Ferrante, Joan M., 33, 44
fin'amor, 13, 68–69, 98, 123
    and suffering, 97–100
First Continuation of the Perceval, 16, 98
Fis Adamnáin (Book of the Dun Cow), 53
folie, aimer par folie, aimer follement, 73,
    78–79
Folie Tristan d'Oxford [Fo], 1, 2, 9, 16, 18,
    20, 22, 25, 29, 30, 31, 32, 33, 35, 36, 39,
    40, 41, 44, 45, 46, 49, 50, 51, 52, 53, 54,
    55, 57, 59, 60, 61, 62, 66, 69, 70, 71,
    72–86, 87, 89, 90, 91, 92, 93, 94, 95, 101,
    102, 107, 109, 110, 111, 116, 117, 118,
    119, 120, 124, 128, 130, 131
    the celestial palace, 53
    the *chasse à l'envers*, 45, 81, 82

fantastical *contes*, 45, 81–82, 91
    the *funteine ki ben surt*, 89, 92, 108–10
    Tintagel, 54–55
    the wild man, 90–95
Folie Tristan de Berne [Fb], 1, 2, 6, 9, 18, 20,
    22, 32, 35, 36, 44, 45, 46, 51, 52, 53, 54,
    55, 57, 59, 60, 62, 65, 66, 67, 70, 71,
    72–86, 94, 100, 101, 102, 106, 108, 109,
    110, 116, 118, 119, 124
    the celestial palace, 53
    fantastical *contes*, 81–82
    madness and melancholy, 108
    miracle at Cana, allusion to, 110
Foulet, Alfred, 17
Fourrier, Anthime, 10, 104, 112
Frappier, Jean, 10, 34
French prose *Tristan* (dominant version)
    [R], 1, 6, 9, 10, 16, 18, 19, 21, 28, 32, 33,
    39, 40, 46, 47, 65, 72, 76, 77, 81, 86,
    93–94, 100, 101, 102, 109, 110, 112, 113,
    119, 120, 126, 132
    Tristan the wild man, 93–94, 128, 130
French prose *Tristan* (variant version of
    MS. B.N.fr. 103) [MS. B.N.fr. 103], 1, 8,
    9, 10, 16, 18, 21, 44, 51, 72, 74, 79, 81,
    91, 93, 94, 101, 106, 110, 112
    madness and punishment, 74
French Tristan poems, 1, 3–4
    intertextuality and meaning, 2–4, 127–32
    literary and biblical allusions in, 1–2,
        107, 110
    narrative structure, 8–11, 36
        episodic poems, 2, 9–11
        return episodes, 9–11, 127
    self-referentiality, 2, 128
    source(s), 10–11, 127–32
    symbolic content, 3
Friedman, John Block, 34
'La Froidors ne la jalee' (R 517), 112
Froissart, Jean
    Méliador, 44, 99
    Paradis d'amour, 43
Frye, Northrop, 57

Gaucelm Faidit, 88
Gautier d'Aupais, 98
Gautier de Coinci, 'De l'empeeris qui
    garda sa chasteé contre mout de
    temptations', 16
Geoffrey of Monmouth, *Vita Merlini*, 92, 94,
    130
Gerbert de Montreuil, *Continuation de
    Perceval*, 31
Giron le Courtois, 28
Gliglois, 98
Gottfried von Strassburg, *Tristan* [G], 1, 9,
    15, 16, 21, 31, 32, 44, 46, 53, 59, 78, 82,
    100, 102, 111, 112